他者のために、他者とともに／Men and Women for Others, with Others

The Role of Jesuit Universities in Asia
アジアにおけるイエズス会大学の役割

A report of the Sophia International Symposium on the occasion of the centenary celebrations of the foundation of Sophia University held on December 7, 2013

共編：髙祖敏明／サリ・アガスティン
Eds. Toshiaki Koso / Sali Augustine

Sophia University Press
上智大学出版

刊行にあたって

コーディネーター：サリ・アガスティン
〈上智大学〉

　「全世界に行って、すべての造られたものに福音を宣べ伝えなさい」。マルコ福音書16章15節に記されているこのイエスの言葉とそれによる派遣が、キリスト教の2000年以上におよぶ宣教とそれにともなうキリスト教精神に基づく教育の源です。そして、「弟子たちは出かけて行って、至るところで宣教した。主は彼らと共に働き、彼らの語る言葉が真実であることを、……はっきりとお示しになった」（マルコ福音書16：19-20）。福音とは、人々の「救いのための良い知らせ」です。この福音を時のしるしと受け止めたイエズス会は、すべての人の「救い」につながる教育を会の活動の1つに位置づけ、「全人的教育」を目指して努力を重ねてきました。

　第二ヴァチカン公会議後のカトリック教会は、アジアのような多文化、多宗教的状況の非キリスト教世界においても、いまもなお「キリスト教的価値観」に基づいて教育を行うように努めています。つまり、イエスが示したメッセージと価値観（特に弱い立場の人々への助け）を、現代において自分たちの置かれた場所で行えるような人を育てることを目指し、「他者のために、他者とともに」という教育理念の実現に力を注いでいるのです。また、経済的利益や消費のみを重視した競争社会の中で、イエスは「私は道、真理、命」（ヨハネ14：6）であると教え、回心を呼びかけたことにならって、全人的救いに導く価値観を基本とした教育活動を行っているのです。グローバルな現代において、多様性を受け入れた社会には正しいリーダーシップと価値観を備えた人材の育成が必要ですが、教育もまた1つのビジネスになって競争に走る現代において、カトリック教育のアイデンティティと役割を再確認しなければならない時が来ていると私は考えます。そこで上智大学創立100周年を良い機会ととらえ、アジアのイエズス会大学が自らへの問いかけを試みたこのシンポジウムの内容を皆さんと分かち合いたいと思います。

　フィリピンのアテネオ・デ・マニラ大学の歴史と現状を再確認することによっ

て、カトリック教育が果たして来た役割を検証したホセ・クルス氏は、「これは歴史的意味合いだけではなく、今日でも教会が教育と学問研究活動によって社会の発展に尽くしていることに他ならない」と述べました。

　台湾の高等教育の現場である輔仁カトリック大学の歴史を検証したルイス・ジェンドロン氏は、「イエズス会は台湾の輔仁カトリック大学再建の主たる貢献者でありながら、キャンパスにおける会の存在感は低下している」ことを懸念しながらも、「キャンパスにおいてイグナチオの霊性を保つことには希望」をもち、「完全に独立した学院である聖ロベルト・ベラルミーノ輔仁神学校のみが、台湾における唯一のカトリック神学院であり、これまでも、そして今後のイエズス会の優先順位の中心となる」と指摘しました。他方、イエズス会員の減少、協働による運営や、中国の歴史的展開の困難さの中でも、「イエズス会高等教育の伝統に精通した一般の教職員が大半を占める」ことを伝えています。

　川村信三氏は、創立100周年を迎えた上智大学を念頭に置きつつ、明治期以後の日本のカトリック教会の歴史を三期に分けて分析し、カトリック教育も3つの変化を遂げたことを指摘しました。カトリック教育は、「社会とは別に」魂の救いを目的とした草の根的努力を果たした時代から、「社会に近づく」方法で国枠主義と偏見との間を生きた時代を経て、戦後の日本では「社会の中で」独自の地位を構築する時代へとアイデンティティが変化していることを指摘し、これからのカトリック大学の方向性について示唆を与えました。

　インドネシアのサナタダルマ大学のクントロ・アディ氏は、インドネシアのような多民族・多文化・多宗教社会における宗教間対話を、大学教育の中で考察・実践するプログラム等を紹介し、カトリック大学のアイデンティティに由来する重要な特徴を強調しました。

　ベネディクト・ユン氏は、「教育熱」の高い韓国社会において1960年代から教育活動に邁進している西江大学を例に、韓国のカトリック学校が社会的・政治的そして文化的課題とどのように関わって来たかを検証し「韓国におけるカトリック学校の現状を踏まえれば、カトリック教育のユニークかつ特別な使命を全うするための理に適った献身的方法を見つけ出し」、「カトリック教育の現状に関する正しい理解と解決策が必要だ」と指摘し、いくつかの建設的動きを紹介しました。彼はイエズス会教育の中心にある「他者のために他者とともに」と「信仰における正義への奉仕」の精神を指摘し、「カトリック学校は多様性、選択肢と思いやりのある異なった学校教育モデルを考えなければならない」と

述べました。

　このようなアジアにおけるイエズス会大学の現状分析を踏まえたうえで、さらに進むであろうグローバル化の中で、カトリック大学がすでに取り組んでいるプロジェクトを紹介しながら、本学副学長の杉村氏は、特にアジアにおける高等教育の1つの方向性として学際的・学融合的な教養教育を軸とする国際高等教育のモデルを提示しています。

　教育は「伝える」ことから始まる活動です。本当に人を生かし、新しい命に輝き、喜んで生きていくことこそ、「他者のために、他者とともに」となるのです。グローバル化が進む中で「行って福音を宣べ伝えなさい」との主イエスの派遣にふさわしいカトリック教育が行われているのかどうか、その「ミッションには今もなお意義があるのか」を考え続けなければなりません。上智大学創立100周年を記念して開催されたこのシンポジウムは、アジアにおけるイエズス会大学教育の現状を多面的に検証するうえで、まことに有意義なものでした。

　最後にご講演くださいました先生方お一人お一人に、またシンポジウム開催とこの出版に携わったすべての関係者の皆様に感謝申し上げます。特にコメンテーターの南山大学学長ミカエル・カルマノ先生、司会を務めてくださったアントニ・ウセレル教授と杉村美紀教授、翻訳に関わった酒井麻里奈さんに感謝いたします。またこのシンポジウムが上智学院理事長、髙祖敏明先生のアイデアとイニシアチブ、上智大学学長（当時）滝澤正先生のご協力によって実現されたことを記して、感謝の意を表します。

目　　次

刊行にあたって　　　　　　　　　　　　サリ・アガスティン　……1

序　上智国際シンポジウム「アジアにおけるイエズス会大学の役割」
　　　　　　　　　　　　　　　　　　　　髙祖　敏明　……7

第1部　アジア5大学からの報告と展望

フィリピンにおけるイエズス会教育
　——アテネオ・デ・マニラ大学の歴史と未来
　　　　　　　　　　　　　　　　　　　　ホセ・クルス　……12

日本近代社会におけるカトリック・アイデンティティとカトリック教育
　　　　　　　　　　　　　　　　　　　　川村　信三　……22

イエズス会中国管区における高等教育
　——突然の終結、新たな再開、改められた宣教の様相
　　　　　　　　　　　　　　　　　　　　ルイス・ジェンドロン　……48

サナタダルマ大学とイエズス会の全人教育
　　　　　　　　　　　　　　　　　　　　クントロ・アディ　……55

韓国におけるカトリック教育
　——1960年以降の課題への応答の歴史
　　　　　　　　　　　　　　　　　　　　ベネディクト・カンユップ・ユン　……65

第2部　コメントとディスカッション

コメントに代えて　　　　　　　　　　　　ミカエル・カルマノ ……90

アジアにおける高等教育の国際連携とイエズス会大学の役割
　　　　　　　　　　　　　　　　　　　　杉村　美紀 ……95

パネルディスカッション ………………………………………… 106

質疑応答 …………………………………………………………… 113

執筆者一覧 ………………………………………………………… 253

序

上智国際シンポジウム
「アジアにおけるイエズス会大学の役割」

髙祖　敏明
〈上智学院理事長〉

　本書は、「上智大学創立 100 周年記念事業」の一環として開催された国際シンポジウム「アジアにおけるイエズス会大学の役割」の報告書です。2013 年の上智大学創立 100 周年にあたり、2013 年 11 月 1 日には、天皇皇后両陛下ご臨席のもと、教皇フランシスコから派遣された特使ファリーナ枢機卿の出席を得て記念式典を執り行いました。この創立 100 周年記念事業を貫くコンセプトは「叡智が世界をつなぐ」(Sophia‒Bringing the World Together) です。

　この言葉は上智大学が積み重ねてきた歴史の要約であり、同時に、本学が 21 世紀に果たすべき使命を要約したものでもあります。今回の国際シンポジウム「アジアにおけるイエズス会大学の役割」は、このコンセプトを活かそうと構想されました。本書は、これを手にする一人ひとりにとって実り豊かなものとなりますように、とりわけ大学使徒職に関わる人々が、個人としても、大学全体としても、自らが招かれている使命をより深く理解し、その使命をよりよく果たしていくことができますように、そして、それによって世界をつなぎ、人類家族により仕えることができますように、との祈りをもって、主催者としての挨拶といたします。

　上智大学は、16 世紀半ばのイエズス会宣教師フランシスコ・ザビエルの「日本のミヤコに大学を」という願いを創立の原点としています。ザビエルの時代から 350 年も経った 20 世紀初頭、当時の教皇ピオ 10 世が明治天皇に親善使節を送り、日本にカトリック大学を開設する可能性を調べさせたところから、ザビエルの夢の実現、つまり日本におけるカトリック大学設立に向けた本格的な動きが始まりました。使節から「カトリックの名に値する世界に開かれた大学であれば大いに見込みがある」との報告を得た教皇は、大学設立をイエズス会に要請し、イエズス会は 1908 年、ドイツ人（インドと中国思想の専門家）、フランス人（上海フランス学院院長）、イギリス人（アメリカ・バッファローミッ

ションの宣教師)の3人の神父を日本へ派遣しました。こうして日本人神父や教授の協力のもと、西欧、インド、中国、アメリカの思想文化が日本に集い、同時に、日本の思想文化をそれらの世界各地に発信する、双方向でつなぎ合う仕組みが作られました。ここに「叡智(ソフィア)が世界をつなぐ」という役割を担う上智大学が誕生しました。1913年春のことでした。

以来上智大学は、とりわけカトリック精神に基づく教育と研究が広く認められた第二次大戦後、「人類の希望と苦悩を分かち合い、世界の福祉と創造的進歩に奉仕」(「上智大学の教育理念」より)すべく、教育と研究、社会貢献、国際貢献に励んできました。とはいえ、激動する世界の中で、またカトリック人口が1%にも満たない我が国にあって、カトリック精神に基づき人材養成を目指すその歩みは、まさに「山あり谷あり」で、試練の連続でした。しかし、ありがたいことに日本国内はもとより、世界各地のカトリック信者をはじめ、多くの善意の人々のご厚意に援けられ、おかげで今年、創立100周年を祝うことができました。

その意味では、このシンポジウムは上智大学創立100周年を記念する「感謝の集い」ですが、企画としては過去と現在をつなぎ、さらにアジアの将来を展望するものです。

皆様もカトリック大学の世界的なネットワークについてはよくご存じのことと思います。事実、世界カトリック大学連盟(International Federation of Catholic Universities)やその傘下の東南アジアおよび東アジアカトリック大学連盟(ASEACCU)、またアジア太平洋イエズス会大学連盟(AJCU-AP)とのつながりは、本学が国際性を発揮し、「叡智(ソフィア)が世界をつなぐ」という使命を果たしていくうえで、まことに大きな支えとなっております。

例えば、数年前から、AJCU-APのネットワークのもとで毎年夏に、学生参加のサービス・ラーニングのプログラム、また、韓国の西江大学、台湾の輔仁大学、フィリピンのアテネオ・デ・マニラ大学、それにインドネシアのサナタダルマ大学と上智の5大学が協力して学生を育てる「グローバルリーダーシップ・プログラム」を実行しております。

もうお気づきのように、今回のシンポジウム「アジアにおけるイエズス会大学の役割」は、この5大学の国別事例報告に、この地域に詳しいミカエル・カルマノ南山大学学長がコメンテーターとして加わるという構成です。ここでの問題意識は、以下のようです。

東南アジアや東アジアに設立されたこれら5大学は、それぞれ創立された時代や国の状況は異なります。例えば、カトリック信者が国民の80％を超えるフィリピンを別にすれば、韓国を含む他の4カ国ではカトリック人口がいずれも少数です。とりわけ、インドネシア、台湾そして日本は、カトリック人口が極めて少ない国です。そこで、第一に、カトリックが少数であるアジア諸国におけるカトリック大学、イエズス会大学は、歴史の中で一体どのような役割を果たしてきたのか。時代と地域からどのような挑戦を受け、それらとどう対決したのか、ないしはしなかったのか。

第二に、各大学が自国の歴史の中で果たしてきた役割についての自己点検評価には、何らかの共通点が見られるのかどうか。またそれらの自己点検評価は、カトリック国といわれるフィリピンのイエズス会大学の場合とは、どのような相違があるのか。

第三に、20世紀の終盤から、イエズス会大学の共通の教育目標として "Men and Women for Others, with Others" が掲げられていますが、グローバル化が進行する21世紀の今日、具体的には何を自らのミッションととらえ、何をどのように果たそうとしているのか。そこには、アジア5大学が協力して一緒に果たせる役割があるのか。あるとすれば、それは何か。

こうした期待を込めた未来志向のものとしても開催された国際シンポジウムの内容が本書を通してより多くの人へとつながることを願っています。

第1部

アジア5大学からの報告と展望

フィリピンにおけるイエズス会教育
アテネオ・デ・マニラ大学の歴史と未来

ホセ・クルス
〈アテネオ・デ・マニラ大学〉

　16世紀半ばから19世紀半ばまで、フィリピンにおける教育はカトリック教会が担っていた。1863年にスペイン植民地政府が各州の教育に対する責任を重くする法律を公布してから1946年にアメリカがフィリピンの独立を認めるまで、国内の教育はスペイン・アメリカそして日本政府によって行われていた。フィリピンが独立を勝ち取った1946年以降現在に至るまで、フィリピン政府がその責務を担っている。とはいえ、16世紀からずっとそうであったように、教会の関係機関や組織の教育への参画は続いている。今日国内で最高レベルの4大学のうちの3校が修道会により運営されている。

　16世紀から、主に初等学校という形で行われていた教育は、宣教活動の主要な柱であった[1]。17世紀以降には、教育の主眼は信仰教育から社会の発展というより大きな関心にとって代わられた。高等教育機関が設立され、その後すぐに大学が創立された[2]。フィリピンにイエズス会員がやってきて2年後、マニラ司教は首都にイエズス会学校を創設することを国王に提案した。認可が下りるまでには長らくかかった[3]。

　1592年、イエズス会はフィリピンに到達してから11年後、ヴィサヤ諸島のイロイロにあるティグバウアンに、読み書き・歌唱・楽器演奏を教える小学校を創設した。その主な目的は信仰教育であった[4]。

　同様の学校がセブ島にも創設された。この学校はのちに読み書き・算数・宗教を教える聖イルデフォンソ・カレッジとなった[5]。生徒はフィリピン人のほか中国人とスペイン人の男子であった。イエズス会はのちにセブ島以東のレイテ島とサマル島にある4つの地区に小学校を創設した。

　同時にルソン島では3つの小学校がつくられた。17世紀の初めの10年にはマニラを含め、列島には複数の小学校があった。マニラの学校は前述の司教の仲介で1595年に開校した。これは中等教育学校である[6]。同様に、聖ヨセフ・

カレッジが 1601 年に開校した。

　17 世紀終わりから 18 世紀初頭にかけて、学校の設立はゆっくりではあるが着実に進んでいった。オーストリア人イエズス会員アンドレアス・マンカーが友人にあてた手紙には、ヴィサヤ諸島イエズス会が活動している地区では、典型的特徴として男子校と女子校が 1 校ずつあることだと記されている[7]。イエズス会員で歴史学者のペドロ・ムリーリョ・ベラルデは、1616 年から 1716 年にかけて、イエズス会の小教区には 14 歳までの男子と女子の学校があることが典型的だと述べた。1743 年、イエズス会は主にヴィサヤ諸島内の 134 の町で活動していた。

　1752 年、スペイン植民地政府は学校教師の給与を公的予算から支払うよう命じた。1752 年から 1863 年の間、小学校教員の給与は政府から支払われるのが一般的であったが、学校の運営や土地・設備の確保は地域の小教区に一任されていた。しかし 1863 年前後の政府財政の不安定化により、学校の運営に必要な費用は事実上管区の負担となっていた。

　19 世紀初めの 10 年のフィリピン社会に関する研究者は、町には必ず基本的な初等教育学校があったと述べている。1930～60 年代には、学校はさらに広まっていたが授業への出席率は低いとの報告がある。しかしそのような不完全な点はさておき、大変高い評価も時には見られる。例えばフランス人のジャン・バプティスト・マラーは島を 3 度訪れた後、「どこに行っても人々が支えている小学校があり、タガログ人のほとんど全員が読み書きができる」と述べている[8]。

　19 世紀中頃までには、宗教・読み書き・算数・歌唱を教える小学校が 600 の町や村にあったことはほぼ間違いない。フランス人旅行家ジャン・バプティスト・マラーは「インディオ（現地の人）の教育水準はヨーロッパの大衆と比べて少しも引けを取らない」との評価を下している[9]。

　小学校の普及は、適切だと思われる所にはどこにでも学校を創設するという修道会の方針によるものだった。イエズス会以外の修道会も学校を創設した。1611 年、ドミニコ会が創設した学校はのちに王立・教皇庁立の聖トマス大学となった。1640 年にドミニコ会の指導下で創設されたスペイン人男児のための学校は、のちにレトランの聖ヨハネ・カレッジとなった。スペイン人女児のための寄宿学校も女子修道会によってマニラに開校された。1591 年開校の聖ポテンシアナ学院と 1632 年開校の聖イサベル学院である[10]。

19世紀半ばになって追放されたイエズス会員らが戻ってきた時には、国内の多くの地域に数多くの学校があった。その中には長い歴史をもつものもあり、高い水準の学校もあった。

アテネオ・デ・マニラ大学の歩み

■ 1859〜1959年

学校は偶然が積み重なって設立されたが、私たちはそれが神の摂理であったと深く信じている。

1767年、イエズス会の創設から227年ほど経ったころ、スペインのカルロス3世がすべてのスペイン領からイエズス会員を追放すると布告した。それに伴い、翌年その政令がフィリピンにもたらされた時、イエズス会員らは逮捕され、所有物も没収された。

1773年、教皇クレメンス14世は世界中のイエズス会を禁止した。教皇の動きにより政変や弾圧が引き続いて起こった。

1880年には、イエズス会はスペイン国で再び公認された。1852年、ある政変の直後、女王イサベル2世はイエズス会スペイン管区に対し、フィリピンに戻ってミンダナオとスルでの宣教を再開するよう命じた。

1859年2月4日、ホセ・クエバス神父を筆頭に、6名の司祭と4名のブラザーが乗った船がカディエスから出航した。一行は4月14日にマニラに上陸した。イエズス会員が到着してまもなく、マニラ市議会は政府が助成している男子小学校であったエスクエラ・ピアを運営するよう要請した。クエバス神父は当初これを断った。しかし市長は、クエバス神父が、ミンダナオ行きを指示した本国政府の命に反したことの責任を持つことにより、彼を説得することに成功した。

1859年12月10日、校長のドン・ロレンソ・モレノ・コンデは正式に、新しいイエズス会員の教員に学校の運営を委ねた。学校はエスクエラ・ムニシパル、すなわち市立学校という新しい名称になった[11]。

1862年には、マニラの市議会が学校を昇格させて中等教育課程を含めることを提案した。これは1865年に実現した。まもなく、商学、地形測量、産業機械学といった職業訓練課程が創設された。学校がアテネオ・ムニシパル・デ・マニラと改名されたのはこの時であった。

エスクエラ・ムニシパルはもともとスペイン人男子のために創設されたが、

イエズス会は当初からフィリピン人も学校に通えるようにした。19世紀末には、生徒の9割が現地人の子どもかメスティーソ（現地人とスペイン人の間の子ども）であった。

　1865年、アテネオ・ムニシパル・デ・マニラで教鞭をとっていたフランシスコ・コリナとハイメ・ノネルという2人のイエズス会員の学者が、当時町の近くを通過した台風に関する考察を地元紙に発表した。自分たちで組み立てた気象測定器を使用して台風の接近と通過進路を事前に予測することで、生命と財産を守れるということを示したのである。実業界はこの技術の利便性を即座に認め、イタリア人イエズス会員のアンジェロ・セッチネ神父が設計した連続気象記録計の購入を手配した[12]。記録計が届くと、科学に興味をもっていたイエズス会員フェデリコ・ファウラ研究員の手によって組立てと操作が行われた。マニラ観測所と呼ばれる気象観測所が設置された。観測所が初めての台風警報を発令したのは1879年のことである。

　1884年、スペイン政府は観測所を公的機関とし、列島に補助観測所を点在させてネットワークの構築をはかった。地震観測中継所が1880年に加えられ、磁気部門が1887年、そして1899年には天文学部門が加わった。

　文学士の学位が初めて授与されたのは、1870年に10人の学生が5年制の高校と大学の合同課程を修めた時である。この過程はのちに6年制となり、1921年には8年制に延長された。当時は高校と大学の区別が現在ほどはっきりしていなかったのである[13]。

　1898年、アメリカがスペインに代わって植民地支配者となった。アメリカ植民地政府はマニラ観測所を政府機関として維持することを決定したが、学校への政府助成金は取りやめられた。その結果、アテネオ・ムニシパル・デ・マニラは私立学校となり、その位置づけになったことを示して、名称をアテネオ・デ・マニラと改称した。

　1908年、アテネオ・デ・マニラは文学士の学位および商学・速記・電気工学・地形測量の資格を授与する権限を得た。

　教育手段として英語が徐々にスペイン語にとって代わり、イエズス会の基本的理念や教授法を犠牲にすることなく、アメリカの公立学校の教育システムへの適応が進んだ。

　1914年には、学校は3つの課程に再編成された。3年間の初等教育課程、6年間かけて人文主義および科学を学ぶ高等専門学校、そして商学・測量学・

機械学と電気学の授業を学ぶ応用課程である。選択科目には絵画・音楽・地形測量学・タイプライティングと体操があった。

やがて社会環境の変化により、学問の再編だけでなくアメリカ人の教師が必要とされていることが明らかになった。1921 年にメリーランド・ニューヨーク管区のイエズス会員がアテネオ・デ・マニラで教えるために派遣された。アメリカ支配下で、文学士課程は 4 年に延長され、組織的な体育の授業が導入され、また課外活動、特に社会的要素をもつものが重要視されるようになった。後者の例を挙げると、チェストン・エヴィデンス・ギルド（Cheston Evidence Guild）のほか、講義・ディベート・議論・ラジオ番組を通して時代の抱える問題へのカトリックからの解決策を模索するカトリック・ラジオアワーなどである。

1932 年 8 月 13 日、火災で校舎が全焼し、アテネオ・デ・マニラは市壁の中から外へと場所を移した。

しかし火災にもめげることなく、学校は強靭さと活力を見せた。ヴィサヤ諸島の砂糖農場者らの度重なる要請に応えて 1925 年にスタートした製糖技術の課程は、産業技術の学科として枝分かれした。まもなく法科大学院と商学科大学および大学院が創設された。第二次世界大戦が勃発した時、アテネオ・デ・マニラは大学昇格に向けての道を順調に歩んでいた。母国のために戦ったアテネオの学生と卒業生は尊い英雄としてたたえられている。1945 年 7 月、戦争が終結すると借地で高校の授業が再開された。翌年学校は市街の城壁の外側、もともと学校の建物があった瓦礫の上に建てられた仮設教室に移った。1952 年、法科大学院と他の大学院を除いて、アテネオ・デ・マニラは現在のメインキャンパスであるケソン市のロヨラ・ハイツに拠点を移した。

■ 1959～2013 年

1959 年 12 月、100 年目にしてようやくアテネオ・デ・マニラは大学としての地位を与えられた。

公立学校として開校されたことを強く意識して、大学は常に社会的目的のために存在していると考えてきた。国民的英雄であるホセ・リサルが卒業生であることを学生に思い起こさせている。

1960 年代から 70 年代にかけて、社会運動に携わる市民が社会の根本的改革を求めた時で、多くのアテネオの学生と教職員は持たざる者への正義を模索す

る愛国運動に関わった。地域文化のより正しい認識と、大学運営におけるフィリピン人の指導的役割を強めることが目的であった。1970年代と80年代には、アテネオの学生・教職員と卒業生はフェルディナンド・マルコスが展開した戒厳令政への反対運動に深く関わった。その時代には大きな政策転換が行われ、女性も大学に進学できるようになった。近年では、大学は2つの格差をなくすことを主眼に置いて自らのミッションとアイデンティティを構築してきた。その2つの格差とは、フィリピン社会における貧富の差と、より多くの定員と資金をもつ海外の大学とアテネオとの格差である。

　このような意識はアテネオ医学・公衆衛生学部の設立にも通じている。

　現在およそ1万2000人の学生が8学部で学んでいる。人文学部、社会科学部、経営学部、理工学部、法学部、ビジネス学部、政治学部、医学・公衆衛生学部である。

　健康は人生における大切な要素であるため、医学部開設の提案は長きにわたって出されていたが、強い反対に会い続けた。国内にはすでに多くの医学部が存在していたため、理事たちは新たな医学部は無用であると考えたのである。

　しかし、特別な種類の医者を訓練する学部の設置が提案されると、反対派は提案を熱烈に支持する声に折れた。卒業生は熟達した技術と個人の健康のニーズに応えるいつくしみの心をあわせ持つ優れた臨床医であること、臨床医がその技術を発揮できるようシステムと資源を総合的に動員することのできる専門性をもつ大胆な指導者であること、病気と貧困の組織的問題を解決し、質の高い保健医療が万人にゆきわたるよう社会的な働きをする人物であることが求められる。

　2007年の創設から、この学部は優れた臨床医を輩出し続けることと、健康とは何か、また発展途上国内でどのように医療をゆきわたらせられるかを再定義するリーダーシップをとる役割があると考えてきた。興味深いのは、この学部の学生は医学博士MDと経営学修士MBAの2つの学位を取得して修了することである。

　医学・公衆衛生学部の他にも、アテネオのミッションとアイデンティティを特徴づける多くの方針や決定がある。例えば、授業料として徴収した収入の15％を自動的に奨学金に充てることなどである。

第1部　アジア5大学からの報告と展望

■2013年以降

　大学は今後どのような方向性を求め、どのような問題や新分野に焦点とエネルギーを傾注していくつもりであろうか？

　それは、イエズス会総長アドルフォ・ニコラス神父が述べた今日のイエズス会高等教育における課題に関連している。総長は３つの異なった、しかし互いに関連する課題を挙げた。1）思考力と想像力を深めさせること。2）イエズス会高等教育（の分野）における「普遍性」を再発見し適用すること。3）高等教育司牧へのイエズス会のコミットメントを新たにすること[14]。

　さらに関連しているのは３つのポイント、すなわちa）使命と特色、b）国家建設、c）環境と発展に中心をおいた大学の戦略計画である。

　2010年に行われたイエズス会大学に向けての講演の中で、アドルフォ・ニコラスイエズス会総長は急激に拡大する世界の相互連鎖について、世界とイエズス会の高等教育における使命を理解するための新たなコンテクストとしてとらえた。

　彼は学生たちが自らの望みを叶え、スキルを磨き、また真理に関わっていく決意をかため、そして最も深い真理に入っていくことができるようにイエズス会大学を奨励した。その始点というのはいつも、感覚ですぐに感じ取ることができるものである。しかし学生はその先へ、つまり見聞きし、さわり、香りをかぎ、感じることができる神の隠れた存在と業へと導かれなければならない。真理の深みや、現実世界での神の働きとの出会いの経験は、学生の人格の深い部分を変える力強い可能性を秘めている。

　これに関して、ニコラス総長はイエズス会大学に次のように問いかけた。「われわれの学校を卒業する人のうちどれほどが、専門的能力と同時に、大学在学中に自分の最も深い部分が変えられていくという現実との深い関わりをもつ経験をしているだろうか？　ただ単に優秀で能力のある希薄な人間を世界に輩出するだけではないということを確実にするために、イエズス会大学はさらに何をしていくべきだろうか。」

　アテネオ・デ・マニラ大学にとって、この問いかけは挑戦でもあり手痛い指摘でもある。というのは、目標を達成できなかったことも数知れず、またイグナチオ的意味で深まりのある目標を意識しないまま冒険を続けてしまったことも同様に何度もあるからである。

　しかしそれでも、大学の構造は、学生の知識と人格を育てることができるよ

うデザインされている。例を挙げると、リベラルアーツの重点的プログラムや、学部生全員が専攻に関係なく学ぶ勉強とは直接関係のない人格形成プログラムである。

　現在のアテネオ戦略計画の10の目標のうちの1つは、イグナチオ的な霊的形成を強化することである。これはつまり、イグナチオの霊性を強調し、知的活動、異文化との対話、困っている人への援助、環境への責任を駆り立てる原動力にするということである。これは全人的育成にほかならない。

　思考力と想像力の深みを促進することに加え、ニコラス神父はイエズス会大学が社会に入り込み、専門家を養成するだけでなく、真実・徳・発展・平和を社会の中で訴え実現していく文化的な力となるよう願った。彼は大学を社会的プロジェクトととらえている。

　アテネオ戦略計画では国家建設に主眼が置かれている。これはつまり、大学は変革の触媒となり、戦略的思想家を育み、文化形成を推進することであり、社会変革に貢献するということである。変革を推進する人は、社会変革に携わる集団を動員し集約を促進する。戦略的思想家としては、貧困やその他の社会的悪を永続させる原因である複雑で文化結合的な、さらに非線形のメカニズムの解決に必要とされる高度な思考に精力を注ぐ。また文化形成者としてはさらに国を理解し、大事にする心を生み出す。

　環境と開発は大学戦略計画のもう1つの柱である。従来のように環境資源を使い続けることを前提とした開発モデルのリスクを評価・管理する方法の発案と、持続可能な開発への代替的方法の設計図を作成し、そしてそれを地域的に学内で適用するという課題が挙げられている。最近アテネオ・インスティテュート・オブ・サステイナビリティ（アテネオ持続可能性研究所）を設立した。

　ニコラス総長はさらに、イグナチオ的遺産に忠実であるためには、大学における研究は常に「高等教育司牧」の意味合いで理解される必要があると示唆した。この意味するところは、質の高い研究を求めるだけでなく、研究が神の国と人類への奉仕となるように方向づけを行うということである。

　ニコラス神父は、知識に手が届くかどうかによって人格・文化・社会の発展が著しく左右される「知識社会」の到来を認識している。グローバル化は知識とその恩恵にあずかることができるかどうかにより新たな格差を生み出した。イエズス会大学に対し、知識格差に向き合い、誰のための知識を生み出しているのか、また誰がその知識を手に入れることができるかを明確にすることを求

めた。アテネオ戦略計画はこの課題にも言及しているが、前途に広がる膨大な課題に今後も投資していかなければならない。

総長はイエズス会大学についての考察を、イエズス会員に対する次の質問で締めくくった。「もしイグナチオとその最初の同志たちがイエズス会を今日また創始するとしたら、彼らはミニストリーの一環としてやはり大学教育に関わり続けるだろうか？」

総長はこの答えは次のような関連した質問を投げかけることで見つかるかもしれないと言う。「教会と私たちの世界のニーズは何か、私たちが最も必要とされているのはどこか。そして、どこで、いかにすれば最善の奉仕ができるか。」

同じ調子で、彼はもう1つ質問を重ねた。「われわれが今日の世界で再びイエズス会を創設するとしたら、どのような大学を、何に重点を置いて、どのような方向性をもって運営していくか？」

アテネオ・デ・マニラ大学は今後も、ミッションとアイデンティティの問題について組織を挙げて精力的に取り組んでいかなければならない。そのための財源もいくらかあり、現代においてイエズス会大学であるとはどういうことかを識別する大いなる決意をもっている。

フィリピンにおける教育と、その中でカトリック教会が果たしてきた重要な役割は長く、多彩な歴史がある。これは歴史的な意味合いだけでなく、今日でも教会が教育と学問研究活動によって社会の発展に貢献しているということにほかならない。アテネオ・デ・マニラ大学は1859年の学校創立当初から、その歴史の範例となっている。

1万2000名の学生数という比較的小さな規模と、54年間という浅い歴史にもかかわらず、アテネオ・デ・マニラ大学は大変強い影響力を発揮している。卒業生のなかには国の現在の大統領、最高裁長官、下院議長、マニラ大司教、産業界・政府・非政府組織やその他多くの分野のトップリーダーがいる。

これが誇りと喜びの源となっていることはもちろんである。しかしわれわれは常に、真のイエズス会大学・カトリック大学であり続けるためにはいかにすべきかを自問し続けている。

注

1 フィリピンにおける教育についての調査には以下のものがある。Encarnacion Alzona, *A History of Education in the Philippines 1565-1930*, Quezon City: University of the Philippines Press, 1932; Evergisto Bazaco OP, *History of Education in the Philippines*, Manila: University of Santo Tomas Press, 1939.
2 John N. Schumacher SJ, *Readings in Philippine Church History*, Quezon City: Loyola School of Theology, Ateneo de Manila University, 1979, pp. 141-152.
3 Thomas B. Cannon SJ, "History of the Jesuits in the Philippines," *The Woodstock Letters* 65, no. 3.
4 Henry Frederick Fox, "Primary Education in the Philippines, 1565-1886," *Philippine Studies* 13, no. 2, 1965, 207-231.
5 Horacio de la Costa SJ, *Readings in Philippine History*, Manila: Bookmark 1965, p. 75.
6 William Charles Repetti SJ, *The Beginning of Jesuit Education in the Philippines*, Manila: Manila Observatory, 1940.
7 Fox, p. 222.
8 Jean Mallat, *Les Philippines*, Paris: A. Bertrand, 1846, II.
9 同上、p. 246.
10 参照：Fidel Villaroel OP, *A History of the University of Santo Tomas: Four Centuries of Higher Education in the Philipines, 1611-2011*, Manila: University of Santo Tomas Publishing House, 2012.
11 Jose Arcilla SJ, "The Escuela Pia, Forerunner of the Ateneo de Manila," *Philippine Studies* 31, no 1, 1983, 58-74. In addition to schools for the youth, the Jesuits also established a school to train teachers. See James J. Meany, "Escuela Normal de Maestros," *Philippine Studies* 30, no 4, and Arcilla, Jose S. SJ, "La Escuela Normal de Maestros de Instruccion Primaria, 1885-1905," *Philippine Studies* 36, no. 1, 1988, 16-35.
12 John N. Schumacher, "One Hundred Years of Jesuit Scientists: The Manila Observatory 1865-1965," *Philippine Studies* 13, no. 2, 1965, 258-286.
13 James J. Meany, "Ateneo," *Philippine Studies* 4, no 2, 1956, 167-171. このセクションにはリベラルアーツが1つの学問分野として成り立つのか、という議論が含まれている。
14 Adolfo Nicolás SJ, "Challenges to Jesuit Higher Education Today" remarks made for the conference "Networking Jesuit Higher Education: Shaping the Future for a Humane, Just Sustainable Globe" held in Mexico City on April 23, 2010.

日本近代社会における
カトリック・アイデンティティとカトリック教育

川村　信三
〈上智大学〉

はじめに

日本におけるカトリック教会の歴史は、16世紀のフランシスコ・ザビエルをはじめとするイエズス会宣教に遡る。この100年に満たない宣教の歴史は、宣教師たちがヨーロッパに送り届けた報告書簡によって世界中のカトリック信者に知られ、「宣教への情熱」を呼び起こすために多大な役割を果たした。その宣教時代も江戸幕府による禁教令によって250年以上もの弾圧と迫害の歴史を経て、19世紀の新しい宣教時代を迎えた。

本稿は、日本が開国し、近代国家の仲間入りを果たした明治期以後のカトリック教会のアイデンティティとその教育について歴史学的な解釈を試みるものである。

考察の方法

カトリック教会とその教育について、アメリカ合衆国社会との関連のコンテキストで考察したロバート・T．オゴーマンの図式（Format）を用いることとする。宗教教育を専門とするオゴーマンは、1790年から現代までのアメリカ合衆国におけるカトリックの歴史を3つの段階に区分し、それぞれの時代に次のフォーマットを当てはめ考察した[1]。

アメリカ合衆国のカトリック史の第1期（1790～1920年）は、「米国文化と対峙した（against culture）時代」と位置づけられた。この第1期はカトリック教会がWASP（ホワイト・アングロサクソン・プロテスタント）社会からの差別や迫害にさらされ、ゲットー的な様相を呈した時期である。第2期（1920～1960年）は「米国文化を超越した（above culture）時代」とし、米国社会へのカトリックの影響を高めようと燃えた時期だったとされた。第3期（1960

ロバート・オゴーマンの図式 (Format)

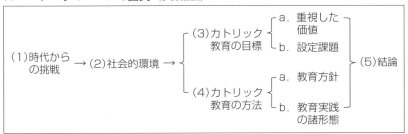

年〜現在）は、「米国文化の真っただ中に（in the culture）『パン種』として入り込んだ時代」であった。すなわち、米国社会と文化を内側から支えたり、預言的批判を加えたりする時期であったとしている。そうした時代区分を明確に設定したうえで、上記のフォーマットが各時代に当てはめられていく。

各時代の考察は、いくつかの問いの形となって分析は続く。

1）時代からの挑戦（Challenges）。その時代、カトリック・アイデンティティに問い直しや再構築を迫るものが何であったかの問い。

2）社会的環境（Social Environment）では、その挑戦の背後にあって、時の教育目標や教育方法に影響を及ぼした文化・経済・政治・社会的要因は何であったかの問い。

3）カトリック教育の目標（Ends）の見定め。その際、重視した価値（Values）、すなわちそうした社会的環境の中で教会が何を重視して時代の課題に対応したのか。設定課題（Tasks）では、この評価に基づいて、その時代のカトリックのアイデンティティを保持するために設定された、教会として解決を要する課題は何であったのかが問われる。

4）方法（Means）としてどのようなものが実施されたか。ここでも、教育方針（Policies）として、これらの課題を解決していくためにとられた時代の政策は何であったか、そして教育実践の諸形態（Structures）として、その政策が実現するために用いられたカトリック教育の具体的形態や方法、そして内容がどのようなものであったかが問われる[2]。

オゴーマンの分析は、あくまでアメリカ合衆国の歴史考察のためであった。しかし、各項目の質問は、世界のいかなる地域においても、あらためて問いただされるべき課題をうまくまとめている。特に、世俗化傾向を顕著に示す社会の中にあって、伝統的なカトリック教会はどのような対応を迫られたのかを分

析するためには大きな手助けとなる。そのうえで、社会の中のカトリック教会の考察を軸足として、様々な出来事を取り上げ考察することが重要である。それゆえ、このフォーマットは日本の近代カトリック史を整理するうえでも有効であろう。オゴーマンのフォーマットに従って、明治開国期の日本国家とカトリック教会の関係性、カトリック内部のアイデンティティの変化、そして総合的に結論づけることのできるカトリック教育の方向性を明らかにしていきたい。

近代日本の中のカトリック史の3つの時代

近代日本カトリック史は、日米和親条約の締結による江戸幕府の開国（1854年）から現在に至るまで、3つの段階がそれぞれ明確な特徴をもって区別される。

第1期（1854～1890年）社会とは別に──個人の魂の救いを草の根的努力
　　　　　　　　　　　　　　　によって実現した時代
第2期（1890～1945年）社会に近づく──国粋主義と偏見の間で生きた時代
第3期（1945年～現在）社会の中で──独自の地位を構築する時代

第1期は、江戸幕府の治世も終盤の1844年、パリ外国宣教会のテオドール・オグスティン・フォルカード[3]神父が琉球に到り、開国直前の日本入国を試みた年をはじめとする。米国人ペリー艦隊が浦賀に来航した翌年の1854年、江戸幕府は「日米和親条約」の締結によって250年の「鎖国」政策を取り下げ開国した。1859年、「安政の五ヵ国条約」により長崎や横浜などが開港した際、パリ外国宣教会の宣教師が各港に入った。その前年の1858年には日仏修好条約によりフランス人居留地内で信教の自由が認められていた。以後、明治期の日本カトリックはパリ外国宣教会司祭の独占状態となった。この時期の主な特徴は、再来日を果たしたカトリック教会が、社会の大勢とは別に、自らのカトリックとしてのアイデンティティを貫こうとしたことである。日本社会とカトリック教会はまだ接触を始めたばかりで、大きく相互に関連づけられてはいなかった。

第2期は1890年に始まる、それまでの宣教方針をあらためて見直す時期である。この年は、現代日本カトリック史上の「分水嶺」とされる。日本社会の側から見れば、開国当時に締結された不平等条約の改正が実現する時期である。また、大日本帝国憲法が発布され、近代国家としての体裁が整った。さらに、

明治政府の富国強兵の国造りが日清、日露両戦争の戦勝（1894年および1905年）への頂点に達するまで勢いづく。カトリック教会側の視点からすれば、1870年から71年に開催された第一ヴァチカン公会議の理念を具体的に日本に適用するための模索の時期であった。この公会議は、「ローマ中心主義」、「聖職者中心主義」的な決議をなし、それを世界中の「地方教会」に広げようとしていた。第1期で形成された「天皇と国家神道を中心とする国造り」とカトリシズムは、この時期の後半期、すなわち1930年代に最も重大な対立図式を示す。

第3期は、1945年の敗戦によって「天皇と国家神道を中心とする国家造り」が終焉した時期である。これまでの対立的な関係から、日本社会とカトリック教会は相互補完とでもいえるような良好な関係を築く好機を迎えた。そうした社会の中、復興日本とともに、民主化の潮流に乗り、諸外国からの援助を受けつつカトリック教会が進展を遂げる。アメリカ合衆国をはじめとする連合国の占領や冷戦構造の中、民主主義国家の建設に、キリスト者への期待が高まっていた。民主化、国際化の波は外国からの人と物の交流を可能とするカトリックにとって追い風となり、社会から歓迎される気運が高まった。カトリック教会は多くの外国人宣教師や修道者の来日を得て活気づく。その時期にカトリック教会や教育の面で大きな変化を示した。

現在の日本におけるカトリック信徒数は、日本の総人口の0.3％、すなわち40万人を前後して推移している。プロテスタント教会の総信徒数を合わせても1％に満たないキリスト者数は、実際は日本社会においてマイノリティーと呼びうる程度の数字である。しかし、数的な現実とは別に、キリスト教が社会に与えた「質的」な影響力という点で、キリスト教学校、そしてカトリックのミッション校が提供した学校教育の果たした役割は決して小さくない。それは、言い換えれば、キリスト教徒（カトリック信徒）は数的には増加しないものの、信者とはならないが、カトリック教育によって育てられた日本人は極めて多く、教会が一般日本人に与えた影響力は無視できないということである。日本人は、宗教としてのカトリックを受け入れたがらない。すなわち洗礼を受けることはしないが、「一流校」を生み出すカトリック学校のシステムには共感するという現実があった。

以上の3つの時期に、それぞれオゴーマンが示した図式を用いて、詳細に検討していくこととする。カトリック教会はどのような社会にいたのか。社会からどのような挑戦を受けたのか。それに対応するため、どのような方法や手段

をとったのかを見ていきたい。

I　第1期（1854～1890年）の考察——邪宗門の末裔　敵対的雰囲気の中の「魂の救い」と「信徒集団の育成」

I−1　第1期に特徴的な時代からの挑戦
キリスト教「邪教」観の継続と増幅

　日本のキリスト教会が、1549年から約100年の宣教期を経て、禁教、迫害、潜伏の時代を過ごしたことは重要な前提である。明治開国以後のカトリックの再宣教はこの前提をおおいに模範にしようとしている。

　イエズス会の宣教師たちのミッション地として、さらにフランシスコ会、ドミニコ会、アウグスチノ会の諸修道会も加わった、いわゆる「キリシタンの世紀」は、最盛期で50万の信徒を数え、禁教令発布前後に少なくとも4万人以上の殉教者を生み出す歴史を刻んでいる。

　江戸幕府が250年間、キリスト教に「邪教」の烙印を与えつづけたため、日本人にとってキリスト教は受け入れがたい悪として印象づけられた。したがって、キリスト教は、日本の近代国家としての出発期、すなわち明治開国期にあって、ゼロからどころか、マイナスの領域から出発せざるを得ない状況であった。キリスト教への嫌悪、軽蔑、忌避感はどのように払拭されるのかが第一の課題であったといえよう。

　キリスト教への偏見と嫌悪の情は、遠い過去のキリシタン時代の記憶にとどまらない。明治政府も同様にそのイメージを保持しようと懸命であった。邪宗門としてのキリスト教敵視は引き続いた。邪宗門としての迫害は終わったが、敵視が強まる段階が続く。すでに、幕末において、仏教や民間宗教に対する恐れが広がっていた。その反動として、水戸学や復古神道などから仏教への批判が相次ぎ、神国論が説かれ、神道の祭祀による人心掌握の機運が高まった。こうした流れは、明治政府に受け継がれた。1867年の長崎浦上信徒の検挙、捕縛および流刑（浦上四番崩れ）は、明治政府が江戸幕府の方針をまったく変えなかったことのしるしである。また、1869年の「五榜の掲示」（国家の運営方針を5箇条にまとめたもの）では、キリシタン禁制の継続が謳われている[4]。1873年、「信教の自由」を近代国家の絶対条件として掲げていた欧米諸外国の圧力に押され、明治政府は江戸幕府の高札を撤去した。これは一般にキリシタ

ン禁制の撤回と誤解されているが、実はそうではなかった。政府は「信教の自由」を受け入れる姿勢を示したが、キリスト教信仰者の増加を容認する気は毛頭なかったのである。

Ⅰ-2　第1期に特徴的な社会的環境
天皇および神道中心の国家政策

　明治政府は、欧米諸外国からの文物の流入が避けられない状況であることを直視した。政府は欧米の文物をキリスト教と切り離して積極的に取り入れる方針をとったが、同時に流入してくるキリスト教の国内における影響増大は避けられないと考えた。そこで、日本人民衆に対し、思想的にキリスト教に対抗できるような何らかの信念体系を植え付ける必要性を認めた。それゆえ導入されたのが、「神道中心の宗教政策」である。

　1872年、明治政府は仏教の教化能力に期待し、キリスト教「防禦」のための運動として、三教（神道・儒教・仏教）合同の大教宣布運動を開始した。キリスト教信仰は、キリシタン禁制を宗教政策の柱としていた江戸幕府のもとで完全に私事化されていた。しかし、「天皇と神道を中心とした国家」を建設したい明治政府を脅かす危険な存在として再登場した。ここに、キリスト教と「天皇の権威を基盤とした国家神道が公的宗教化した近代日本国家」の対立図式が明確に示された。両者の緊張関係は1945年まで形を変えながら継続する。つまり、明治新政府は、国是としての国家神道を基盤に国造りを行い、キリスト教の外国的要素（精神的・内的影響）を排除しようとした。神道の強調は、裏を返せば、政府がキリスト教信仰のもつ人心掌握の潜在的な能力を認めていた結果であり、外来のキリスト教が新たな民衆秩序構築への妨げとなるとの危機感の現れでもあった。

Ⅰ-3　第1期のカトリック教育の目標
個人的な「魂の救い」への参与および社会の底辺層の信徒育成

　ある研究者の指摘によれば、明治初期のカトリックは、社会一般への関心が希薄であったという[5]。同時期に日本で宣教を始めたプロテスタント教会のような、新生日本社会に強くコミットメントしようとする姿勢を、カトリックは示さないという特徴がみられた。青年たちを、高等教育を通じてキリスト教化していこうとしたプロテスタントとの違いは歴然であった。この時期、カトリッ

ク教会、特にその指導的立場にあったパリ外国宣教会の宣教師によって重視された価値は、人びとの「魂の救い」（help of souls）である。それは慈善活動と結びつく初等学校教育や、個人や家族を対象とした「信徒集団の育成」へと道を開いた。

　フランス革命を経験したヨーロッパのカトリック世界は、19世紀の半ばには、教皇自らが旗手となって「反自由主義」「反近代主義」の態度を硬化させた時代にあった。1864年に教皇ピウス9世によって出された『シラブス』（近代主義の誤謬表）はその対決姿勢に満ちあふれた文書として有名である[6]。教会トップとしての教皇自身や教皇庁に近代社会への敵対的姿勢が貫かれた時代であった。その傘下にある司祭、修道者、信徒らはその姿勢を当然のごとく自身の日常生活へも反映させていた。社会変革ではなく、隣人の救いに向かったカトリックは内面的で個別的な信仰活動を重視した。特に、開国期に日本宣教に携わったパリ外国宣教会のフランス人司祭たちは、時代固有のこだわりを有している。すなわち、革命でカトリック教会が壊滅的危機に直面したフランスのカトリック教会には、「聖俗二元論」的な考え方が強く、世俗主義、合理主義、自由主義など当時の社会の動きを極度に警戒し、社会に対して自らを閉ざす方向に動いた。これはヨーロッパカトリック教会の一般的な傾向であった。明治のカトリック教会は、そのフランス教会に全面的に依存していた。

　カトリック信仰にとっての最も根本的な行動は、「目の前にいる人びとの救い」すなわち「魂の救い」であった。こうして、明治前期のカトリックの活動は、ほぼ例外なしに「慈善」的活動へと向かっていた（設定した課題）。教育の観点からすれば、第1期、カトリック教会は、孤児となっていた乳幼児などの世話に奔走したため、初等教育レベルの問題解決に集中し、パリ外国宣教会をはじめ、様々な活動の中で、中高等教育はほとんど考慮されなかった。

　キリスト教には、初代教会以来の「隣人愛」とその実践を促す「慈悲の業」の思想が根強くあった。マタイ福音書25章における「最後の審判」の場面で、善人とされるのは、「最も小さな人（貧しい人）」を隣人として受け入れた人びとであった。これがカトリックの伝統的愛徳の聖書的根拠である。ヨーロッパの中世を通じて、ハンセン病者、旅人、孤児を手厚く保護することはキリスト教の最高の徳とされた。13世紀以後になると、「兄弟団」（confraternitas）と呼ばれる信徒集団がそうした活動の主な担い手となり、我が国でも盛んとなった「慈悲の組」（ミゼリコルヂア）の活動となって栄えた[7]。キリシタン時代

の教理書『どちりなきりしたん』においても「七つの慈悲の業」が丁寧に解説されている。「飢えたるものに食を与え、渇したるものに飲ませ、旅人に宿を貸し、裸のものに着せ、病人を見舞い、牢獄の人をたずねてなぐさめる」。これがキリスト教カトリックの「慈悲の業」の基本として大切にされた。こうした伝統が、カトリックの実際の慈善活動として途絶えることはなかった。フランス革命において絶体絶命の危機においやられたカトリック教会の中で、特に19世紀に創設された数々のフランス系女子修道会にはその精神が特別に生き残った。その人びとが来日するやいなや、具体的に設定した目標は、今日私たちが目にするカトリック・ミッション校の姿ではない。当初の目標は、日本の開国期における「最も小さな人」と思われる孤児やハンセン病者を対象とする「魂の救い」だったのである。

Ⅰ-4　第1期のカトリック教育の方法

「慈善活動」（Philanthropic activities）と結びついた「初等教育」

　インドのコルカタで活動したマザーテレサは、自身とその姉妹たちの活動が「社会事業」と呼ばれることを好まなかった。路上で倒れた人びとを宗教に関係なく、その死まで看取る。「目の前に助けを必要としている人がいるかぎり手助けする」。一信仰者として当然のことを為したまでであるとマザーテレサは考えたのであろう。

　明治初期、総体的に日本人は貧しかった。この時期のカトリックの諸々の活動を見ていると、パリ外国宣教会の宣教師にせよ、それを手助けした日本人女性たちにしろ、その目指すところは、16世紀の「慈悲の組」（ミゼリコルヂア）のものであり、またマザーテレサのものと同じであった[8]。明治初期の日本といえば、近代国家の仲間入りをしたことが強調される希望に満ちた時代のように言われることが多い。しかし、日本各地では疫病が蔓延し、貧困者の群れが都市の周辺に集まる現実があった。長崎では、明治中頃までに、頻繁に蔓延する腸チフス、痘瘡、コレラ、赤痢などの疾病が人びとを苦しませた。横浜も状況は同じである。

　パリ外国宣教会は、外国人居留地の中に拠点をもつ傍ら、政府による外国人の行動制限（40km）の範囲いっぱいに行動した。いわゆる「歩く司祭」として、貧しさに喘ぎながら誕生したばかりの近代国家日本に足跡を残した。カトリックに限れば、1872年、長崎の大浦天主堂で創設されたフランス人神父による

養護施設である聖嬰会や、横浜のサン・モール修道女会[9]の「仁慈堂[10]」、1874年に岩永マキらによって長崎に始まる浦上養育院など、例外なく孤児や身寄りのない病者を世話する施設であった。

　なかでも、注目すべきは横浜のシスター山上カクと長崎の岩永マキという二人の女性の存在である。シスター山上カクは、プチジャン神父やジラール神父などの最初期のパリ外国宣教会神父の招聘を受け横浜に上陸したサン・モール修道会のシスター・マチルドの手助けをした、最初の邦人会員の一人であった。シスター・マチルドは横浜の山手3番地に多くの孤児を収容できる施設である「仁慈堂」を設立した。これは横浜最初の孤児院である。シスター・マチルドの助手であったシスター山上は横浜中を私服で歩き回り、貧者、病者を見舞い、捨て子を集め、戸籍のない子を自分の戸籍に入れ山上姓として世に送り出した。漢方を調合し、ハンセン病者を発見しては修道院の小屋に収容し食事を運んだ。彼女の生涯で洗礼に導いた者は568人、世話した孤児は3,600人に及んだ。山手の仁慈堂は1897年には482人の孤児を収容し、横浜の人びとから「尼寺の孤児院」と呼ばれて親しまれた。1902年5月に発布された「私立学校令」により、孤児救済事業は、小学校に類する各種学校の扱いを受け、「仁慈堂」は「菫女学校」と改称した。関東大震災で施設は大きな打撃を受け、1924年、「菫女学校」は財団法人の管轄となり、50年におよぶ「仁慈堂」の流れはここに消滅した。

　長崎では、横浜のシスター山上と同様の活動が、信徒の岩永マキの手によって始められた。浦上四番崩れの際、追放された岡山藩鶴島の流刑地で過ごした岩永は、帰還後の長崎でパリ外国宣教会ド・ロ神父（De Rots）の指導を受けながら、本原で幼児教育を始める。当時の長崎は台風による災害や疾病による死者の多さから、多くの孤児を生み出していた。ド・ロ神父の指導の下、信徒の高木仙右衛門は、自分の家屋、土地一切を岩永らが創設した「十字会」に寄付した。岩永マキをリーダーとする女性たちの「十字会」（通称「女部屋」）は、修道会の三誓願はたてないが、同じ精神で生きようとする信徒の会であった。ここで最も重要視されたのは、やはり16世紀に長崎で活動した「長崎ミゼリコルヂア」の伝統であった。

　1877年には、フランス系修道女会の第二陣であるショファイユのサン・アンファン・ジェジュ（幼きイエズス会[11]）らが「神戸女子教育院」や「大阪養育院」（1879年）などを設立した。これらはやはり乳幼児養育のための施設で

ある。1878 年には、シャルトル聖パウロ修道女会[12]が函館に上陸し「聖パウロ会暁の星園」を創設している。現在では、カトリック系女子中高等学校の運営で有名な諸修道会が、ほぼ例外なく、孤児の世話から出発している事実に注目したい。

　明治初期のカトリック教会は、学校という施設に関心をもったが、それは主として「孤児」たちの育成を助ける「初等学校」であった。この時、英雄的な活躍をしたシスター山上カクや岩永マキのような人びとは、決して学校という社会事業を創始したのではない。むしろ、彼女たちの姿勢は、「目の前の最も小さな人びと」に奉仕するというキリストの望みに一致したものであった。そうしたプロセスも、やがて初等学校が公立の小学校として政府の管理下に移されるにつれ、次第にその役割を終えていった。

　この時、カトリック教育にとって重大な変化が意識されていた。女子修道会は「小学校」経営を存続させるべく努力したが、日本社会におけるカトリック学校のイメージは貧者や孤児のための施設に密接に結びついていたということである。したがって、中・上流家庭はカトリック学校を敬遠したため、入学希望者の獲得が困難となった。初等教育のレベルで、カトリック学校は明治初期、次第にその数を増したが、1880 年以後は、生徒数、学校数ともに減少するか伸び悩んでいたことが統計上明らかに表れている[13]。1889 年以後、カトリック学校数および生徒数は増加しなかった（全国の小学校は 1873 年の段階で 24,000 校を数え現在とほぼ同数となっていた）。以下の数字には、小学校ばかりでなく孤児院や養育院も含まれている。その領域の区分は 1885 年の「小学校令」まで曖昧であった。

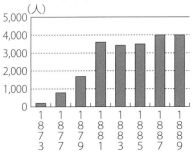

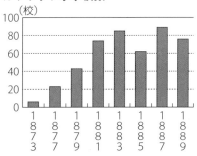

カトリック教会が貧しい人びとと結びつくイメージは、小学校のみではなかった。「目の前」の「魂の救い」を重視するカトリック教会の姿勢は、孤児ばかりでなく、他の分野でも発揮されたためである。パリ外国宣教会の神父たちは、明治初期、宗教センターを自ら作り、そこに人びとを集めるという方針を主にしたわけではなかった。むしろ、外国人の活動制限の範囲ぎりぎりまで歩きまわり、現地で出会った人びとの中に信仰共同体を根付かせた。明治中期までにそうした活動は、民家や人びとのあいだで育つ「カテキスタ」の協力を得ながら、ホーム・チャーチ方式として根付いていた。1889年、ジェルメン・レジェ・テストヴィド[14]神父によって創設された日本初のハンセン病院や、八王子の信徒共同体などはこのように誕生し維持された。

この時期の日本カトリックの特徴は、社会の底辺で苦しむ人びとに接触してはいたが、その人びとを生み出す社会そのものには触れていなかったことである。これをある人びとは、カトリック教会の「ゲットー化」という言葉で表す。しかし、「魂の救い」を優先したことはカトリック活動の正攻法であり、それ自体はおおいに誇りうることである。それがある時期に方向転換された事実にカトリック内の態度がみられ、今後議論されるべき点であろう。

II　第2期（1890〜1945年）の考察
——社会との接点を模索

1880年代の後半となり、「邪教」であり「非合法」としてのカトリック教会のイメージは影を潜めつつあった。しかし、社会の底辺層に結びついたカトリック教会のイメージは、引き続き日本社会一般から歓迎されないという状況を生んでいた。そうしたなか、1890年という年は、日本社会にとっても、カトリック教会にとっても、明治初期に始まった様々な事柄が新局面に移り変わる時、転換の時の始まる「分水嶺」と位置づけられる。

II−1　第2期に特徴的な時代からの挑戦
「教育勅語」および「文部省訓令一二号」

明治政府は、1887年頃まで欧化政策を推進していた。そのため、キリスト教はその恩恵を受けていた。欧化政策の推進者井上馨は同時に「条約改正」交渉を継続していた。しかし、交渉が行き詰まると、社会には次第に国粋主義的

な日本主義が広まり始め、結果的に反キリスト教の風潮が強まった。

1889年、大日本帝国憲法が発布された。この憲法は条件付きの「信教の自由」を認めた。しかし、神社神道は特別の地位を与えられ、他のあらゆる宗教から超越した立場となった。

1890年に発布された「教育勅語」は、天皇と臣民の密接な関係を教育現場で強化させ、天皇のために忠誠を尽くすのが臣民の根本的あり方であると規定した。すなわち、日本国の天皇支配を徹底したのである。これは「教育文書」というよりは、擬似宗教文書の役割を担うものであった。1887年の統計ではカトリック学校はすでに93校、生徒数4,780人を数える規模となっていた。もちろん、それはすべて初等・中等教育の分野である。1889年の「教育勅語」の発布後、カトリック学校の数は急激に減少した。1909年の統計では、カトリック学校は26校となった。

そして、カトリック学校教育にとっての最大の挑戦は文部省発令の「訓令一二号」[15]となって表明された。1899年、条約改正により、外国人居留地がなくなり、外国人の「内地雑居」[16]が始まった。時の文部省は、日本国内にキリスト教が広がることを懸念し、「訓令一二号」という法令を出した。それは、公立・私立を問わず、学校における宗教教育と儀式を禁止したものである。宗教教育を継続するならば、文部省認可の学校資格を剥奪するとした。その結果、高等学校への入学資格、徴兵猶予、官吏任用の受験資格などの特権を失うこととなるため、宗教教育を行う学校に入学志願者は集まらない。この措置は事実上、キリスト教学校の宗教的影響を排除しようとするものであり、プロテスタントおよびカトリックの学校にとっては大打撃となるものであった。

Ⅱ-2　第2期に特徴的な社会的環境

国粋主義と欧米列強との対等な関係構築の狭間で

第2期の社会的環境は、天皇と神社神道を中心とした国家造りが政府により強力に推進される時代である。また、日本社会が欧米列強により近代国家としての承認を受けることが優先された時期であった。したがって、国内的には国粋主義的な傾向をもつ一方、欧米諸外国に対しては常に肯定的な態度を保持する必要のある時代であった。日本におけるカトリック教会もそうした政府の二面性に翻弄された。

カトリック学校は宗教上の中立という道を選択した。1889年、日本最初の

男子カトリック学校として「暁星学園」がマリア会によって東京に創設された[17]。文部省の教育における国粋主義政策が出される直前のことである。ただし、全国のカトリック学校の生徒数は 5,520 人となり、若干の増加をみているため、多くの小規模な初等学校が統廃合され、より規模の大きな学校が創設されたことを示している。カトリック学校の宗教的中立の立場は、良くも悪くも成果をもたらしたといえる。

カトリック教会側の変化——第一ヴァチカン公会議理念の徹底

　この時期、カトリック教会に生じた最大の変化は、日本国内ではなく、海外からもたらされたものである。1869 年から翌年にかけて開催された第一ヴァチカン公会議による決議が、それまでの反自由主義、反近代主義的なカトリック教会のあり方をさらに強化した。そして、ローマ教皇を中心とする中央集権化、聖職者中心主義を世界に押し広げようとしていたことであった。

　第一ヴァチカン公会議の決議を受け、1879 年 6 月に、教皇庁布教聖省の教令が出され、宣教地ごとに地方教会会議の開催が要請された。すなわち、ローマ教会の中央集権化を地方教会に徹底させるための措置であった。これを受けて、日本のカトリック教会は、1890 年 3 月、長崎の大浦天主堂において地方教会会議を開催した。この会議は日本と朝鮮半島のカトリック教会との共催となり、日本の三司教と朝鮮半島の司教代理 1 名のほか、神学顧問として日本人宣教師 7 名が出席した。ラテン語で書かれた決議文は 93 年布教聖省に認可され、同年香港で出版された[18]。決議文の構成は以下のとおりである。

　　第一章：聖職者と神学生（De Clero et Seminariis）
　　第二章：修道者（De Religiosis et Sanctimonialibus）
　　第三章：伝道者（De Catechistis）
　　第四章：信徒（De Christianis）
　　第五章：求道者（De Catechumenis）
　　第六章：書籍（De Libris）
　　第七章：学校と孤児院（De Scholis et Orphanotrophiis）
　　第八章：信仰宣布の手段（De Mediis ad Fidem propagandam）
　　第九章：教会財産等のあり方（De bonis Ecclesiae temporalibus）（全九章）

長崎地方教会会議の決議を一瞥すると、この時期のカトリック教会がいかに社会に対し、唯我独尊的に硬化していったかがわかる。近代社会に対する閉鎖的な対決姿勢、ローマ教皇とその代理者である司教、司祭に対して信徒の従順などが強調された。これまでヨーロッパの枠内にとどまっていたカトリックの社会に対する対決姿勢が全世界に波及する。世界のカトリック教会が細かい法規によって画一化された。

　日本のカトリック教会においては、長崎教会会議以前には、外国人宣教師よりも日本人信徒のほうが有利な立場にあり、一般信徒の中には、自宅を信徒や求道者のための集会や祈りの場として提供する者がいた。「草の根的」な教会共同体が形成されていた。宣教師は主としてそうした自発的に集う信徒たちの共同体を巡回することで宣教活動を行っていた。しかし、この会議以後は、教会聖堂を中心とするカトリックのヒエラルキー制度が重要視された。そのため、日本のカトリック教会は、明治前期に実施していた「草の根的」、「水平的」な活動方針を変えて、「垂直的」、より「官僚的」な教会運営へ方向転換を余儀なくされた。

　この結果、カトリック教会において特に顕著な変化が、洗礼者数に表れた。会議後、洗礼準備の重要性が強調され、長期の準備期間が必要とされたので、これまで「カテキスタ」を中心に行われていた洗礼式が制限され、成人洗礼者数が減少した。統計は、宣教師一人につき成人改宗者数の減少を顕著に示している（下表）[19]。

　長崎教会会議は日本のカトリック教会の方針をも変えた。一般信徒の家を教会の代わりとして使用することが禁じられ、必ず教会のミサに参加することが求められた。また、日本の教会は画一的な西洋風の教会に変貌し、信徒たちも教導職の指導に従順で規則を守り、困難にあってもひたすら耐え忍ぶ、自主性の乏しい受動的な存在へと変わっていった。

司祭一人あたりの年間授洗者数（全国平均）

1874～1880 年	40～60 人
1887 年	37.3 人
1888 年	34.4 人
1890 年	24.4 人
1891 年	20.7 人
1900 年	9.9 人

II−3　第2期のカトリック教育の目標と方法
カトリック教育——中・上流社会層重視へのシフトチェンジ

　日本政府の方針、世界的なカトリック教会の方針転換に応じ、日本のカトリック教育においても大きな変化がみられた。長崎教会会議の影響は教育の分野にも波及した。カトリック学校は「宗教学校」としての性格（主として初等教育の分野）を放棄し、中立的立場をとらざるをえなかった。さらに、ローマからの指針によって、さらに決定的な方針の転換が求められた。この時期の目標は、カトリック教会の中高等教育への進出と、社会におけるエリート、良家子女の教育へと転進せざるをえない状況に直面した。

　1899年、「私立学校令」の公布によって、外国人経営の学校に対する監督が強化され、教育と宗教の分離が訓令された。それを受けて、暁星学園（マリア会）は、直接的な宗教教育をせず、中立的な教育の実施を打ち出した。カトリックの宣教、つまり受洗者の獲得は、もっぱらパリ外国宣教会の宣教師に委ねられることとなった。すなわち、「教育」と「布教」、「一般子弟教育」と「カトリック教理教育」の区分が明確に行われるようになった。

　1890年代のカトリック教会は、社会の下層に位置する人びとを対象とした司祭たちの「歩く宣教」から、知識人、中流・上流から信者を獲得するべく学校教育事業に宣教方針の重心を移した。この点では、明治初期から社会への関わり、一般青年の教育に従事したプロテスタント教会を模範とすることが必要であった。カトリック教会は、貧者や初等・中等教育に集中する方針から、高等教育へのコミットメントへと大きく舵をきった。

　時の政府の方針においても、カトリック教会に高等教育を求める機運が高まっていた。日露戦争後の世にあって、日本政府内では、ヨーロッパとの交流を促進する機運が盛り上がっていたためでもある。これまでの草の根的で、フランス人のみが影響力をもつカトリック教会とは別の視点が求められていたことは確かである。その結果、日本政府はオコンネル枢機卿を特使とする派遣団を受け入れ、明治天皇への拝謁を許した。オコンネル枢機卿は、日本におけるカトリックの評判と高等教育機関設置の可能性を探り、それをローマ教皇ピウス10世に報告している。その後、東洋学者であったイエズス会のヨーゼフ・ダールマン神父が、1903年の来日を機に、東京におけるカトリック高等教育機関の設置を構想し始め、直接ピウス10世に謁見し、その可能性を力説した。

　1908年のイエズス会と聖心会の来日は、日本のカトリック教育の歴史で大

きな転換点を示す出来事となった。イエズス会は大学設置のため、聖心会も女子の高等教育機関設置のために日本に派遣された。イエズス会は1913年に日本最初のカトリック大学である上智大学を開校し、聖心会は1915年に聖心女子学院専門学校を開校した。日本の高等教育分野では、「大学令」により、大学認可を受けるのは官立大学のみであった。上智大学は、当初「専門学校」として出発せざるをえなくなった。開校時、宗教教育は許されないが、倫理教育は可能ということで認可が下りた。キリスト教系大学は、法律、外国語など、なにがしかの「専門」を強調する学校として生き残る道を模索した。

　一般社会に影響力をもとうとするカトリック知識人たちの活動が活発化するのもこの時期である。特に、岩下壮一神父の活動は注目に値する。岩下神父は、東京帝国大学で講義し、各大学にカトリック研究会を設立し指導した。また『カトリック新聞』や雑誌『声』の編集長や主筆となって、積極的に日本人の知識層にカトリシズムを紹介した。その結果、1920年代から30年代にかけて、吉満義彦らのカトリック思想家を標榜する人材が育った。

　しかし、1930年代の日本は、国粋主義、国家主義の最盛期であり、カトリックへの反発が強まった時期でもある。そして、この時期を象徴するかのような事件が、1930年代初めに、上智大学および暁星学園を中心とするカトリック学校において起きていた。「靖国神社参拝拒否」事件である。この事件を契機に、上智大学は消滅の危機に瀕した。大学にとって最も苦しい時期は1945年の終戦まで続いた。問題の要点は、カトリック教徒が神社内で「敬礼」できるかどうかであった。ただ、靖国神社に「敬礼」する行為が、「宗教」として行われるのか、それとも祖先への尊敬や国家への忠誠の印など「習慣」として行われるのかが問題であった。1932年9月、東京教区のジャン・アレクシス・シャンボン大司教[20]は鳩山一郎文部大臣に書簡を送り、神社「敬礼」は愛国的な意義をもつもので、宗教的な意義をもつものではないことを明らかにしてほしいと願った。これを受けて、神社参拝は教育上の理由によるもので、要求されている「敬礼」は愛国心と忠誠を表すものであるとの答えが文部省より通達された。これによって、カトリック教会は、カトリック信徒の学生、生徒、児童が神社参拝の際に行う「敬礼」を「愛国的行為」で「何等宗教的意味を有さぬもの」として許可し、問題解決をはかった。

反共という接点

しかしながら、この時期、カトリック教会には、国家の圧力に積極的に対抗するための確固たる信念が貫かれなかった矛盾した事実をも指摘すべきであろう。それは、当時のカトリック教会が抱いていた強烈な「反共主義」という立場である。当時の国粋主義とカトリックは「反共」という立場でははからずも一致していた。そのため、カトリックの態度が曖昧になった事実は否定できない。1934年、教皇庁布教聖省は、1932年に建国された「満州国」を承認した。そこには、満州南下を目論むソビエト・ロシアへの対抗勢力としての日本への期待があったためである。教皇回勅『ディヴィニ・レデンプトリス[21]』は共産主義の脅威を明記している。「反共」という接点は、国家方針に全面的に反対できない不徹底さをカトリック教会の中に生み出していたといえる。

明治初頭以来、「魂の救い」を重んじ、慈善事業の実行を通して歩みを始めたカトリック教会は、第2期に入って、日本の中・上流階級や知識人にも目を向け、さらには、イエズス会の上智大学、聖心会の高等専門学校の設立によって、本格的に高等教育分野での活動を開始していた。しかし、前述のとおり、国家主義、官尊民卑の風潮の中、関東大震災などの財政困難なども加わり、カトリック高等教育は幾度となく窮地に追い込まれた。もしも大戦が10年長く続いていたなら、上智大学は存続できなかったのではないだろうか。

Ⅲ 第3期（1945年〜現在）の考察
——社会の中で独自の地位を構築

1945年8月15日、日本国民は、ポツダム宣言受諾を伝える玉音放送において初めて天皇陛下の肉声を聞いた。それが敗戦を告げるものと即座には理解できなかったものの、天皇自らの語りに戦いの終わりを察した。米国戦艦ミズーリー号上での無条件降伏文書への調印をもって、日本は敗戦国として連合国司令官の下、占領統治下に置かれた。社会の規範となっていた国家神道や天皇への忠誠などの価値観が崩れ、人びとは精神的に困窮した。日本人は精神的な支えを必要としていた。日本人の将来は、連合国総司令官ダグラス・マッカーサー率いる総司令部に委ねられた。第1期以来の、カトリック教会と「天皇の権威を基盤とした国家神道が公的宗教化した近代日本国家」との対立構造はここに完全に消滅した。

マッカーサーはカトリック教会および教育についてどのような見解をもっていたのか。その答えを知る興味深い記録がある。1947年11月10日、米国人イエズス会員で、ジョージタウン大学の外交学部[22]を創設したエドモンド・ウォルシュ[23]神父が来日した。彼はイエズス会総長の命により戦後の日本を巡察するため派遣された。対ソビエト政策や共産主義国家の研究で名高く、ニュルンベルグ裁判ではナチスの宗教迫害の実態について調査した人物である。このウォルシュ神父を、マッカーサー元帥は待ち構えていた。ウォルシュ神父来日の翌日、マッカーサーはGHQ本部でウォルシュ神父を迎え会談をもった。ウォルシュ神父の日記によれば、その際、マッカーサーは次のように語っている。

　　この国民は何か精神的な宗教を受け入れる準備がととのっている。日本人は本質的に神秘を理解する人びとである。いまここでなされることは、これから千年続くような歴史をつくりだすことになるだろう[24]。

　マッカーサーはプロテスタントを自認し、フリーメーソンとも深く関わったとされている。その念頭には、東西冷戦構造が顕著となりつつあった時、日本における、共産主義の台頭が最大の懸念事項としてあった。マッカーサー自身はカトリシズムを信奉していなくても、カトリックには多くの期待を寄せた。その最大の理由に、この「反共」の橋頭堡としての日本の再生があったといえる。そのために、唯物史観とは一線を画し、かつ国家神道のような単独の統制ではない、精神主義の宗教を尊重する心を日本人に植え付けようとしたのであろう。プロテスタント教会とともに、カトリック教会も占領期にGHQをはじめ諸外国から大きな援助を受けることになる。それは、新たに作り出された「冷戦構造」の中の、言い換えれば西側陣営の中の、キリスト教の重要性を裏付けることにもなっていた。

　マッカーサーは、ウォルシュ神父を通して、戦後日本復興におけるイエズス会への期待を語り、この国の将来設計の一助としてのカトリックの教育活動に信頼を示した。ウォルシュ神父は1948年2月に上智大学内のSJハウスにおいてイエズス会管区会議を招集し、今後のカトリック活動の方針策定に向かった。

Ⅲ-1　第3期の特徴的な時代からの挑戦
敗戦国・三流意識と外国コンプレックス

　この時期の最大の挑戦は、敗戦国民となった人びとの意識そのものであった。すべてを失った人びとは、新生日本に期待するよりも、より多くのトラウマを抱えていた。占領国、三流国扱から生じた「外国コンプレックス」は少なからず国民を支配していた。「外国コンプレックス」は、占領されていながら日本国民が直接外国と交流することを妨げられていることから一層の深手となった。そうした意識からの脱却なくして、新しい展望は生まれない。日本国民は米国のもたらす民主主義的自由、世俗主義などを受け入れつつ、日本国民としての誇りを回復するきっかけを待ち望んだ。カトリック教会もカトリック教育機関も、この意識改革の道を進むことが求められていたといえる。

　日本人は敗戦によって、史上経験したことのない「諸価値の再認識」のプロセス（a process of revaluation of values）に置かれていた。伝統的価値のいくつかが崩壊し、「民主主義」、「民主的自由」など戦勝国アメリカから新たにもたらされた価値と、日本固有の守るべき価値のあいだで右往左往する国民の姿があった。アメリカ合衆国がもたらしたものはすべてがキリスト教的、カトリック的な価値観に基づくものでないことは言うまでもない。物質主義、プラグマティズム、自然主義、教育分野におけるデューイズムなどが、サブカルチャーの要素とともに一挙に日本社会に流れ込んだ。

Ⅲ-2　第3期に特徴的な社会的環境

　日本社会全体のアメリカ世俗主義化や物質主義的傾向は、敗戦後の復興が進むにつれ日本人の心を支配する大きな要因であった。1953年以後の朝鮮半島の動乱による軍需景気による経済復興は、日本の高度経済成長の引き金となった。

　1955年から74年まで約20年間、日本は高度経済成長期と呼ばれる空前の社会変動期を体験した。しかし、そうした社会にあって国民の中に意識のずれが生じていた。「相対的不遇意識」というものである。「相対的不遇意識」とは、高度成長の恩恵をあまり受けなかった人びと、つまり中小零細企業で働く人びとや中小企業主、日本社会においてマイノリティーとして位置づけられている人びとなどが抱いてきた意識である。こうした人びとが助けを求めたのは、カトリック教会ではなく新興宗教であったと言われている[25]。

　一方、カトリック教会の内部でも新しい時代が始まりつつあった。カトリッ

ク教会にとっての戦後最大の分岐点は1962年に開催され、65年に閉幕した第二ヴァチカン公会議である。公会議は、「アジョルナメント」（今日化）を意識し、従来の聖職者中心主義、ヴァチカン中心主義の考え方を改め、社会により広く開かれた教会のあり方を提示した。それは、これまで世の中の動きにかたくなに扉を閉ざそうとするか、対決姿勢をもって臨んでいたカトリック教会が、教会外の他者を認め、互いに尊敬し合いながら共存する道を探ろうとする試みでもあった。他宗教、他宗派への態度が改められ（エキュメニカル運動）、兄弟・姉妹の関係性が強調された。この態度の変化は、孤立し、唯我独尊的な態度ではカトリック教会の未来はないと洞察されたことにもよるが、やはり、東西陣営の狭間にあって、精神性を重んじるカトリック教会の生きる道が示されたということでもある。こうした、教会自体の変化は、日本のカトリック教会および教育に大きな影響を与えた。

Ⅲ-3　第3期のカトリック教育の目標
社会の中で影響力をもつ人材の養成

　戦争直後から、マッカーサーをはじめとするGHQは、学制改革に乗り出した。新たに6・3・3制により、中等教育が大きく変化した。上智大学を経営するイエズス会は、戦前創設の六甲学院とともに、新たに高等学校を2つ設立した。この時、民主化の波にのって米国式教育が尊重され、外国人との交流機会も増えることから、イエズス会の設立した栄光学園（1947年）および広島学院（1956年）には当初から優秀な志願者が集った。上智大学においても、風前の灯のような志願者数が、640人までに回復し、戦後のスタートを切った。

　これらの学校は、多くの外国人教員を擁する、民主主義日本の象徴のような姿を示すことに成功した。つまり、日本人の意識にあったネガティブな要素を払拭してくれると期待されたことが、順調に優秀な生徒を集めることに成功した要因である。また、人びとから好意をもって受け入れられるとともに、これらの学校側にはある1つの理念のようなものがもたれた。それは、第2期の中・高等教育時代からも潜在的にあったものであるが、ここに新たに花開く機会を得たものである。すなわち、社会の中で重大な影響力をもつ人材の養成という目標である。1947年2月のイエズス会管区会議の席上、栄光学園の設立に尽力したハンス・ヘルベック神父の言葉はそれを象徴的に示している。

日本で、イエズス会が教育の分野で高い評価を獲得できれば、カトリック教会も高く評価されるだろう。その際、イエズス会が学校教育において第一になすべきことは、多くの生徒を洗礼に導くことではない。むしろ、より高い学習レベルを達成し世に示すことである[26]。

ヘルベック師は続けて言う。

多くの信徒のいる平凡でふつうの学校より、少ない信徒であっても、知的面でよりレベルの高い学校を作ることが教会への奉仕になる[27]。

この発言の背景には、「学校」と「宗教」をはっきり区別した第2期のカトリック学校の方針が再強調されているかのようである。「教育の分野で高い評価を得る」とは、この学校からは社会の指導者が多く輩出するという意味であろうか。「より高いレベルの達成」とは、この学校で行われている教育の質が、日本の諸学校の中で第一級のものであるべきということであろう。そうした目的のためには、カトリック学校という名目に固執する必要はない。より一般的な数多くの志願者から、その候補者たちをカトリックの理念によって、徹底して教育するという目標が現れてくる。その結果、もちろん例外はあったが、カトリック学校は、宗教立学校という性格を犠牲にしてでも、一流の一般校化に突き進むことに躊躇しないという態度をもつこととなった。戦後の米国流の民主主義教育の流れの中で、外国人を多数擁するカトリック学校はその最も実現可能なグループとして有利な立場にあった。

ここで意味することは、カトリック・ミッション学校の「エリート化」であるといっても差支えないであろう。その結果、ヘルベック師が目標としたように、カトリック教会自体の評価が高まったかどうかは定かではない。少なくとも、カトリック教育のゆえにカトリック教会に入るというものはむしろ少数派である。多くの日本人は、カトリック学校とカトリック教会の信仰とは区別して考えている。多くのミッション学校の父母は同じ思いを抱いている。「わが子をミッション校へ通わせはするが、洗礼は受けさせない。キリスト教の良さによって学校を選んだのではなく、その学校を卒業することが世間的に有利だからである」と。

Ⅲ-4　第3期のカトリック教育の方法
多数の外国人教員の派遣——語学教育の充実による国際的な人材養成の可能性

　戦後、キリスト教は、カトリック、プロテスタントともに急成長を遂げる。1950年代にはカトリックの受洗者だけでも年間1万人以上を数えていた。急成長は、戦後、海外から来日した多数の修道会による多大な財的および人的投資によって支えられた。多くの教会や幼稚園の建設資金のほとんどが海外から送られてきたものである。来日する外国人司祭の数は日本人司祭数をはるかに上回り、1950年代には日本人の6倍の外国人司祭がいた。日本人司祭が外国人司祭数を上回るのは、1980年代後半になってからのことである。

　戦後の学制改革、民主化、自由主義的雰囲気の中で、カトリック学校は志願者、在校生、卒業生を急激に伸ばした。上智大学は、終戦直後の1948年674人の学生数であったが、20年後には15倍の大所帯となった。1957年、それまでの男子校上智改め、女子学生を受け入れることにより、その急成長に拍車がかかった。特に、外国人による徹底的な外国語教育を通して国際的に活躍できる人材の養成が世間的に評価された。また、少人数教育が実際の効果をあげていた。戦後の団塊世代の大学で少人数制は大きな魅力であった。また、語学的才能に恵まれた優秀な女子学生が押し寄せ、上智大学の「一流化」が始まる。

　上智大学が発展した大きな要因は、外国人宣教師による「人格教育」

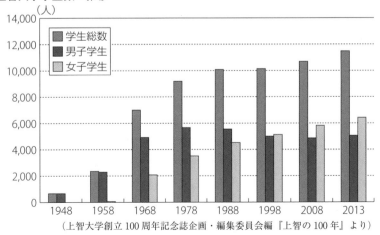

（上智大学創立100周年記念誌企画・編集委員会編『上智の100年』より）

（cura personalis）の実践による。当時の日本にあって、外国人教員を確保することは極めて困難であった。しかし、世界にネットワークをもつイエズス会は、英語圏のみならず、多くの国籍をもつ教員を上智大学に集めることができた。ここに、「外国コンプレックス」を払拭したいとする時代のニーズと結果が一致する理想的な学習環境が整ったといえる。同じことは、イエズス会の高等学校や、他の修道会経営学校にも大なり小なりあてはまることであった。まだ外国渡航も難しく、1ドルを360円で固定していた占領後わずかな年月に、日本に居ながらにして外国との交流ができることは、敗戦によって疲弊した日本人とその家族にとって大きな期待となって映ったことであろう。

　戦後の上智大学を中心とするイエズス会の教育において、外国人宣教師の果たした役割の大きさを統計的に考えてみると、1908年から1945年の40年近い期間に来日した外国人イエズス会員は140名であった。1947年から1949年のわずか2年の間に71名が来日する。そして1950年から65年の間には、218名の宣教師が来日し、主として教育活動に携わった。この15年間の来日が大規模であったという事実は、1966年から99年の30年間の来日数が60名弱であったことからもわかる。特に、1958年、ペドロ・アルペ師が管区長となった時から顕著となる。のちにイエズス会総長として全イエズス会を統括することになるアルペ師は、この頃、世界中を巡り、多くの日本宣教師をリクルートして回った。その結果、上智大学、栄光学園、広島学院等で教鞭をとる宣教師の数が倍増した。彼らの多くは語学教師として、まだ外国渡航の機会のほとんどない日本の若者に、現地にいるかのごとく語学習得と外国を学ぶ機会を提供した。上智大学が一般大学として「一流校」とみなされるようになったのも、ひとえにこの「語学教育」と「国際性を意識した教育」を先取りしたことによってである。そうした教育を受けた卒業生たちは、社会のニーズに応える分野に広く散っていった。

　中高等学校のレベルでいえば、やはり、外国人を多く配置したミッション校は、時代の潮流にのり、名門校の地位を獲得していく。外国人修道女による語学教育や躾教育の徹底は、これまでの日本社会では顧みられなかった新鮮さと効果をもたらすものと期待されていた。いつしか、そうした学校の多くは、外国からの援助がなくなり、外国人修道女や宣教師も激減する中で、従来の時代のニーズへの要請という期待は減少した。その代わり、「偏差値の高い生徒」を集め、有名大学進学に有利な学校という評価に依存する事実は否定できない。

マッカーサーやイエズス会の当局の思惑とは別に、カトリック学校、大学は、教育方法や方針というよりは、時代の要請という面で、日本人の心を掴んだのであって、決して精神的要因が第一であったわけではないのかもしれない。しかし、その中でも、数多くの卒業生が、神父やシスターの懇切丁寧な、「人格教育」（cura personalis）によって、信仰に目を開かれていたことも忘れてはならない事実である。

結　論

最後に、これまでの歴史的考察から、いくつかの問題提起をもって終わる。

第一に、明治初期に行われた「魂の救い」を重視する教育は、残念ながらより社会的効果を目指すために取って代えられた。それゆえ、カトリック教育は方向転換をしたが、その結果をどのようにとらえるべきか。その選択は余儀なくされたものであったとしても、「魂の救い」を重視した教育を、再考し取り入れる余地は現在のカトリック教育にないのか。

第二に、1890年を境に、社会の中・上流や知識人をターゲットにしたカトリック教育は今どのような成果をもたらしたと言えるのか。その際の「成果」の意味は何であるか。カトリックにとっての高等教育とは何か。

第三に、戦後、「外国コンプレックス」の払拭と「外国を学ぶ」という目標に社会が大きく傾いた時、外国人の援助によって語学教育を中心とした学校教育で地位を築いたカトリック学校の姿があった。しかし、国際性や少人数教育など、上智大学が1960年代から70年代に提供し成功したことを、日本社会全般が、同じように提供している今日にあって、カトリック学校の最大の特徴となる新たな特徴は何か。また、戦後高度経済成長期に「相対的不遇意識」をもつ人びとを取り込めなかった結果、多くの人びとが「新興宗教」に向かった事実をカトリックはどう反省するか。

第四に、カトリック教育は、これまでの近代日本にあってどのような成功を遂げたのか。近代日本は、カトリック教育の何を必要としたのか。また、何を必要としなかったのか。

以上の問いを、歴史の考察から引き出し、議論すべきであると思う。

注

1 Robert T. O'Gorman, *Catholic Identity and Catholic Education in the United States since 1790*, A Monograph on the History of Catholic Education in the United States written for the Catholic Education Futures Project, 1987. オゴーマンの論文は、髙祖敏明師によって要約解説がなされている。参照、髙祖敏明「アメリカ合衆国のカトリック教育の行方―R．オゴーマンのモノグラフ『教会、それはかつて学校であった』から―」『カトリック教育研究』第9号、1992年、71-88頁。
2 髙祖敏明、前掲論文、73-74頁。
3 Théodore Augustin Forcade, 1816-1885.
4 明治開国期についての、カトリック教会史の概略は以下を参照した。三好千春「明治以後のカトリック教会の歴史」イエズス会日本管区編『100年の記憶――イエズス会再来日から一世紀』南窓社、2008年、23-40頁。
5 青山玄師の指摘。
6 『シラブス』(近代主義の誤謬表：ピウス9世の数多くの演説、回勅、書簡による大勅書) 1864年12月8日発表。ジンマーマン監修、浜寛五郎訳『デンツィンガー・シェーンメッツァー　カトリック教会文書資料集』エンデルレ書店、441-447頁。
7 この点は次の論考を参照のこと。河原温・池上俊一編『ヨーロッパ中近世の兄弟会』東京大学出版会、2014年。
8 日本での「コンフラリア」の活動については、河原・池上編前掲書の第七章「地中海から日本へ」(川村執筆) を参照のこと。
9 L'Institut des Sœurs de l'Enfant Jesus.
10 マカオに現存する「ミゼリコルヂア」は、漢字名を「仁慈堂」とあてている。サン・モール修道女会は東南アジアを経由して来日した。その際、各地で活躍する信徒組織の名を、横浜での新たな活動のために採用したと思われる。
11 Congrégation des Sœurs de l'Enfant-Jésus de Chauffailles.
12 Congrégation des Sœurs de St. Paul de Chartres.
13 ロジェ・オーベール著、上智大学中世思想研究所編訳・監修『キリスト教史』9 (自由主義とキリスト教) 第11章 (青山玄師執筆箇所) 平凡社、1997年、414頁 (文庫版453頁)。
14 Germain Léger Testevuide, 1849-1891.
15 「文部省訓令第一二号」。私立学校令と同時 (明治32年) に公布された。別名「宗教教育禁止令」。官公私立学校での宗教教育・活動が学科課程・課程外を問わず禁じられた。宗教教育継続を望んだ学校には正規学校の資格が取り消されるか、徴兵猶予、上級学校進学、高等文官試験の受験資格はく奪などの措置をとるとされた。キリスト教系学校にとっては大打撃であり存続の危機さえささやかれた。従来の教育方針どおり、宗教教育を行おうとした学校は青山学院や明治学院などである。
16 「内地雑居」。内地解放とも呼ばれる。外国人居留地など外国人に対する居住・旅行・外出の制限を撤廃して、国内における自由な居住・旅行・営業を許可すること。
17 暁星学園誌等編纂委員会『暁星百年史』1989年。
18 *Acta et Decreta primae synodi regionalis Japoniae et Coreae. Nagasaki Habitae A. D. 1890*. Hong Kong: Typis Societatis Missionum ad Exteros, 1893.

19 ロジェ・オーベール著、上智大学中世思想研究所編訳・監修『キリスト教史』9（自由主義とキリスト教）第 11 章（青山玄師執筆箇所）平凡社、1997 年、417 頁（文庫版 455 頁）。
20 Jean-Baptiste Chambon（MEP）.
21 「ディヴィニ・レデンプトリス」*Divini Redemptoris*（無神論的共産主義についての教皇回勅）
22 Georgetown University, School of Foreign Service.
23 Edmund Walsh. SJ.
24 川村信三「20 世紀日本イエズス会史――再来日前史から戦後」イエズス会管区編『100 年の記憶――イエズス会再来日から一世紀』南窓社、2008 年、89 頁。原文は、Georgetown University, Special Collection, Edmund A. Walsh Papaer, Box 2. に収められているウォルシュの日記より。"The People are receptive and ready for a spiritual religion. They are in essence a mystic people [...]. What is now done here can make history in there parts for the next thousand years."
25 三好千春、前掲論文、38 頁。
26 川村信三、前掲論文、92 頁。
27 川村信三、前掲論文、92-93 頁。

参考文献

青山玄「明治・大正・昭和初期カトリック信徒の宣教活動」『南山神学』10 号、1987 年、177-196 頁。
青山玄「明治期における日本のカトリック教会」上智大学中世思想研究所監訳『キリスト教史』第 9 巻 11 章、平凡社、1997 年、435-461 頁。
三好千春「明治以後のカトリック教会の歴史」イエズス会日本管区編『100 年の記憶――イエズス会再来日から一世紀』南窓社、2008 年、23-40 頁。
横浜雙葉学園八十周年記念誌編集委員会編『横浜雙葉学園 80 周年記念誌』1980 年。
米田綾子『シリーズ福祉を生きる』14（岩永マキ）大空社、1998 年。
泉隆『シリーズ福祉を生きる』20（シャルトル聖パウロ修道女会）大空社、1998 年。
矢島浩『明治期日本キリスト教社会事業施設史研究』雄山閣、1982 年。
フランシスク・マルナス著、久野桂一訳『日本キリスト教復活史』みすず書房、1985 年。
カトリック女子教育研究所『カトリック女子教育研究』別冊（改訂カトリック女子教育史関連歴史年表　1865 年〜2000 年）、2003 年。
イエズス会日本管区編『100 年の記憶――イエズス会再来日から一世紀』南窓社、2008 年。
木越邦子『幕末・明治期キリスト者群像』現代企画室、2012 年。
太田淑子編『日本、キリスト教との邂逅』オリエンス宗教研究所、2004 年。
O'Gorman, Robert, T. (1987). *Catholic Identity and Catholic Education in the United States since 1790*. A Monograph on the History of Catholic Education in the United States written for the Catholic Education Futures Project.
髙祖敏明「アメリカ合衆国のカトリック教育の行方―R．オゴーマンのモノグラフ『教会、それはかつて学校であった』から―」『カトリック教育研究』第 9 号、1992 年、71-88 頁。

第1部 アジア5大学からの報告と展望

イエズス会中国管区における高等教育
突然の終結、新たな再開、改められた宣教の様相

ルイス・ジェンドロン
〈輔仁カトリック大学〉

I 輔仁カトリック大学

I－1 時代の突然の終わりと新天地での再開

　輔仁カトリック大学（以下「輔仁大学」）は1925年に北京で創立され、ベネディクト会によって運営されていた。のちに経営難に陥り、共産党政府が1950年に大学を押収するまでは神言会（SVD）が運営にあたっていた。

　1955年頃には、台湾に移住した輔仁大学の卒業生たちが台湾での大学再建を呼び掛け始めていた。この案はローマの教会権威に快く受け入れられて、1959年にはユー・ピン大司教が台湾の輔仁大学の学長に任命された。大司教は大掛かりな計画をもって教区司祭およびイエズス会（SJ）を含む7修道会の援助を受けて大学の早期再建を目指していた。

　1923年以降、イエズス会は天津で工学と商学専門の高等教育機関を運営していたが、この学校は1951年に共産党政府によって突然閉鎖に追い込まれた。そこでユー・ピン大司教はイエズス会に対し、輔仁で商学部と工学部を創設するよう要請した（イエズス会は1903年に上海でもオーロラ大学を設立していたが、これも1952年に共産党政府によって突然閉鎖させられてしまった）。

　1950年代後半、すでに数名のイエズス会員は台湾の国立大学で教鞭をとっていたため、彼らは輔仁の再建に特別の関心は寄せていなかった。しかし、総長らは協力の方針を決定した。最終的にイエズス会は、神言会と（協力者である）聖霊会、教区司祭らとともに輔仁大学の発展に全面的な尽力をした。

　適切な土地を見つける作業は困難を極めたが、1962年に大学建設地の購入が行われ、イエズス会は法学部と、のちに商学部の創設に責任を負うこととなった。イエズス会は土地購入、学部棟の建設、そして給与支払いにかかった費用

の3分の1を負担しなければならなかった。その時から30年以上にわたって、大学は1つのキャンパスに3つの準自治的カレッジが存在している状態で運営されてきた。学長も教職員らも、それら3つの「セクション」からの助成に頼らなければならなかったのである。最も大きな権力をもっている理事は神言会員、教区司祭、イエズス会員が1人ずつで構成された3人の評議員（独立した副学長的地位）であった。

　輔仁大学の複雑な内部構造（3つの学校が1つになっている）は、カレッジ同士の競争関係を保ちながらうまく機能していた。しかし教育省はこのような組織編成にまったく満足していなかった。教授の中にも、状況を憂慮し、効率の低さに不平を漏らす者がいた。理事会レベルでは、基本的な誤解が生じていた。イエズス会と神言会の神父たちが大学を3つの公平な関係者（司教、SVD、SJ）による共同体として理解していたのに対し、司教は大学は自分たちのものであり、修道会がそれに対して重要な奉仕を行うものだと思っていた。最終的に1990年代後半になって、3つのセクションを最高決定権をもつ1人の学長のもとに統合し、3つのグループ（教区司祭、SVD、SJ）はそれぞれのセクションで貢献を続けるという決定が理事会によって下された。言い換えれば、創立メンバーのグループは決定権を失いながら、中央経営陣への協力を要請され、また、自らの属するセクションで霊的・道徳的影響力を保つこととなったのである。

Ⅰ－2　ミッションの積極的促進

　1980年代に入ると、神言会とイエズス会は、大学がその使命を体現していくためには、彼ら自身がもつ固有の教育理念（カトリック＋SVD、カトリック＋SJ）を積極的に促進することが重要であることに気づくようになった。米国のカトリック大学や世界の他地域でも、同様の努力がなされていた。キャンパスで働く修道者や司祭数の減少やカトリックの教職員・学生数の極端な少なさは、大学の使命をより明確に編み出し、教職員および学生がその使命を生きるのを助けるため、様々な方法を考え出す必要性を生み出した。輔仁では、まず神言会が運営しているセクションで、のちにはイエズス会のセクションで、注目すべき努力がなされた。イエズス会ミッション事務局が設置され、能力のあるスタッフが雇われ、予算申請は承認され、数年にわたって一連の活動が行われた結果、セクション全体の雰囲気や教職員らの間にプラスの効果をもたら

した。これは、根本的な構造改革が検討され、施行されて学長のもとに学部が統合され、セクションの長から大学中央幹部へと経営決定権の移行が行われるのと同時期に起こっていったことである。1つのセクション内で生まれた良い動きは最終的に大学レベルでより促進されることとなった。イエズス会セクションで創始され、のちにすべてのセクションで採用されたのがサービスラーニングである[1]。しかし、セクションのレベルで成功した動きの中には、大学レベルで提案された際には継続困難になったり、その魅力が失われてしまったりした。修道会はキャンパス内、特にもともと経営していた学部内で影響力を行使する力をかなり失ってしまったと感じていた。

I-3　一般信徒のリーダーシップに移行された教育理念

　イエズス会が直面した別の困難は、現地での召命の減少や海外から台湾に来たり高等教育に関わったりすることへの関心の欠如によってキャンパスで働く正規のイエズス会員が減り続けていることであった（しかし中国本土への関心は常に高かった）。そして難しい判断を迫られることになった。イエズス会は輔仁大学の学院メンバーから手を引くべきか、という問題である。この議論は現在でもいまだに続いている。

　現在イエズス会中国管区で検討されている提案は以下のとおりである。

> 大学における会の組織的存在（理事会、評議会、宣教事務局など）は少なくともあと10年は保つ（数年後にはキャンパス内のコミュニティを閉鎖することを検討する）。同時に、協定を結んで聖ロベルト・ベラルミーノ輔仁神学院の事実上の存在感を増す。これは輔仁大学キャンパスに新たにイエズス会員を派遣することなく可能であるとみられている。イグナチオの使徒的協力者をキャンパスで生み出し続け（人々はイエズス会教育の価値観や方法によく通じている）、イエズス会宣教事務局の職員がそのミッション・ステートメントを効果的に実現するための実現可能な計画を立て、周辺環境の変化に合わせてそのプランを改めていくことができるよう、計画的に努力しなければならない。これには追加の予算とコンサルタントの雇用が必要であるかもしれない。すでにイグナチオの霊性に従う共同体のメンバーとなって活動している教職員には、イエズス会的価値観をキャン

パス内で適用できるよう連携することが求められる。目標は、10 年後に万が一イエズス会の組織的存在がキャンパスからなくなったとしても、イエズス会とイグナチオ的教育価値観が大学の多くの人々を鼓舞し続けるよう、強固な構造と優秀な人材が育っていることである。

輔仁大学のセクションの１つは昔はイエズス会の傘下にあったものの、カトリック大学であってもイエズス会大学ではない。カレッジのいくつか、例えば法学部・商学部・社会科学部や医学部の一部などにおいてイエズス会宣教事務局が道徳的リーダーシップをもっているものの、イエズス会の強固なリーダーシップは失われている。イエズス会は、輔仁大学をイエズス会高等教育の空間として作り上げていくことについて越えられない限界を明らかに感じていた。

Ⅱ　より大きなコンテクストで
── イエズス会中国管区と高等教育

Ⅱ-1　中国の神学校の突然の閉鎖──新天地への移転

イエズス会は聖ロベルト・ベラルミーノ神学校（教皇庁立）を 1929 年から経営していた。それは上海（中国）で開校し、1952 年に政治環境の変化で中国からフィリピン（Baguio）への移転を強制されるまで続いていた。当時そこはイエズス会の神学生と司祭のみの学院で、博士課程はなかった。1967 年に神学校は台湾の輔仁大学の隣のキャンパスに移転し、資格を満たした生徒には門戸を開いた。哲学の勉強をしたことがない生徒のために、宗教学研究所を設立した。そして神学博士または宗教学博士の学位も授与するようになった。神学校には現在 200 名以上の全日制課程の学生が在籍しており、その半分ほどは中国本土から来ている。2012 年に神学校は「聖ロベルト・ベラルミーノ輔仁神学校」と名称を変更した。輔仁大学から独立した神学校であるものの、輔仁大学と様々な分野にわたる協力協定を結んでいる。輔仁大学には神学部がないため、神学校は何らかの神学的存在を大学に持ち込もうとしている。

神学校の教授は様々に異なる修道会や教区に属しており、一般信徒の教授も数名いる。イエズス会は神学校のリーダーシップをとっている。私たちはまた、イグナチオの霊操に特に重点を置いた霊性に関するプログラムも提供している。イエズス会はこの使徒職を保つことに力を入れており、これを中国管区の

使徒的最優先事項と考えている。また、輔仁大学において良い影響を与えるべく努力をしている。

II-2　中国での再開――小規模に

イエズス会中国管区におけるもう1つのイエズス会高等教育機関に「北京センター」がある。これは理事会をもつ独立した研究教育機関である。これは小規模な経営形態で、1・2学期を学寮で過ごしながらイエズス会大学（ロヨラ大学シカゴ）の認可した授業を履修する学部生が100名ほど在籍している。大体はイエズス会や他のカトリック大学からくるアメリカ人学生のためであり、高い学術レベルには定評がある。北京センターは15年前に創設され、国際経営経済大学のキャンパス内に位置している。異なる管区からのイエズス会員が北京センターで教鞭をとっている。これは、外国からの生徒に中国（と中国語）の知識の素晴らしい手ほどきの機会を与え、またマテオ・リッチや他のイエズス会宣教師たちの中国への遺産をささやかながらも引き継いでいく方法である。中国、特に北京と上海では、外国からの学生の世話をするセンターが多くある。北京センターは創造性を発揮し、1学期または年間を中国で勉学に励みたいと思っている学生に最良の教育の機会を与えることに大体において成功してきている。

II-3　香港での新たな種類のイエズス会大学――中国のために

中国管区における過去数年間の学問的「冒険」でもう1つ重要なのは、香港においてイエズス会リベラルアーツ・カレッジを創設しようとのプロジェクトである。香港の行政は、香港を極東における高等教育の重要拠点にしようと計画していた。香港大学は世界一の中国の大学と考えられている。また香港にあるいくつかの公立大学も大変レベルが高い。香港政府は全寮制カレッジを含む、私立で自己資金調達を行う大学の設立を促進することを決定した。香港のイエズス会員は香港のイエズス会系高校の卒業生と協力して、過去数年間にわたって同様の考えを発展させてきた。中国領土内にイエズス会のリベラルアーツ・カレッジを設立しようというものである。そのようなイエズス会系リベラルアーツ全寮制カレッジは香港の学生（3分の1）だけでなく、中国本土からの学生（3分の1）、また他のアジアからの学生（3分の1）をも対象とする。香港であればこそ、イエズス会はリベラルアーツの教科課程を実施し、かつ中

国・香港またアジア太平洋諸国の将来のリーダーを育成するために必要な政治と学問の自由をもつ。

　このプロジェクトはイエズス会大学の国際的ネットワークに好評で、イエズス会大学で教鞭をとるイエズス会員や一般の教員たちも大きな関心を寄せた。イエズス会大学数校から集まった専門家が香港を拠点とするチームとともにリベラルアーツ・カレッジについての詳細な要項を立案した。プロジェクトを検分して準備チームと公式に会談を行った国際専門家集団（Institutional Review は 2012 年 6 月 25～27 日に行われた）の推薦を受けて、香港政府（香港学術・職業資格認定委員会）が、2012 年 9 月にはこの新しいカレッジに正式な認可を与えた。2013 年の 1 月には、理事会が初めて開かれた。理事会は多くの海外のイエズス会大学からの 15 名のイエズス会の専門家らと、10 名の香港の専門家と社会指導者によって構成されている。

　香港政府は 3 年前すでに、公的な土地（クイーンズ・ヒル）を私立の全寮制カレッジのキャンパス用地として確保しており、大学創設に最もふさわしい団体に土地を与えると公に発表していた。約 10 の団体が土地利用を申請し、政府の決定を待っていた。同時期、香港では新たな政府指導者が生まれたが、この人物は他の政策を優先しており、これまでのところ決定は下されていない。その結果、イエズス会リベラルアーツ・カレッジのプロジェクトは計画どおりに前進することができないでいる。準備チームは他の選択肢を検討しつつある。それは、土地を購入しキャンパスの建設を始めるというものである。この新計画に沿って行くと、カレッジは少人数でゆっくりと開校するため、イエズス会に土地（クイーンズ・ヒル）が与えられた場合と比べて自らのペースで成長していく自由をもつことができる。このリベラルアーツ・カレッジでは大半の教職員がイエズス会員ではないものの、イエズス会の伝統に深く則るものとなるだろう。

Ⅲ　結　　論
——中国におけるイエズス会教育ミッションの歴史的展開

　イエズス会中国管区の高等教育への関与はまず 20 世紀初頭に中国本土で始まり、のちに 1960 年代から台湾に広がった。イエズス会は台湾での輔仁カトリック大学再建の主たる貢献者でありながら、キャンパスにおける会の存在感

は低下している。キャンパスにおいてイグナチオの霊性を保つことには希望がもてる。完全に独立した神学校である聖ロベルト・ベラルミーノ輔仁神学校のみが、台湾における唯一のカトリック神学院であり、これまでも、そして今後のイエズス会の優先順位の中心となる。近年では中国本土からの生徒の受け入れと相まって（中国には学位を授与できる神学部がない）、発展が進んでいる。この神学院は輔仁大学のキャンパスにも少なからぬ影響を与えている。

　15年前、海外からの学生に中国文化と中国語の手ほどきを与え、また彼らの学ぶ学問分野に中国的なアプローチを与えることを目的として、小さいがエネルギッシュなセンターが北京に設立された。北京センターは主に学部生のためで、4年間の大学でのカリキュラムの一部を担うこととなっている。

　現在、中国管区は香港と中国本土の学生のために香港でリベラルアーツ・カレッジの創設に着手している。これは明確なイエズス会機関となるが、イエズス会員数は最低限で、イエズス会高等教育の伝統に精通した一般の教職員が大半を占めるという点で新たな試みである。

注
1　実際のところ、サービスラーニングの影響は輔仁大学のキャンパスのみにとどまらない。輔仁大学のイエズス会セクションが1990年代にまずサービスラーニングプログラムを開始し、その成功によって他の多くの大学もこの指導法の発展に参画するようになったのである。2007年には、台湾のすべての大学でサービスラーニングプログラムの促進を奨励する目的で教育省が正式に計画を発表した。

サナタダルマ大学とイエズス会の全人教育

クントロ・アディ
〈サナタダルマ大学〉

はじめに

　2010年1月、アメリカのイエズス会大学の学長は、イエズス会大学に固有の特徴と使徒的原理についての合意文書を発表した（AJCU, 2010）。さらに、イエズス会の使徒的ミニストリーに積極的に関与していくうえでの重要な結びつきにも言及した。文書によると、「カトリック・イエズス会大学」であることこそが、学校を独自性ある機関たらしめる特徴であるという。そのような学校の存在意義は、大学が持つべき重要な側面をすべて持ち合わせる"真の大学"であるという事実に見出される。知的使徒としての活動を通して、学生が自らの人生・社会・職業また奉仕活動において良い影響を与えることができるよう導き教育することが大学の使命である。

　イエズス会の大学として、私たちはイグナチオの遺産と、イエズス会教育の際立った特徴を受け継いでいる。聖イグナチオはそのカリスマ性と霊操を通して、私たちの活動と学生に対する教育が、すべてにおいて神を求め、識別力を高め、「状況を思慮深く分析し、経験との対話を通して、反省に基づく評価を通じて、行動そのものを目的とし、そして評価への開かれた心をもって世界と関わっていく」よう私たちを鼓舞している（イエズス会35総会）。

　それぞれの大学が、その活動を通して以上のようなカトリック・イエズス会的特徴を深め適用していく独自の方法をもっている。本稿では、①大学が置かれたコンテクスト、すなわち背景状況としてのインドネシアを見ること、②私たちの教育ミニストリーにおけるキリスト教ヒューマニズム的特徴を考えること、③イエズス会教育における全人教育を理解すること、④現代の課題と争点、

特にインドネシアのような多民族・多文化・多宗教社会における宗教間対話を考察することによって大学のアイデンティティに由来する重要な特徴を強調したい。

I　インドネシアのコンテクスト——サナタダルマ大学

インドネシアには国全体に多様な民族・文化・言語の豊かさがある。この多様性は宗教・社会的人口構成にも反映されている。イスラム教が最も多く信仰されている宗教である。インドネシアの人口の内訳はイスラム教徒が88.1％、プロテスタントが6.1％、カトリックが3.2％、ヒンズー教徒1.8％、仏教徒0.6％、その他0.2％となっており、「その他」には伝統的な土着宗教が含まれている（2010年現在）。

文化的多様性は歴史に基づくものである。1000年間にわたって続いたインド文化の影響はヒンズー教と仏教の文化的融合を生み出し、主要な政治王朝の興亡を引き起こした。14世紀初頭には貿易を通じて、のちにはイスラム教徒の支配者を通してイスラム教が伝播した。19世紀まで続いたイスラムの拡大のプロセスは、17世紀初頭からインドネシアを植民地化したオランダに対する抵抗運動と時期が重なっている（Muller, 1999）。

インドネシアのカトリック教会は比較的歴史が浅い。オランダがインドネシアでの宣教活動を解禁したのは19世紀半ばになってからであった。オランダからのイエズス会員らはまずフローレス島とティモールで宣教活動を行い、20世紀初頭からは主にジャワ島に集中している。

1945年はインドネシア独立派教会にとって新たな時代の始まりとなった。同年にはカトリック教徒は70万人ほどであり、うち10万人はジャワに住んでいた。今日ではカトリック信者はおよそ689万人おり、インドネシアの人口の2.91％を占めている。Muller（1999）の記述によると、教会の驚くほどの成長はカトリック教会がインドネシア的特徴を取り入れたことによる強い魅力を反映したものである。今日ではインドネシア人司教がほとんど独占的に教区のリーダーシップをとっている。インドネシア人司祭、修道女とブラザーの数は増加し続けており、外国人宣教師にとって代わった。それ以降、一般信徒も教会内で重要な役割を果たすようになり、インドネシアは長らく、特に医療と教育の分野で人々に仕える伝統を培ってきた。

サナタダルマは1993年4月から大学となっているものの、その歴史は1955年、イエズス会が教員養成機関を設立しようとしたことにさかのぼる。「サナタダルマ」の名称は「奉仕の賜物」を意味している。この愛の奉仕は国と教会に捧げられる。

　現代社会の必要性にこたえ、科学技術の進歩に後れをとらないため、1993年4月にサナタダルマは大学となった。教員養成・教育学部で教員の養成を続けながら新たな学部を開設した。現在サナタダルマでは7つの学部学科で23の学士課程、3つの大学院課程、2つの専門職課程と複数の語学学習コースが開かれている（Tatang, 2006）。

II　キリスト教ヒューマニズム

II-1　用　語

　「人文主義」、また「人文学」という語は15世紀のイタリア・ルネサンス、そしてストゥディア・フマニタティス（Studia Humanitatis）と呼ばれた教育課程の基盤としての文学作品の推奨に由来している（O'Malley, 2000）。その文学とは、ギリシャ語とラテン語の詩作、修辞学、演劇と歴史のことであり、エラスムスがのちに人格の成熟（*pietas*）という言葉で述べたように、適切に教えられれば、正しくはっきりとした、高潔で社会に貢献する意志をもつ人物を育成すると信じられていた。そのような目標は学生が良い文学を真摯に学ぶことを要求するものであった。このような勉学を通じて学生は雄弁な話術を習得し、また同様に、著名作家の作品において出会う徳の高いふるまいの例に刺激を受けるのである。そして自らの公的生活において実践的な分別、つまり他者に影響を与えることができる知恵を習得していく。したがって、教育の目標とは現代的な意味でとらえれば指導者を育成することであった。

　イタリア・ルネサンスにおける人文主義運動は少なくとも1つの重要な特徴をもっていたということに言及しておきたい。それはキリスト教的なものであった。これが意味するのは、キリスト教の教義や神学の側面と融合する形で修辞学の特定の側面が発達し、それが人間の尊厳という新たなテーマにつながったということである。

Ⅱ-2　ルネサンス人文主義に固有の特徴

モドラスはルネサンス人文主義運動の重要な特徴を以下のように強調した（Modras, 2004）。

1）古典主義

　　人文主義運動はギリシャ語・ラテン語による古典作品への復興を奨励した。古典文学は文学的麗流さと文体の美しさを生み出すものと考えられていたのである。

2）全人の育成

　　ストゥディア・フマニタティス（Studia Humanitatis）という語は、古典文学教育は人間の特別に望ましいあり方、つまり自らの徳を最高に高めた人物を育成するのだという主張を示唆したものである。人々は、良い文学こそは善良で均整の取れた全人を生み出すと信じていた。

3）市民的徳を行動に移す人生

　　フマニタティスの意味するところを最大限に引き出すためには、人は認識的能力だけにとどまらず実用的技術も磨かなければならなかった。人文主義教育の理想的結果とは、修辞学が質の高さだけでなく世論を形成する能力のために賞賛され、それを通じて市民としての義務を果たすことのできる人物の育成であった。

4）共同体内における個人主義

　　ルネサンス文化に生きた人々は、共同体の一員としての強い感覚を養われていた。当時アイデンティティや責任はまだ家族や階級などの共同体のつながりによって決定されていた。しかし同時に、自らの感情や意見を述べることのできる個人としての感覚もまた新たに生まれつつあったのである。

5）人間の尊厳と自由

　　ルネサンス文化は、人間は、本能に支配されていない唯一の生物であると考えていた。人間は自らの運命を決められるという特権と責任を与えられているのである。人間であるとは、道徳的選択に向き合い、徳高く、あるいは堕落した生活を送るということである。

6）真理の調和と統一性

　　人文主義者は信仰と理性、哲学と神学の調和を信じていた。トマス・ア

クィナスがわかりやすい指針を残している。「すべての真理を造られた神は、真理の調和を確実なものとなさる」。この原則が、真理は自らの探し求めるところにある、というルネサンス期に生まれた考え方の源泉となったのである。

Ⅲ 全人を司牧する

ストゥディア・フマニタティスはイエズス会学校や大学で教えられる学問内容の中心要素を形成した。前述のとおり、フマニタティスという用語は、道徳的な善さと真理への献身、そして市民的な善のために行動するという心意気を育んでいく過程と勉学の両方に関連している。

イエズス会の他のミニストリーと同様、教育も全人、つまり認識的能力のみならず人格と道徳に目を向けている。

教育に関するイエズス会の理論は存在しないが、イグナチオ的霊性やイエズス会の慣習に見られる原則で、教育に対する特徴的な観点を記録されているものに、以下の3つの重要な文書がある。『ラツィオ・ストゥディオールム (Ratio Studiorum)』（1599年）、『イエズス会教育の特徴』（1986年）、そして『イグナチオ的教授法』（1993年）である。

a)『ラツィオ・ストゥディオールム』（1599年）
『ラツィオ・ストゥディオールム』はイエズス会組織の中で教育に関わっているすべての人の役割の説明を集めたものである。この文書では運営・カリキュラム・指導法そして生徒指導という4つの重要な分野が論じられている。

本書は仕事を最も効率よく行うことについて述べているが、しかしなぜその仕事が第一に有意義なものと考えられるのかを示す教育哲学にはっきりと触れていない。

であるから、過去30年間にわたって、新しいミレニアムに向けての『ラツィオ』が検討されている。これは1599年の『ラツィオ・ストゥディオールム』を改定しようという自発的な動きが起こったためではない。むしろ、移り変わりの早い世界の真新しいコンテクストが呈した新たな課題に直面した教育者、イエズス会系学校や大学に関わる一般信徒と修道者らの緊急の必要性にこたえようとした一連の応答の結果として生まれたものである（Duminuco, 2000）。

b)『イエズス会教育の特徴』(1986 年)

『イエズス会教育の特徴』はイグナチオの世界観を振り返り、それを今日の人類の必要に照らし合わせて教育に適用していくことから生まれた。これはイエズス会教育の現代的アイデンティティのための文書として役立ってきた。

文書はイエズス会教育の特徴を列挙し、共通のビジョンや目的意識を与え、そしてイエズス会系学校が自己評価を行うにあたっての規準を与えるものである。

文書はイエズス会教育の本質と使命を明確化するのに役立った。しかし問題は、「目標を達成し、原則を根付かせるためには、どのようにこの特徴を教師と学生の交流に生かし、理論を実践し、レトリックを現実にすることができるだろうか？」ということである (Duminuco, 2000)。

c)『イグナチオ的教授法：実践的アプローチ』(1993 年)

『イグナチオ的教授法』は理論を実践に移すための実用的指針を提供してくれる。この文書は、すべての意義ある教授法におけるビジョンと方法論の相乗効果、すなわち学習者の成長と発達を教師が見守る方法を強調している。

最終目標は何であろうか？　目標は、他者のために奉仕する人物（アルペ、1974)、均整が取れており賢く、成長の見込みがあり、敬虔で愛があり、神の民に惜しみない奉仕をもって正義を行うことに力を入れる人物（コルヴェンバッハ、1986)、また、能力・良心と憐れみの心に満ちた人物を育成することである（コルヴェンバッハ、1993)。

イグナチオ的教授法は学問的意味での卓越性をさらに超えようとするものである。それは教師と学生の間、また各集団内で行われる協調的プロセスであり、生涯学習と他者への奉仕を促進するため、自学自習と共同学習、発見と創造性、そして自省を奨励する。したがってイグナチオ的教授法は、教師が生徒に寄り添っていく方法ともいえる。このプロセスはコンテクストや経験、自省、行動および評価の重要性を考慮に入れたものである。学習と成長が途切れることなく繰り返されるサイクルなのである。

『イエズス会教育の特徴』と『イグナチオ的教授法』は合わせて包括的な文書としてとらえることができる。コルヴェンバッハ神父 (1986) は次のように強調した。「それらは決定打でも最終結論でもない。そのようなものは大変難しく不可能である。むしろ、1つの視点、目標、そしてそれに到達する道をも与える道具である。」

IV 現代の課題と問題

IV-1 思考力と想像力を深める

　イエズス会現総長のアドルフォ・ニコラス神父は、2010年4月にメキシコシティで開催された国際イエズス会高等教育会議において、希薄化のグローバル化と総長自身が名付けた現象について述べた。これは私たちの学校で学んでいる何千人もの生徒にもよく当てはまる。希薄化のグローバル化（思考、展望、夢、人間関係、信仰の希薄化）は、カトリック（イグナチオ）の伝統において際立った特徴である思考と想像の深みを、新たな創造的方法で促進するよう私たちを駆り立てている。

　思考と想像力の深みは現実との深遠な関わり、つまり本質を見出すまで諦めないことを求める。神・キリスト・福音という本質的なものとの関わりのための深い洞察なのである。

　私たちの行う教育の深みは何であろうか？　フィリピンにおけるイエズス会教育150周年を記念した際のアドルフォ・ニコラス神父の問いかけがこれに関連している。私たちはどれほど深く学生のニーズに応えられているか？　意味と目的を求める最も深い飢え渇きにどのように答えているか？　物事をよく見て考えるよう深く促しているか？　人格や奉仕の心、信念、信仰と長所をどれほど深く形成しているか？　「内側から決める」——つまり、識別力のある人物を育成できているか？

　ニコラス神父が指摘したとおり、（イエズス会の）教育では、より信仰深く、人間的かつ公正で持続的な世界をつくるために、学習と想像の深みは現実世界での経験と学問的厳格さを集約したものとなっている。

IV-2 普遍性の再発見

　グローバル化という新たな現実は、共通の所属意識と共同責任概念をもたらした。世界にはより普遍的で、私たちの狭い関心を超えて物事をとらえることを可能にする価値観が必要である。ニコラス神父も述べたように、世界の大きな課題を1つの地域や1つの大学だけで解決することはできない。それには、たこつぼ化を超えてともに働くことができるような物の見方と心の広さが必要である。カトリック高等教育の抱える困難は、その所属の広さや問題意識と責

任の大きさに関して、どうすればより普遍的な教育を行えるかということである。

「もし私たちの大学が人格形成と知的活動を深め、それを皆でより協力的かつ普遍的にしていくことができたら、私たちの大学は教会の使命である完全な人間の発展に真に尽くすことになるだろう」(ニコラス、2009)。

Ⅳ-3　宗教間対話の動き——インドネシアのコンテクスト

宗教間対話はイエズス会員とその使徒職にとって重要な問題の1つである。イエズス会総会(32、34、35回)で示されたこの問題意識は、アジアにおける教会の対話の方法とともに神学の現場性を発展させるという課題に適切に対応する。その対話の方法とは、経験の対話、人生の対話、行動の対話と神学的意見交換による対話である(Prakosa, 2011)。

上記の問題意識への応答として、イエズス会アジア太平洋会議はアジア神学発見プログラム(ATEP)という計画を立ち上げた。ヘル・プラコサによると、ATEPの目的とは、第35イエズス会総会が呼びかけたように理解と対話への架け橋となること、アジアのカトリック教会が貧困問題・多宗教化・多文化主義に向き合うという課題に応えること、そして学生やイエズス会神学者が神学の現場性を考え発展させていく機会を提供することである。プログラムの内容は信仰についての枠組み、コーラン、コーランの解説書、ハディース(イスラム教聖伝)、イスラム教の歴史(アジアとインドネシア)、イスラム法、イスラム神学、哲学と神秘、そしてイスラム教徒とキリスト教徒の対話である。

プログラムのダイナミクスは相関性のある4つの秩序だった段階に分けられている。初めにグループで社会の現状を体験するところに始まり、特定の問題を解決するために具体的な行動を起こすことに移る。この転換は社会分析と社会神学の再考によって行われる(Muller, 1999)。これは方法論としては新しいものではない。多くのイエズス会員が、イグナチオ的教授法と呼ばれる「コンテクスト—体験—内省—実践—評価」の方法論を長きにわたって行ってきた。

このアプローチでは、初めの段階(体験)は、参加型の観察によって社会の現状と問題を認識し体験することを目的としている。この段階で重要な活動は没入、すなわちイスラム教徒の共同体での生活や仕事をまず自分で体験することである。この体験によって参加者が体感する共同体の喜びや希望、そして悲しみや不安が彼らの心の琴線に触れることが望まれる。

第2段階(学術的分析)では、体験がより広範囲の社会状況の中でとらえら

れる。この段階では、第1段階での体験を学際的手法（なかでもインドネシアのイスラム教徒に関連する社会学的・経済学的・文化人類学的な手法）を用いて批判的な分析を行う。

　第3段階（内省）は、社会的分析の結果を踏まえて神学の現場性を考える。この段階では、社会的分析で得られたことを、聖書や教会の対話に関する教義も含めた他のキリスト教的慣習と照らし合わせる。言い換えれば、社会の現状を福音的観点から理解するのである。

　第4段階は実践である。前段階で分析・再考してきた社会問題に対して信仰を実践する。この実践が示すものは自分が信じている事は日常生活に影響をもたらすということである。

　プログラムの責任者であるヘル・プラコサ（SJ）神父が2011年と2012年のATEPプログラムを振り返って、ペサントレンで過ごした1週間は大変貴重な経験になったと述べた。参加者はイスラム教に関して授業や本で得た情報の真偽を確かめることができた。それに続く内省の段階では、サナタダルマ大学神学部で神学の教鞭をとるキエサ（SJ）神父の指導のもと、イスラム教徒との生活とイスラム教の理解をキリスト教神学とイグナチオの霊性的観点から再考した。このプログラムは価値のある洞察と豊かな視点を与えることで、参加者が生活し働く場所をよりよく理解する手助けをしている。

結　論

　学生に人類、文化の最良のものを学ばせ、それを自らの霊的成長と神の体験に結びつけ、知識を共通善のために使わせ、すべての人々の幸福に向けてグローバル文化の市民として自らをとらえさせるイエズス会の教育は、私たちの現在の教育的要求に大きな関わりをもっている。

参考文献

Arrupe, Pedro, SJ. (1974). *Men For Others*, Washington, D.C.: J.S.E.A.

Association of Jesuit Colleges and Universities (AJCU). (2010). *The Jesuit, Catholic Mission of U.S. Jesuit Colleges and Universities*.

Duminuco, Vincent J. (ed)., (2000). *The Jesuit Ratio Studiorum: 400th Anniversary Perspectives*. New York: Fordham University Press.

Kolvenbach, P.H., SJ. (1986). *The Characteristics of Jesuit Education*. Rome: Jesuit Curia.

Modras, Ronald. (2004). *Ignatian Humanism: A Dynamic Spirituality for the 21st Centu-*

ry. Chicago: Loyola Press.

Muller, Banawiratma, SJ. (1999). "Contextual Social Theology — An Indonesian Model," *East Asian Pastoral Review*.

Nicolás, Adolfo, SJ. (July 13, 2009). *Challenges and Issues in Jesuit Education*. On the Occasion of the 150th Anniversary of Jesuit Education in the Philippines, Ateneo de Manila University.

Nicolás, Adolfo, SJ. (April 23, 2010). *Challenges to Jesuit Higher Education Today*. Remarks for "Networking Jesuit Higher Education: Shaping the Future for a Humane, Just, Sustainable Globe," Mexico City.

O'Malley, John W., SJ. (2000). "From the 1599 Ratio Studiorum to the Present: A Humanistic Tradition?", in Duminuco Vincent J. (ed). *The Jesuit Ratio Studiorum: 400th Anniversary Perspectives*. New York: Fordham University Press.

Prakosa, Heru, SJ. (1993). "Building Interreligious Dialogue as Survivors in Line with Local Wisdom" *Ignatian Pedagogy: A Practical Approach*. Rome: Jesuit Curia.

Prakosa, Heru, SJ. (2011). *ATEP: Asia Theological Encounter Program — A Report*.

Tatang, Iskarna. (2006). *Sanata Dharma Prospectus*. Yogyakarta.

韓国におけるカトリック教育

1960 年以降の課題への応答の歴史

ベネディクト・カンユップ・ユン
〈西江大学〉

教育の目的は、空っぽの心を開かれた心に変えることである
——マルコム・フォーブス

I　序　　論

　1960 年代から、社会経済発展を伴う韓国の「圧縮された現代化」(compressed modernity) は世界の注目を集めてきた。この発展は、ほとんど宗教的ともいえる韓国人の教育への熱意と、政府による入念な教育制度の整備によるものである。「教育熱」が韓国の政治経済発展の根本要因となったことは確かであるが、その一方で、韓国の教育界は教育熱の原因および結果である一連の問題に対処してこなかった。また同時に、政府の教育への強い関与によって、カトリック学校を含む宗教関連校に他の公立校との差を際立たせる余裕を与えなかった。
　本稿は、1960 年に西江大学が設立されてから、韓国のカトリック学校が社会的・政治的そして文化的課題とどのように関わってきたかに焦点を当てる。次節では韓国におけるカトリック教育が置かれていた社会経済状況に考察を加え、続いて韓国とカトリック教育の課題を指摘する。次にカトリック教会とその教育機関が課題に対応するためにとった措置を、主に社会教育面に絞って概観する。最後に、教育問題を緩和し、カトリック教会の教育的関与を高めるための集合的知恵を引き出すことを目的として、いくつかの論点を提示する。

II　社会と教育の発展と課題

II−1　韓国教育の発展と特徴
　韓国教育の発展に特徴的なのは、教育と経済成長の不可分なつながりである。

経済発展と教育の役割に関していえば、後者が前者の触媒となっている韓国は経済学者や教育関係者の強い関心を集めている（Chung, 2010; Y.H. Kim, 2010; Lee, Jung & Kim, 2006; OECD, 2001; Seth, 2002, 2005）。1960年以降、発展の各段階で必要となる労働力を確保するため、韓国政府は人材育成政策に基づいて教育政策と工業化戦略を調整してきた[1]。

教育と工業化政策の相互対応は、「シークエンシャル・ボトムアップ・アプローチ（Sequential Bottom-up Approach）」と呼ばれる韓国教育のもう1つの特徴を生み出した。急速な工業化とそれに伴って増加した熟練労働力の需要は、初等教育から高等教育を受けるものの人口が相次いで拡大した。このアプローチによって政府が設定した経済発展段階に応じた必要な労働力を供給することが可能となった。しかし教育機会の急速かつ連続的拡大は韓国人の教育への並々ならぬ情熱によって加速したのである。

韓国人の教育への情熱は世界でも他に類を見ない。教育への情熱――「教育熱」（Seth, 2002）と呼ばれる、教育への過剰な期待――は、儒教的な教育観に深く根ざしたものである教育は人々が成熟し完全なものとなる助けであり、国を治めるうえで必要な技能を身につけるための真の方法と考えられている。韓国の教育熱は韓国における教育の発展の第一義的要因となったが、一方で望ましくない反動も出ている。教育熱による親の子どもへの過剰な期待が子どもの多大な負担となっていることは言うまでもない。

さらに韓国の学生と親は、幼稚園に入るとすぐに大学受験地獄に巻き込まれることが明らかになっている。入学試験のためにすべての労力と方策が費やされる。毎年11月の試験日には、国中が固唾をのんでそれを見守る。この日は韓国人の人生にとって最も大事な日であるため、聞き取り試験の最中は、飛行機も発着を控えるのである。選択肢式の一度きりの試験で得る点数が、「高名な大学での学位を得ることによって社会的地位の維持ないしは上昇につながる」（Seth, 2005, p.24）とされるほどに生徒の将来を左右する。この過酷な入学試験は、過剰な家庭の教育支出（影の教育）、貧富の差による社会的不一致（二極化）、学歴がものをいう社会の促進（学歴主義）、および大学入学希望者が通らなければならない「試験地獄」といった否定的な社会効果も生み出している。

II－2　課題と社会環境

これを背景として、韓国の教育制度が直面している種々の問題は、政府の喫

繁の課題となっている。これに加えて、カトリックの教育機関など私立の宗教関連校に特有の問題も取り上げる。

A　韓国における教育の一般的課題

a）影の教育

大変皮肉なことに、教育熱、つまり教育の過熱は諸刃の剣である。経済成長の第一要因となった韓国人の猛烈な教育熱は影の教育につながった。この影の教育は私費教育を増大させ、一般の学校教育制度への信頼は失われた[2]。

『韓国統計年鑑』（スタティスティクス・コリア）(2013)によると、2012年に小学校から高等学校までの生徒に費やされた影の教育費用はGDPの1.6％にもあたる190億米ドルにも及んだ。生徒1人当たりの月々の平均出費は23万6000ウォン（210米ドル）であり、全生徒の69.4％が影の教育を受けていた[3]。このデータからは韓国の親が子どものために多様な影の教育を用いていることがわかる。住居や年金、娯楽といった他への出費を犠牲にしてまでも、世帯収入の多くが私費教育に充てられているのである[4]。

b）グローバル化と知識社会の到来

グローバル化は韓国の教育制度の痛いところを指弾する鬨（とき）の声であり、2つの課題を突き付けた。それは「国際市場における国家の競争力を支え……人材発展の課題に見合うよう教育制度を再編すること」(Lee, Kim, Kim & Kim, 2006, p.66)であった。かつては際限のないつめこみと機械的な暗記という厳しい訓練の波にのまれていた韓国の教育は、知識社会の到来によって、生徒の創造性を伸ばし、より率先的に学ばせる制度と環境を整えることを余儀なくされた。

c）学校崩壊

米国では、「学校の失敗」は学校が社会的平等を達成できず生徒の学力が上がらない状態を指す。しかし韓国における「学校崩壊」はこれとは異なり、生徒が教師への敬意を持たず、規律が乱れ、授業への関心が薄まっているという状態を意味する。影の教育や私費教育の問題にも絡み、教室で生徒に向き合うことを「戦場」と表現する欲求不満のたまった教師たちにとって、これは厄介な問題である。そういった点で、教室での学びは機能不全に陥っている。生徒が教室での学びへの意欲を失う要因は3つ挙げられる。「情報技術と消費を中

心とする社会への効果的適応ができていないことによる学校教育の限界と、世代間の不一致や若者文化と学校文化の衝突……（そして）教師の権威と生徒の掌握力の低下につながった近年の教育方針の失敗」(M. Kim, 2003, p.143) である。

公立学校教育への根強い不満は、初等教育から高等教育のいずれの段階においても、子どもを海外へ送り出す親の増加につながっている。小学校から高等学校までの年代で留学する生徒の数は、特に2008年以降の世界規模の景気後退によって減少しているものの、高等教育においてはその数は増加している。2011年には、高等教育段階で約16万5000人、小学校から高校で1万6500人の韓国人学生が海外で勉強していた。初・中等教育段階における留学生数が減少する一方で、高等教育におけるその数は増加している（表1）[5]。海外留学のために使われた費用の合計は毎年40億米ドルを超え、2011年には約44億米ドルであった（図1）。

表1　海外留学生数　　　　　　　　　　　　　　　　　　　　　　単位：人

	2006	2007	2008	2009	2010	2011
小学校	13,814	12,341	12,531	8,369	8,794	7,477
中学校	9,246	9,201	8,888	5,723	5,870	5,468
高等学校	6,451	6,126	5,930	4,026	4,077	3,570
大学	113,735	123,965	127,000	151,566	152,852	164,169

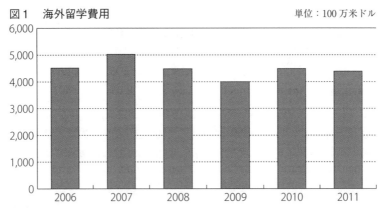

図1　海外留学費用　　　　　　　　　　単位：100万米ドル

出所：e-country indicator
http://www.index.go.kr/egams/stts/jsp/potal/stts/PO_STTS_IdxMain.jsp?idx_cd=1534

d）社会と教育の二極化

近年、教育と社会そして政治の場で問題となっているのは、教育格差をどのように縮め解消するかという問題である。この教育格差は 1995 年 5 月 31 日に施行された教育改革が、新自由主義的教育手法と 1997 年のアジア通貨危機によって加速したことに端を発するといわれている。

e）多文化主義の発展

つい最近まで韓国は民族的・言語的に極めて均質であったため、政府は容易にかつ効率よく全国共通のカリキュラムを組むことができた（Y.H. Kim, 2006, p.354）。しかし、10 組に 1 組ともいわれる国際結婚の増加や、移民労働者の大量流入は韓国の人口構成に変化をもたらした。1995 年に約 27 万人であった外国人の数は、2005 年には 75 万人となっている。2009 年にはその数は 110 万人にも上り、人口全体の 2.2％を占めるまでになった。この割合で増加が続くと、2050 年までに外国人の数は 400 万人となり、全人口の 10％を占めるとされている（Park, 2009, p.20）。国際結婚から生まれた子どもが差別されがちであることに照らしてかんがみると、多文化教育がいかにすれば国際結婚夫婦や外国人の子どもを伝統的に均質な韓国社会に溶け込ませる一助となりうるのかは捨ておけない問題である。

f）人口の変化と大学改革

韓国は OECD 加盟国の中で過去 50 年間の出生率の低下が最も著しく、またアジアにおいて私費教育費の割合が最も高い（Anderson & Kohler, 2012）。低出生率と私費教育費拡大の強い相関性からは、子どもの数を 1 人または 2 人に抑えることで、子どもに競争力をつけさせ成功させたいという親の強い願いが窺える。低出生率は韓国の教育制度と社会、特に短大と大学に大きな損失をもたらしている。政府の見込みでは、出生率低下の結果、2018 年以降、高校を卒業する生徒の数は大学の定員数を下回る。人口の変化がもたらした厳しい状況下で、教育省は 2015 年以降、大学の定員を減らし制度を再編するという計画に対する各大学の対応を迫ることを決定した（K.H. Lee, 2013）[6]。

B　カトリック教育特有の課題

カトリック学校は学問と宗教の教育を行う 2 つの役割を担っており、それは

「全人的育成を促進する優れた方法」であるだけでなく、「教会の救いの使命の一部」でもある（The Catholic School, 1977, #8-9）。しかし韓国の教育制度一般とカトリック学校の現状には大差がない。おびただしい数の研究がカトリック教育の直面している課題や問題を理解するために多くのページを割いている（Han, 2007; Ahn, 1998 も参照のこと；Kang, 1999；カトリック学校法人連合会, 1999, 2007）。

a) 試験中心型教育

大学入試への執着によって、カトリック学校も、どれだけ多くの生徒を有名大学へ進学させることができるかという激しい競争の波に乗らざるをえなくなった。創造性よりも丸暗記、また人格形成よりも試験に重点を置いた歪んだ教育のあり方が是正されるべきであることはカトリック学校も認識しているが、保護者や生徒からの圧力は無視することができない。韓国の学校教育環境が出世主義と学歴主義にとらわれている限り、ひとりカトリック学校だけが人格形成に力を注ぐことは困難である。

b) 政府の教育方針：すべてを1つの枠組みへ

公的な責任と教会の役割というカトリック学校のもつ2つの機能を考えれば、公的教育機関としての政府の指導管理は理解できる。しかし教会の役割と機能は政府の方針によって簡単に封じ込められてしまい、カトリック教育の使命が脅かされることになる。共通の教育課程と政府による教科書検定に加え、教育熱の抑制を狙いとする一連の教育改革は、カトリック学校の生徒選抜の独自性の減少につながった[7]。

標準化政策と私立学校法の改定は私立学校の自主性よりもその公的役割を際立たせるものであり、私学の自主性と特殊性、また各校の使命をうやむやにしてしまった。私学はカトリック学校の建学の精神に見合う生徒を入学させることができず、またその精神を反映した特殊なカリキュラムにも制限がかけられている。

c) 経済的危機とアイデンティティ・クライシス

私学を統制するもう1つの手段は助成金である。標準化政策によって、私立学校の経済的独立性と持続性の問題が露呈した。政府は私学が授業料を独自に設定する権利を取り上げ、公立校と同じ授業料を徴収するよう強制した。政府

は1971年から私立中学を対象に、また1979年からは私立高校を対象に助成金を与え、公立・私立どちらの生徒にも平等な機会が与えられるようにした。助成金は私学が被った経済赤字を補うためのものであった。2006年には私学への助成金は35億米ドルにも上り、中学と高校の年間予算に対してそれぞれ73.7%と44.3%を占めた。政府がかじ取りをしているため、私学は際立った特徴や多様性をもたない、にせの、あるいは準公立校となってしまった（The Ministry of Education & Human Resources Development, 2007）。

d) 宗教教育への制限

1992年、宗教教育が選択科目として一般カリキュラムに導入されるようにするため、政府は「宗教科免許制度」を導入した。政府が私学の独自性と特殊な地位を考慮したという点でこれは画期的であったかのように見えた。しかし政府による宗教教育への介入はそれだけにとどまらず、宗教教育の公認と制度化に続いて、様々な介入政策や規制が行われた。例えば宗教科教員の養成と認定や、宗教科の教科書の内容や選定における指導などである。宗教科教育に政府の規制は重くのしかかり、いまやカトリック学校は「カリキュラムの全体的補足の必要性、教材の不足、適切な教師の不足、教師間に広がる落胆の念、（そして）予算の問題」にあえいでいる（Han, 2007, p.40）。

e) 教会内の協力体制の欠如

私立学校のアイデンティティを象徴する最も重要な存在理由はその建学の精神にあり、これは生徒の「学校を選択する権利」および学校の「カリキュラムを設定し生徒を選抜する権利」を保障するはずであった。政府の干渉政策に応答するという点において、カトリック学校とカトリック教会は時宜にあった協力体制をとることができなかった。

カトリック学校法人連盟（Association of Catholic Education Corporations）がやっと設立されたのは1986年のことである。これはカトリック教育機関同士の協力的パートナーシップを強化するため、2005年にはカトリック学校法人連合会（The Federation of Catholic Educational Foundation）となった。韓国カトリック司教会議（CBCK）は、私立学校法の改正が議論をよんだ2006年以降、より積極的に教育に関わるようになる。

Ⅲ　カトリック教育と応答

Ⅲ-1　カトリック教育の位置づけ

　カトリック教会は韓国の教育の歴史に少なからぬ貢献をしてきている。1865年、初の現代的な学校となった聖ヨゼフ神学院が韓国東部のバエロン（Baeron）に設立され、1911年にはベネディクト会が初の教員養成大学であるスンシン教育大学を開設した（The Federation of Catholic Educational Foundation, 2007）。

　1963年時の韓国教育制度の統計データから、全学校・私立校・カトリック学校の数がわかる。学校の数について、カトリックの幼稚園・小学校・中学校・高等学校そして大学はそれぞれ全国の学校数の15.4％、0.2％、2.8％、4.5％、8.6％を占めていた。カトリックの幼稚園に入園した園児の数は全国の園児数の20.7％にあたり、大学は2.0％であった。私立学校に占めるカトリック学校の割合はそれぞれ15.6％、17.4％、6.9％、10.4％、14.7％であった（表2）。

　その約50年後となる2012年には、幼稚園と高校、大学の数は増加したが（それぞれ213、38、10校）、小学校と中学校の数は減少した（各6、28校）。生徒数については、1万8,377人から1万5,915人への減少をみせた中学校を除き、総じて増加している。幼稚園と大学の生徒数の増加には目を見張るものがある。幼稚園の入園児数は3,853人から2万2,903人（493％）に増加し、大学では2,192人から4万3,450人（1880％）になっている（表3）。しかし、1963年から2012年にかけて、カトリック学校の数とその生徒数が全学校の数と生徒数、また私立学校の数に対して減少していることには留意しなければいけない。

Ⅲ-2　カトリック教会の応答

　カトリックの教育機関がカトリック教育を行うことができなかったのには主に2つの理由がある。1つはカトリック学校の自治と独自性を許さなかった政府による教育システムの規制、もう1つは大学入試に重点を置き、宗教教育よりも一般科目の勉強に焦点を当てる社会風潮である（Kang, 1999）。カトリック学校は、全人教育のための課外科目を教えることに関して説得力のある理論的根拠を親や生徒に示すことができないでいる。一定の授業料、規制の多い教育方針、カリキュラムの統制、また生徒選抜の権利の制限による独自性の欠如によって、カトリック学校は準公立校となってしまった。同時に、カトリック学

表2　1963年における韓国教育の統計

	学校数の合計（校）			生徒数の合計（人）		
	計	公立	私立	計	公立	私立
幼稚園	363	4	359	18,668	246	18,422
小学校	4,835	4,789	46	4,421,541	4,407,977	13,564
中学校	1,114	662	452	665,760	387,080	278,680
高校	669	381	288	365,020	208,493	156,527
大学	58	24	34	109,063	35,370	73,693
短大	36	3	33	14,423	577	13,846
	カトリック学校	合計に占めるカトリック学校の割合	私学の合計に占めるカトリック学校の割合	カトリック学校の生徒数	全体に占めるカトリック学校の生徒の割合	私学に占めるカトリック学校の生徒の割合
幼稚園	56	15.4%	15.6%	3,858	20.7%	20.9%
小学校	8	0.2%	17.4%	2,598	0.1%	19.2%
中学校	31	2.8%	6.9%	18,377	2.8%	6.6%
高校	30	4.5%	10.4%	11,133	3.0%	7.1%
大学	5	8.6%	14.7%	2,192	2.0%	3.0%
短大	データなし			データなし		

表3　2012年における韓国教育の統計

	学校数の合計（校）			生徒数の合計（人）		
	計	公立	私立	計	公立	私立
幼稚園	8,538	4,525	4,013	613,749	127,347	486,402
小学校	5,895	5,819	76	2,951,995	2,909,999	41,996
中学校	3,162	2,517	645	1,849,094	1,519,004	330,090
高校	2,303	1,356	947	1,920,087	1,072,986	847,101
大学	199	43	156	2,122,747	477,960	1,644,787
短大	142	9	133	769,888	16,792	753,096
	カトリック学校	合計に占めるカトリック学校の割合	私学の合計にしめるカトリック学校の割合	カトリック学校の生徒数	全体に占めるカトリック学校の生徒の割合	私学に占めるカトリック学校の生徒の割合
幼稚園	213	2.5%	5.3%	22,903	3.7%	4.7%
小学校	6	0.1%	7.9%	3,674	0.1%	8.7%
中学校	28	0.9%	4.3%	15,915	0.9%	4.8%
高校	38	1.7%	4.0%	32,280	1.7%	3.8%
大学	10	5.0%	6.4%	43,450	2.0%	2.6%
短大	1	0.7%	0.8%	1,864	0.2%	0.2%

出所：Korean Educational Development Institute: http://cesi.kedi.re.kr
　　　Catholic Bishops' Conference of Korea: http://cbck.or.kr

校はより依存的になり、カトリック教会の教育理念に基づいて学校運営を行う力と意志を失った。この状況下で、イエズス会第29代総長のコルヴェンバッハ神父（2001）が本会が行うべき「学問的・職業的・精神的・道徳的そして霊的な"全人"を教育する」（p.23）努力について述べたことを考えても、全人的形成はもはや幻想のようにも思える。

遅々としたものではあるが、カトリック教育とカトリック機関はそのアイデンティティに疑問をもち、福音的価値観をもった生徒をどのように教育するかを考え、課題に対して体系的な応答を始めている。それらの応答の効果にはまだ疑問が残るが、カトリック教育者、CBCK、CBCK内の教育委員会、西江大学の4つの異なる主体による応答を挙げることができる。

A　カトリック教育関係者
　a) カトリック学校法人連合会（http://www.cascfe.or.kr/cascfe/）

1986年10月11日、カトリック教育機関の理事会長らは西江大学に集まって各校が抱えている問題について話し合い、福音的価値に基づいて各校の使命が守り果たされるよう、協力関係を強めて共同で問題解決にあたることに合意した。同年12月6日には、のち2005年からのカトリック学校法人連合会の前身であるカトリック学校法人連盟を設立した。この連盟の設立目的は「管区や修道会のもとにあるカトリック教育機関が現在抱えている問題を議論し、協力関係を強めて共同でカトリック教育の使命を果たしていくことである」。連盟は数名の司教、司祭、修道女によって構成され、一般信徒は理事会に含まれていない。連合会とCBCKの教育委員会は密接な協力関係を保ちながら、複数の事業計画に携わっている。

　b) カトリック教育者連盟

2010年、西江大学で開催された第2回カトリック教育関係者会議の締めくくりとして、カトリック教育者連盟が正式に設立された。この組合には、カトリック教育の方向性を定め、教育問題を扱う方法を決定することが期待される。

B　韓国カトリック司教会議（http://www.cbck.or.kr/）
　a) 教育委員会の設立

1972年10月、カトリックの教育理念に基づいた福音的価値観を育て、韓国

の教育制度の発展に寄与することを目的として、CBCK は教育委員会を設立した。ユースミニストリーの重要性が増すにつれて、2008 年、CBCK は教育ミニストリーからユースミニストリー委員会を切り離した。

b）カトリック教育憲章

CBCK は、カトリック教育が韓国の教育制度に与えた歴史的貢献にもかかわらず、教会が歴史と教育の観点からカトリック教育の役割を評価してこなかったということに気づいた。カトリック教育理念を確立し、学校運営を行ううえでの助けとなるような教会の公文書さえ存在しなかったのである。この状況を受けて、2006 年 10 月、CBCK は韓国カトリック学校憲章をマグナカルタとして採択した。

憲章にはカトリック学校は 2 つの特徴をもつものと明記されている。1 つは教会的特徴で、「キリストの生涯を手本として、キリスト者としての価値観を持って教会の宣教の使命に尽くす」ということであり、もう 1 つは一般的な特徴で、「他の学校と同じように、知識と情報を伝え、文化的遺産を伝え、深い人間性を養う」意味がある（カトリック教育憲章 1.1）。憲章は、カトリック学校の使命は「宣教と全人教育に尽くすことである」（カトリック教育憲章 1.2）としている。

c）韓国におけるカトリック学校教育の指針

2011 年、CBCK は憲章の精神がすべてのカトリック学校で実現されるようにとの期待のもと、「韓国におけるカトリック学校教育の指針」の最終版を発表した。指針はカトリック学校教育憲章にさらに詳細な情報と内容を盛り込み、拡大したものである。

この指針は関係者、つまり生徒・親・教職員にカトリック学校の長所と独自性を理解させ、カトリックの機関が効果的かつ継続的にカトリックの教育精神を広めることを目的としている。それに加え、カトリックの教育哲学と学校の自立に関して公私いずれも妥協しようとする動きに対して、カトリック機関と個人が適切な応答ができるよう法的な基盤を与えるものでもある。

d）幼稚園におけるカトリック教育のガイドライン

CBCK は現在「幼稚園におけるカトリック教育の指針」を作成中である。

指針はカトリック学校教育憲章を反映するもので、カトリックの信仰の精神に基づいてどのようにカトリック幼稚園を運営すべきかを示している。

C　イエズス会の応答──西江大学（http://www.sogang.ac.kr/english）
a）イエズス会の教育理念

　イエズス会の学校は、学校の２つのひな型を融合させているという点で他に類を見ない。その２つのひな型とは、理性を訓練する中世の大学と、人格形成のためのルネサンス人文主義高等教育学校である『イエズス会教育へのポケットガイド、イエズス会の学校はなぜこんなにも成功を収めたのか？』。教育における成功については、イエズス会教育方法のいくつかの特徴が以下のように挙げられる。

- 自己認識と自律
- 自他の経験から学ぶ姿勢
- 人生の方向性を神に信頼する
- 知能と理性を真理発見のための道具と考え敬意を払う
- とるべき行動を見分けるスキル
- 才能や知識は他者を助けるための賜物であるという確信
- 問題解決における柔軟性と現実主義
- 目標は高く
- すべてに神の御業を見いだす

　現代のイエズス会の教育界は２つの重要なイエズス会原理により彩られている。１つは「他者のために」である。イエズス会第28代総長アルペ神父は1973年のヨーロッパのイエズス会学校の卒業生への講話で以下を強調した。「今日、我々の教育の最も重要な目的は、他者のために生きる人を育成することでなければならない……」（Arrupe, p.9）。もう１つは「信仰への奉仕と正義の促進」である。1975年、第32イエズス会総会は、当時の使命の本質について重要な記述を残している。その使命とは「信仰への奉仕、その中でも決定的に必要なのは正義を促進すること」（第32総会、４§２）であり、かつ「（正義を行うという信仰への奉仕は）我々のすべての活動を集約するものでなければならない……」（第32総会、２§９）。これらのイエズス会の金言は多くの書物やスピーチの基礎となっており、今日のイエズス会教育界の気風をつくっている。それはイエズス会教育の現代版憲章であり、カトリックの中でもイエ

ズス会の学校を認識するためのリトマス試験紙となっている。

　西江大学の使命は全人を育成するというイエズス会の教育理念を引き継いでおり、さらに、カトリック、イエズス会、また韓国の人間の発展および世界に尽力するという方向性をもつ伝統をも備えている。

b) 西江大学学内および学外でのプログラム

　2005 年、イエズス会韓国管区の 50 周年を記念して、コルヴェンバッハ神父（2005）が西江ファミリーに向けて行った講演でイエズス会の教育目標を要約した。「つまるところ、目標とすべきは、学生が地域社会に奉仕するリーダーとなれるよう完全な成長を促すことです。イグナチオの教育は能力・良心・思いやりに満ち溢れた男女を育成することを目指します」。これらのイエズス会教育とその目標に見られる特徴を受けて、西江は様々な研究と奉仕活動のプログラムを提供している。

b.1　イエズス会大学としてのカリキュラム

　西江は当初、人格形成という目的のため、卒業に必要な 160 単位のうちの半数を一般教養科目に充てていた。1970 年代に入り、一般教養科目の必要単位数は減り、教養科目の選択科目が拡大された。現在では、一般教養単位は最低 22 単位、最高で 31 単位履修することになっている。

b.2　キャンパスミニストリー（http://kyomok.sogang.ac.kr/）

　キャンパスミニストリー局には 5 人のイエズス会員、2 人の修道者と 2 人の一般信徒が働いており、イエズス会の教育理念を厳密に反映した 4 つの分野の多様なプログラムや活動を行っている。

b.2.1　養　成

　カテキズムの講座、学生のための聖書勉強会、英語・スペイン語・フランス語による聖書勉強会が行われている。現在学生向けに 21、外国人向けの 2 つの聖書勉強会が行われている。2010 年以降、「愛への飛び石」という名称の、新入生とその親を対象としたプログラムが行われている。このプログラムは親が子どもに対して、手書きの手紙とともに人生の教訓が詰まった本を薦めるというものである。

b.2.2　学生・教職員による組織

関係者向けの学内組織には、祭壇奉仕者、フィアット（FIAT）聖歌隊、主日ミサ奉仕を行う主日ユースコミュニティ、グラシアス（Gracias）聖歌隊、主日英語ミサのための典礼委員会、そしてボランティア活動を行うイグナティウス会などがある。マリア会（Legion of Mary）は教職員のためのグループである。それに加え、典礼ダンスや黙想ヨガのグループも積極的に参加者を受け入れている。

b.2.3　国際イマージョン経験とボランティア奉仕

第三世界の恵まれない人々の歴史と文化を学び、ボランティア奉仕を通して「他者のために」の精神を実行するため、西江はカンボジアとフィリピンでイマージョン経験プログラムを行ってきている。

2008年に開始されたAJCU-APサービスラーニング・プログラムは、同地域のイエズス会大学の学生が3週間にわたって地域奉仕を実際に行いながら、イグナチオの教育学をどのように日常生活に活かせるのかを学ぶサービスラーニングの場となっている。

またその他にも、国内でのボランティア奉仕も2種類用意されている。1つは北朝鮮からの亡命者の子どもたちのためのもの（Firefly Teachers Council）、もう1つはハンセン病患者のためのものである。

b.2.4　ボランティア社会奉仕センター

コルヴェンバッハ神父（2001）は、将来の全人教育は「社会的に、豊かに現実世界で貢献するための社会と文化についての教養ある認識、またすぐれた教養に裏付けられた一致によって」（Kolvenbach, 2001, pp.23-24）育成されなければならない、と強調した。この言葉を受けて、センターでは6つのボランティア奉仕組織の活動計画と資金面への支援を行ってきた。さらには、地域奉仕の授業も開講され、地域奉仕認定制度を運営している。

b.3　イグナチオ夜間学校

1978年以降、この学校は社会的・経済的に恵まれない学生が西江大学の学生を先生として勉強する機会を得る場となっている。西江イエズス会コミュニティの主任司祭が学校長として運営を援助している。

c）西江の将来

1960年の創立以来、西江大学は韓国における高等教育の先導役となり、革新的な計画を導入して模範的教育モデルとなった。西江の創立当初からの特徴である国際的かつ体系的な教育課程、全人育成に焦点を当てた必修一般教養、厳格な学問管理と生徒のためのクラ・ペルソナリス（cura personalis）のおかげで、西江はこんなにも短期間のうちに一流大学へと成長することができた。しかし、高度な集中的経済成長とグローバル化は、より大規模で競争力のある地域に根ざした大学との競争ともあいまって、西江のアイデンティティと持続可能性に影響を与えた。西江は教育の向上のためのみならず、イエズス会の教育理念を生き生きとみなぎらせるために、主に3つのプロジェクトを企画している。

c.1　一般教養の再編と霊性のためのチュルウー・マンレサ（Chulwoo Manresa）センター[8]

西江は地域奉仕・リーダーシップ・実習を含む一般教養科目を拡大して、叡智・人格・霊性を備えた全人的育成をめざす。この計画達成のための1つの方法として、ソウル郊外にチュルウー・マンレサ霊性センターが創設された。合計96の教室と寮を備えたこのセンターは、学事年度2015年から、全新入生を対象にした霊性教育に使われる予定である。

c.2　第2のキャンパス：GERBキャンパス

ソウルにある西江のメインキャンパスは手狭になってきている。西江はソウル東部郊外のナムヤンジュにGERB（Global Education Research & Business）のキャンパスを建設することを計画している。このキャンパスは教育・研究・文化そして産業界との結束を強化するための高等教育設備として使われる。

c.3　SOWUUS（恵まれない学生のための西江世界大学）

第三世界における人間の発展に貢献しようと、西江は第2キャンパスに恵まれない学生のための西江世界大学を創立し、社会的・経済的に恵まれない学生を毎年一定数全世界から受け入れ、無償で大学教育をすることを計画している。第30代イエズス会総長ニコラス神父は、「より人間的で公正で、持続的かつ信仰にあふれた世界」（Nicolás, 2010, p.13）を築いていくために共に努力すること

の重要性を説いている。イエズス会大学として西江がもつ利点を積極的に利用することで韓国の大学に新たなパラダイムを切り開く。言うまでもなく、その利点にはイエズス会大学の世界的ネットワークも含まれる。西江はユネスコや国連と連携し、韓国の教育・科学技術分野での発展の経験に基づいた学びの機会を若者に与えることで、彼らが帰国後に祖国の経済や人々の発展に貢献できるようにしていく。この計画の鍵となるのはイエズス会大学の広いネットワーク、国連、ユネスコ、NGO と企業の連携である。

Ⅳ　将来に向けてのカトリック教育の課題

　韓国におけるカトリック教育は、全人教育と宣教の価値と意味を兼ね備える展望や使命を全うしようと、重要だが困難の多い道を歩んできている。山積する問題とその原因と影響は、創造的解決策を早急に求める動きを生み出した。韓国のカトリック学校の現状を踏まえれば、カトリック教育のユニークかつ特別な使命を全うするための理に適った献身的方法を見つけるまでには長くかかるだろう。カトリック学校の基礎となる使命を考えれば、カトリック教育の現状に関する真の正確な理解と解決策が本当に必要とされている。以下の提案を議論のためのものとして提示する。

A　ルーツと伝統の新しくより深い理解

　「カトリック学校が存続のためにできる唯一のことは、カトリック学校の教育目標に忠実であることだ」(The Catholic School, 第85条) とされている。学校の教育目標がその使命、展望と教育理念を表すことは疑いようもない。それらは学校が計画し実施するすべての方針の内容と性質に関わり、学校の進むべき方向を示す重要な指標となる。

　しかし、教育目標は学校がその時々で置かれている新たな状況をより深く顧みて、学校がよりよい役割とサービスを果たせるよう再考されなければならない。学校関係者や社会に変化をもたらす新たな状況に教育的使命がどう対応するか考えることは、創立時からの霊的遺産の本質を時代にふさわしいものへと改めていくこととなる。新たな雰囲気を考慮することなく安易に現状に満足してしまう傾向には常に危険が潜んでいる。

B　市場との対話

　重要なことは、市場を避けるのではなく市場との対話を続けることである。大学で働くイエズス会の召命は「教会が世界に出会い、世界が教会に出会う境界線に生きること」であり、その挑戦は「境界線が常に変化していること」である（Murray, 1966, p.10）。教皇フランシスコは『チビルタ・カットリカ』（イタリア雑誌）の編集長とのインタビューで、現状維持を求めたり「フロンティア開拓を抑制」したりする誘惑への警告を発した（Spadaro, 2013）。

> 私がフロンティアと言うとき、私は特に、文化的世界で働く人々が、自らが働き考えるコンテクストの中に入り込む必要性のことを指しています。研究室の中で生きていくという危険が常に潜んでいます。私たちの信仰は研究室のためのものではなく、旅路に対する歴史ある信仰です。神は抽象的真実の概論としてではなく、歴史として自らを顕しました。私が研究室を恐れるのは、研究室で問題に向き合い、それを家に持ち帰って人工的に色付けすれば、問題をコンテクストの外に出してしまうことになるからです。フロンティアを持ち帰ることはできません。境界に生き、大胆でなければいけません。（Spadaro, 2013）

　指導者層はどのようにすれば市場の力に流されずに教育目標や価値観を保持し強化することができるだろうか。奉仕と憐れみの精神をもつ市民をつくり出すよりよい教育のための教育環境をつくる努力をして市場に参画するよりも、居心地よく挑戦を受けることのない象牙の塔に立てこもる方が危険で害が大きい。問題は、大学指導部が市場の圧力に対して、どのように大学の公的責任とのバランスを取るかということである。

C　地元、地域そして世界規模でのネットワーク作り

　地域的なレベルでは、ネットワークの発展はカトリック学校と関係者らの協力的パートナーシップ強化のために行われるべきである。ネットワーク構築は1つの問題に対して様々な思慮深い観点を得るのに役立ち、建設的な相乗効果をもたらす1つの方法として社会により良い影響を残すことができる。

　西江はイエズス会のネットワークを通して国際的な関与を拡大できる。ニコラス神父は、「希薄化のグローバル化——思考・展望・夢・関係・信念の希薄」

のもたらす問題に対処するため「より深い分析・熟考・洞察力」を求めた(Nicolás, 2010, p.9)。彼は続いて、イエズス会高等教育機関のより普遍的、創造的そして効果的な国際的ネットワークを提案した。

> 各大学が社会的プロジェクト(proyecto social)としての働きを通して社会に大きな善を還元できるとすれば、すべてのイエズス会高等教育機関がグローバルな社会的プロジェクトのようになれたら、われわれの世界への奉仕の範囲はどれほど広がることでしょう[9]。(Nicolás, 2010, p.15)

アジア太平洋地域でのイエズス会連盟では、高等教育のアジア太平洋イエズス会大学連盟(AJCU-AP)と、中学・高校のJEC-APがネットワーク構築の良い例である。AJCU-APのいくつかの加盟校の学生と教職員のためにAJCU-APによって創始されたサービスラーニング・プログラム(SLP)、また上智大学と西江の間で行われているスポーツと文化交流プログラムのSOFEXも例として挙げられる。

D　カトリック教育理念の正当化に向けての法的な制定と社会批准

前述のとおり、宗教をもつ私立学校は、政府による法律、規約、方針の締め付けという過激な干渉と規制にさらされてきた。法律による規制はカトリック教育の根底にある哲学の実現を危うくした。2005年と2007年の私立学校法改正にもかかわらず、宗教校の自主性はまだまだ確保されていない。カトリック教育の発展は、宗教をもつ学校の独特の役割を規定する法的措置に一部依拠している。カトリック学校のより自主性のある運営と識別された教育を保証するためには、私立学校法などの関連する法律を改正する努力が大いに求められている。

E　学校法人の役割の強化

どのような学校法人にも、主に3つの役割と責任がある。それは学校に経済的援助をすること、創立時の教育理念が保たれているか確かめること、そして教育の質を保証することである。

　・現時点で、学校の長所と短所は何か。

・学校はどのようなチャンスと脅威に直面しているか。
・学校の長期的戦略計画はどのようなものか。
・学校指導部がカトリック・イエズス会の教育理念と特徴を促進するため、学校はどのような方針をとっているか。
・学校指導者の権限を強化するため、学校はどのような人材と財源を確保しているか。

F　教会の使命を一般の大学と共有するために

　教会は、教会の使命を果たす中での一般信徒の役割と存在価値を認めている。教会の救いの使命の働き手として、信徒一人ひとりはつねに「キリストの司牧・預言・そして王としての役割を共有する人物」であり、さらに彼らの使徒としての地位は「教会の救いの使命そのものへの参画」である（Lay Catholics in Schools, 1982, #6）。同じ傾向で、イエズス会の第34総会ではイエズス会の使命達成における一般信徒の役割を強調した。「一般信徒との協力は、我々の構成要素でもあり、個人的・地域的そして組織的な見返りを求める恵みでもある。一般信徒のミニストリーの奉仕、宣教において彼らと協力関係を持つこと、そして将来の協力の創造的方法にオープンであるよう我々に求める。」（第34総会, 13, #26）

　しかし教師や一般信徒の役割に関するこれらの宣言と裏腹に、現実には、韓国のカトリック教会で組織の方向性や理念を決定するレベルでの一般信徒の関与は驚くほど小さい。例えば、すでに述べたように、韓国カトリック学校法人連盟の理事会に一般信徒は1人もいない。集合的知能や協力体制を通して、一般信徒の参画が増えるようにすべきである。同時に、学校法人を含む学校指導部は教職員が学校の教育理念を肌で感じ日々実践していくために手助けするプログラムを行うべきである。新入職員や契約職員と教員対象の研修や卒業生向けのプログラムが考えられるだろう。

G　創造的市民参画

　市民参画という面で、カトリック教育の制度がどれほどの可能性をもちうるかについて真剣に考えなければならない。多様性を認めない現在の韓国の教育制度には試験準備に直接つながらないような特色ある教育への余地は残されていない。カトリック学校は多様性・選択肢と思いやりのある異なった学校教育

第1部　アジア5大学からの報告と展望

モデルを考えなければならない。それは最終的にカトリック教育の価値を高めることとなるだろう。以下の問題は再考に値する。

・社会正義・平和・環境を改善するために宗教教育を用いる最良の方法は何か。
・恵まれない人々の教育面での強みを増やすために何ができるか。
・特に多文化家庭の子どもたちに対して、どのような対策が適切か。
・地方などの辺境地域との文化的・教育的格差はどうすれば縮められるか。

注
1　1960年代、労働力集約的な軽工業に重点が置かれた時代には、初等教育の全国的普及によって労働者の供給が確保された。1970年代には、資本集約的な重化学工業に重点が移り、中等教育や技術・職業訓練が重視されるようになった。1980年代、最先端工業が技術集約的、また知識・情報集約的工業へと移ったため、高等教育が急速な広がりを見せた。
2　影の教育の定義は「学校外で行われる月謝制のレッスンで、学校で学ぶ科目について補足的教育を行い、公立教育制度で行われる一か八かの試験に備えさせるもの」(Lee & Jung, 2010, p. 514) である。
3　2010年のGDPに占める教育機関への韓国の支出割合は、OECD加盟国34カ国のうちデンマークとアイスランドに続いて第3位であった。韓国はGDPの7.6%を教育に充てており、これはOECD平均の6.3%よりも高い。
4　韓国政府は教育熱が社会と家庭の支出にもたらす悪影響に注目している。
5　2012年には、韓国からアメリカへの留学生数は中国とインドにつづき第3位であった。
6　教育省の提案は以下のとおりである。1）2015年からすべての大学を5つのカテゴリーに分類する。2）第1グループの大学は現状維持を認めるが、他の4グループの学校は定員を削減する。3）学校評価が低ければ定員削減幅を引き上げる。4）第5グループはペナルティとして閉校する。
7　中学校入試の廃止（中学校無試験入学、1969年）、高校の標準化政策（高等学校標準化政策、1973年）、私立学校法人の定款の改正（私立学校定款改正、1975、1981、2006年）、そして高等学校の成績の内申制（内申制、1981年）。
8　西江カトリック高等マネジメント・プログラム（Advanced Management Program）の卒業生であるチュルウー・リー氏は、このセンターがイエズス会の教育理念に基づく人格教育の場となることを願って、西江に多額の寄付をした。
9　1989年にエルサルバドルで殺されたイエズス会神学者のイグナチオ・エラクリアが提唱したproyecto social（社会的プロジェクト）という言葉を巡って、ニコラス神父（2010）は「豊かな叡智と知識、才能、展望とエネルギーを用いて、信仰の奉仕と正義

の促進へのコミットメントを動機として、専門家を訓練するだけでなく、真理・徳・発展と平和を社会にもたらす文化的力となるために社会に溶け込もうとする」(p.14) 大学であると定義している。

参考文献

Ahn, B.C. (1998). 가톨릭 학교 운영의 현황과 문제 및 미래 전망 [Catholic School Management: Current Status, Problems and Prospect], 사목 [Samok], 8: 71-89.

Anderson, T.M. & Kohler, H-P. (2012). *Education Fever and the East Asian Fertility Puzzle: A case study of low fertility in South Korea*. Retrieved September 20, 2013 from http://repository.upenn.edu/cgi/viewcontent.cgi?article=1037&context=psc_working_papers

A Pocket Guide to Jesuit Education (n.d.). Retrieved September 23, 2013 from http://www.bc.edu/content/bc/offices/mission/publications/guide.html

Arrupe, P. (1973). *Men for Others: Education for Social Justice and Social Action Today*. Rome: S.J. Press and Information Office.

Chang, K.S. (1999). Compressed modernity and its discontents: South Korean society in transition. *Economy and Society* 28 (1), 30-55.

Chung, J.Y. (2010). Social Dynamics and Educational Change in Korea. In C.J. Lee, S.Y. Kim & D. Adams (Eds.), *Sixty years of Korean Education* (pp. 444-475). Seoul: SNU Press.

Han, M.S. (2007, May). 가톨릭 학교의 교육 현실 [Status of Catholic School Education]. Symposium conducted at the meeting of the Education Week Seminar. Nonsan, Korea. Retrieved October 5, 2013

John Paul II (1992). *Ex Corde Ecclesiae*. Retrieved September 28, 2013 from http://www.vatican.va/holy_father/john_paul_ii/apost_constitutions/documents/hf_jp-ii_apc_15081990_ex-corde-ecclesiae_en.html

Kang, T.J. (1999). 교육개혁과 가톨릭 학교교육 [Education Reform and Catholic Education]. In the Federation of Catholic Educational Foundation (Ed.), 한국의 가톨릭 학교교육 [Catholic Education in Korea] (pp. 135-156). Seoul: Catholic Cultural Center.

Kim, J.Y. (2013, March 7). Education spending gap reaches a 10-year high, *The Korea Joongang Daily*.

Kim, M. (2003). Teaching and Learning in Korean Classrooms: The Crisis and the New Approach. *Asia Pacific Education Review* 4 (2), 140-150.

Kim, Y.H. (2010). Education and Economic Growth in Korea 1945-1995. In C.J. Lee, S.Y. Kim & D. Adams (Eds.), *Sixty years of Korean Education* (pp. 326-359). Seoul: SNU Press.

Kolvenbach, P-H. (2001). The Service of Faith and the Promotion of Justice in American Jesuit Higher Education. *Studies in the Spirituality of Jesuits* 31 (1), 13-29.

Kolvenbach, P-H. (2005). Speech at the 50th Anniversary of Sogang University, Seoul,

Korea.
Kolvenbach, P-H. (2005, September 10). Interview with the Sogang Alumni Newspaper. 서강옛집 [The Sogang Alumni Newspaper].
Lee, C.J. & Jang, H.M. (2010). The History of Policy Responses to Shadow Education in Korea: Implications for the Next Cycle of Policy Response. In C.J. Lee, S.Y. Kim & D. Adams (Eds.), *Sixty years of Korean Education* (pp. 512-545). Seoul: SNU Press.
Lee, C.J. & Jung, S.S. & Kim, Y.S. (2006). 한국교육의 발전 전략과 새로운 과제 [The Development of Education in Korea: Approaches, Achievement and New Challenges]. 教育行政學研究 [The Journal of Educational Administration]. 24 (4), 1-26.
Lee, C.J., Kim, S.K., Kim, W.J. & Kim, Y.S. (2006). A Korean Model of Educational Development. In C.J. Lee, S.Y. Kim & D. Adams (Eds.), *Sixty years of Korean Education* (pp. 53-106). Seoul: SNU Press.
Lee, K.H. (2013, November 12). 대학평가 5등급 체제로… 재정지원도 차등화 [5 Levels of the University Evaluation]. 아시아 경제 (*The Asia Economy Daily*).
Murray, J.C. (1966). The Vatican Declaration on Religious Freedom. *The University in the American Experience* (pp. 1-10). New York: Fordham University.
Nicolás, A. (2010) Depth, Universality, and Learned Ministry: Challenges to Jesuit Higher Education Today. In F. Brennan (Ed.), *Shaping the Future: networking Jesuit higher education for a globalizing world* (pp. 7-21). Washington, DC: Association of Jesuit colleges and universities.
O'Brien, D.J. (2008). Conversations on Jesuit (and Catholic?) Higher Education: Jesuit Sí, Catholic….Not So Sure. In G.W. Traub (Ed.), *A Jesuit Education Reader* (pp. 217-231). Chicago: Loyola Press.
OECD (2001). *The Well-Being of Nations: the Role of Human and Social Capital*. Paris: OECD.
Park, C.U. (2009). 다문화 교육의 탄생 [The Genesis of Multicultural Education]. Ansan: Borderless village press.
Piderit, J.J. (1999). Managing Jesuit Universities After GC 34. In M.R. Tripole (Ed.), *Promised Renewed: Jesuit Higher Education for a New Millennium* (pp. 43-61). Chicago: Loyola Press.
Seth, M.J. (2002). *Education fever: Society, Politics, and the Pursuit of Schooling in South Korea*. Honolulu: University of Hawaii Press.
Seth, M.J. (2005). "Korean Education: A Philosophical and Historical Perspective." In Y.K. Kim-Renaud, R.R. Grinker & K.W. Larsen (Eds.), *Korean Education* (pp. 3-15). Retrieved September 30, 2013 from http://www.gwu.edu/~sigur/assets/docs/scap/SCAP24-KoreanEd.pdf
Spadaro, A. (2013, September 30). A Big Heart Open to God. *America*. Retrieved October 4, 2013 from http://www.americamagazine.org/pope-interview
Statistics Korea (2013). 2012년 사교육비조사 결과 [Survey Results on the Expenditure for Shadow Education]. Retrieved September 24, 2013 from http://kostat.go.kr/

survey/pedu/pedu_dl/1/index.board?bmode=read&aSeq=271849

The Catholic Bishops' Conference of Korea (2006). *Charter of Catholic School Education*.

The Catholic Bishops' Conference of Korea (2011). *Guidelines for Catholic School Education in Korea*.

The Catholic Bishops' Conference of Korea (n.d). *Guidelines for Catholic Education in Kindergarten*.

The Federation of Catholic Educational Foundation (1999). 한국의 가톨릭 학교교육 [Catholic school education in Korea]. Seoul: Catholic Cultural Center.

The Federation of Catholic Educational Foundation (2007). 가톨릭 학교 관련 법제의 현황과 발전 방안 [The Current Status of Laws related to Catholic Schools and Suggestions]. Seoul: Catholic Cultural Center.

The Ministry of Education & Human Resources Development (2007). 사립학교 재정결함 지원 제도개선 방안 [Proposal for Improvement of Financial Deficit Subsidies for Private Schools].

The Sacred Congregation for Catholic Education (1977). *The Catholic School*. Retrieved September 23, 2013 from http://www.vatican.va/roman_curia/congregations/ccatheduc/documents/rc_con_ccatheduc_doc_19770319_catholic-school_en.html

The Sacred Congregation for Catholic Education (1982). *Lay Catholics in Schools: Witness to Faith*. Retrieved September 23, 2013 from http://www.vatican.va/roman_curia/congregations/ccatheduc/documents/rc_con_ccatheduc_doc_ 19821015 _lay-catholics_en.html

The Society of Jesus (2009). *Jesuit Life & Mission Today: The Decrees & Accompanying Documents of the 31st-35th General Congregation of the Society of Jesus*. St. Louis: The Institute of Jesuit Sources.

第2部

コメントとディスカッション

第2部　コメントとディスカッション

コメントに代えて

コメンテーター：ミカエル・カルマノ
〈南山大学学長〉

　本日のシンポジウム、「アジアにおけるイエズス会大学の役割」に対する枠組みとして適切と思われる2つのキャッチフレーズについて見解を申し述べるところから私のコメントを始めさせていただきます。1つは上智大学を表すモットーである「他者のために、他者とともに」、もう1つは上智大学が100周年記念にあたって公式テーマとして掲げた「叡智（ソフィア）は世界をつなぐ」です。

　私はどちらも好きです。何故ならどちらも理解できるからです。ですが、それと同時に何となくしっくり来ないものを感じます。アジアはもちろん世界の重要な地域ですが、今日ここで話しているのは、2つの修道会から来たたった6人の男性だけです。つまり、1人の神言会員がイエズス会員によってなされた発表にコメントをしています。とはいえ、私は（少々おこがましいかもしれませんが）これらの修道会の名前は、アジアと世界の他の地域における私たちの使命が何であるかを端的に示していると信じています。それは、イエスとともにイエスのために奉仕する人々に加わることがいかなる意味をもつのかを表現し、また神言に耳を傾ける人とともに、そして彼らのために奉仕することです。

　ご想像のとおり、この使命を表現するのに、Societas Jesu（イエズス会、SJ）と Societas Verbi Divini（神言会、SVD）は同じ方向性をもちながら異なった言葉を用いています。私がここで申し上げたいことは、また逆も真なりということです。つまり、イエズス会大学の役割について話すことは、同じ言葉を使いながらまったく異なる現実について話すことになるかもしれないということです。私たちは共通の使命をもっていますが、同時に、共通の言葉やコンセプトで表現される共通の話題について話す時、疑いもなく同じ霊によりつき動かされていながら、違う話をしているということに気づかされるのです。

　そういうことが起こるのは、高等教育においてカトリック精神を実践しようとする様々な努力が、実に多様で時には敵意に満ちた環境で行われているとい

う単純な事実によると本日の発表は明白に示してくれました。したがって、差異に焦点を当てることで平坦な逃げ道を選んでしまいそうな誘惑が常にあります。例えば、日本が西洋諸国とまったく異質で、西洋人には理解しがたいということはよく知られています。私自身、国際カトリック大学連合（International Federation of Catholic Universities, IFCU[1]）主催のシンポジウムで発表した時などに、「日本は特別」というカードを切ってしまったことがあります。"One size (mission) fits all" の手法は立ち行かないし、カトリック大学についての使徒的憲章の中心的メッセージもそれではありません。しかし私たちは今日、歴史や環境の差異の中でも、霊性を保つための家族が必要だということにも気づいたはずです。私たちは同じ霊によって突き動かされる共同体であり、今日のこの場は私たちの内に働くその霊を感じる良い機会であったと思います。ただ単に情報交換をしているのではなく、情報を通して同じ霊性を共有しているのです。

■ホセ・クルス教授（アテネオ・デ・マニラ大学）の発表について

　クルス先生が発表の初めに「私たちの学校の創立は偶然が積み重なった結果だ、いや、私たちの中では神の摂理によるものだと信じられている」とおっしゃったのを聞き、とてもうれしく思いました。イエズス会であるかどうかにかかわらず、これこそカトリック高等教育機関についての話に必要とされる視点です。現実的な目標設定と健全な経営は大変重要ですが、同時に、教育ミニストリーに対するイエズス会の責任を再定義し新たにするという課題が常にあります。修道会が学術的ミニストリーに関わることで差異を生み出すことができるのは疑問の余地がないのですが、その責任の意味は定期的に議論し再検討していく必要があります。

　私の注意を引いたもう1つの点は、植民地時代がフィリピンにおける高等教育ミニストリーの一部にとり重荷ととらえられていることです。このような歴史は、はびこる経済格差とあいまって、近い将来カトリック高等教育に立ちはだかる大きな壁となり続けるでしょう。

■ベネディクト・カンユップ・ユン教授（西江大学）の発表について

　韓国のカトリック大学は、他とは異なる性質の敵対的な環境に直面しています。大変厳しい政府の統制と非常に競争の激しい入学試験の文化（教育熱と呼

ばれるもの）に代表されるように、カトリック高等教育の課題は、そのような画一性の強調に対抗して自らの特別な使命を表現する方法を見つけ出すことです。それに加えて、非常に低い出生率、国際結婚率の高さ、そして韓国で職を求める大量の移民も問題となっています。

　しかしこのような制限された条件の下でも、イエズス会大学は社会に真の貢献をするプログラムを主導しています。国内外から恵まれない学生を連れてきて学ばせるというSOWUUS（恵まれない学生のための西江世界大学）に特に注目したいと思います。グローバル化した市場経済の枠の中でそのようなプログラムを行うのに必要とされる心の広さは、教皇フランシスコがインタビューで語った言葉に表れています――そしてこれは繰り返して申し上げる価値があると思います。「私たちの信仰は研究室の信仰ではなく、旅路の信仰、つまり歴史的な信仰です。神はご自身を歴史としてあらわされました。抽象的な真理の概念としてではありません。……ですから、境界線に生き、大胆でなければなりません」。

■ルイス・ジェンドロン教授（輔仁大学）の発表について

　これまで、困難な環境の例は主に教育機関にはコントロールすることができない外部要因から生まれたものでした。しかしときには、カトリックの高等教育機関が直面する課題は、例えば大学の創立者ら（修道会と教区などの）の間の協力の欠如といった内部問題から発展していることもあります。このような状況は（世界中で召命が減少しているために）高等教育分野で働く十分な数の正規のイエズス会員がいないという事実によって悪化しています。また同時に、輔仁大学の例は、より的を絞ったイエズス会の関与のための機会を示すものでもありました。例えば、輔仁大学神学部（台湾で唯一の神学部）が果たしている重要な役割や、香港にイエズス会のリベラルアーツ・カレッジを創設しようとしている取り組みなどです。

　私が大変重要だと思ったのは、カトリック大学共通の必須科目（一般教養）、つまり学生（および教職員）が様々な学問領域を越えて率先して対話するための共通基盤を作ろうとする一致に基づく努力の強調です。様々な学部や領域で深く教育研究を行いながら、共通の人間性の核心部分の重要性を何度も何度も強調していくこと、もしかすると、これはイエズス会大学がアジアで果たすよう求められている役割の1つかもしれません。

コメントに代えて

■クントロ・アディ教授（サナタダルマ大学）の発表について

　カトリック大学の中心的価値観の強調については、しばしば、アディ教授が用いた「イエズス会教育——全人教育」という表現で表されます。言うまでもなく、このフレーズを教育活動の指針としているのはイエズス会だけではありませんし、アディ教授はそのことも大変明確におっしゃいました。「私たちはカトリックのイエズス会大学として同じアイデンティティを共有している」と。私はこれを、人は同時にカトリック信者にもイエズス会員にもなりうるのだという、明快な肯定の言葉として受け取りましたが、同時に1つの疑問をもちました。今日のパネリストに代表される数多くの異なった環境の中で、同じアイデンティティを保つことができるのでしょうか？　初めに申し上げたように、「カトリック大学」または「イエズス会大学」という言葉は、大学が設立された環境によって様々に異なる現実を意味します。

　私は、私たちの努力を結びつける共通のアイデンティティを維持し、今日さらに再確認することは十分可能だと思います。そのことについて、以下、川村教授の発表を用いて見ていきたいと思います。

■川村信三教授（上智大学）の発表について

　川村教授はキリスト教を日本における分裂的な要素と特徴づけました。これは伝統的な神道の枠組みの中で天皇の全能性を強調した日本政府の方針を混乱させたもの、という見方です。ある意味で、私は、これこそ私たちの大学がそれぞれの国で果たすべき使命ではないかと思います。クライトン・クリステンセンが名づけた表現を使うと、私たちの使命は、伝統にとらわれたかのように見える社会に「分裂的革新[2]」をもたらすことです。私たちがカトリック精神のこのような側面を、常には意識してこなかったことは確かです。その代わりに、私たちは直面する前途多難な環境を、私たちが本当に達成したいもの、ないしは成し遂げたいことを「混乱させる」ものとしてとらえる傾向があります。

　このような例は数多くあります。1890年の教育勅語はミッションスクールの宗教教育に重大な影響をもたらし、軍事政府の靖国神社をめぐる方針は、上智大学の学生に深刻な問題を突き付けました。同時に、川村教授が指摘されたように、反共主義は政府と教会の間につながりのようなものを生み出しました。今だから言えることですが、カトリック大学は無神論的コミュニズムと狭量な軍事ナショナリズムの双方にとってより分裂的な力をもっていたであろうこと

がわかります。

　多国籍企業がグローバル化した市場経済を席巻している状況は、私たちに似たような課題と機会を与えてくれます。その良い例は、イエズス会総長ニコラス師が挙げた4つのチャレンジと完全に適合しているアテネオ・サステイナビリティ研究所だと思います。これは、政治的・歴史的・経済的環境が多様な21世紀のアジアで、特にカトリック大学が考えるべき役割です。そのような立場はカトリック大学の存続を特に保証するものではありませんが、個人的には、今すぐにカトリック精神の維持か大学の存続かという二択を迫られることはないだろうと思います。しかし、私たちをカトリックたらしめる精神を定義し、その精神に忠実であるよう折に触れて確認するというチャレンジは常に付きまとっています。

　私は川村教授の発表の結論がとても良いと思いました。発表の最後には結論ではなく疑問[3]やジレンマが残る。しかしそれでも、私たちの大学は偶然でなく神の摂理によって創設されたものですから、悲観的になる必要はありません。疑問を投げかけ続ける限り、たとえ過去の方法を手放すことになろうとも、私たちは人類に奉仕する分裂的な力であり続けることができるでしょう。

注

1　"The Catholic University Today: Nanzan University." Actes du premier symposium du projet: Unversité, Eglise, Culture. D'un paradigme à un autre, l'Université catholique aujourd'hui. Université Saint-Paul, Ottawa, 20 avril 1999.（Pierre Hurtubise, ed.), Paris: Fédération internationale des universités catholique, 2001, pp. 213-236.

2　クリステンセン自身もこの考え方を教育に適用している。Clayton M. Christensen, Michael B. Horn, Curtis W. Johnson, *Disrupting Class: How Disruptive Innovation Will Change the Way the World Learns,* McGraw-Hill, 2008.

3　『ピーナッツ』の漫画に出てくる私のお気に入りの言葉に「答えを出せないときは、その疑問に疑問をもつべきだね」というものがあります。

アジアにおける高等教育の国際連携と
イエズス会大学の役割

モデレーター：杉村　美紀
〈上智大学〉

はじめに

　アジア諸国では1990年代以降、教育需要への対応と人材育成の必要性から高等教育改革を進めている。その過程で大学や政府は、欧米諸国をはじめとする海外大学との協力や連携を図ることで戦略的に国際化を進め、国境を越えた教育プログラムを構築し、学生や研究者、スタッフの交流を促すことによって文化交流拠点を創ろうとしている。他方、キリスト教のミッションに基づく高等教育機関においては、国際化に焦点が当てられるはるか以前から国境を越えた教育活動を展開してきた。本稿では、国際化が進む今日、こうしたキリスト教系大学が、これまでの教育の実績と伝統をもとに、どのような役割を担うことができるか、あるいは担うべきかを、カトリックの男子修道会であるイエズス会の大学に焦点を当てて検討する。以下では、はじめにアジア諸国での高等教育の国際化が、国際競争を加速させる一方、国際連携という高等教育の新たな可能性を生んでいることをキリスト教系大学の国際連携の事例を通して紹介したうえで、2008年よりアジアで実施されている学生交流プログラム「イエズス会グローバルシップ・プログラム」を取り上げ、学際的・学融合的（inter-disciplinary / trans-disciplinary）教育を軸とする国際高等教育のモデルを提示する[1]。

I　高等教育の国際化がもたらす２つの側面
　　　──競争と国際連携

　アジアの高等教育における1990年代以降の国際化進展の背景には、高等教育の大衆化と進学志向の伸びがある。これをうけ、「頭脳流出」（brain drain）

問題を抱えてきたアジアの各国政府は、自国の高等教育の拡充と発展を図り、「頭脳還流」(brain circulation) の手段として教育競争力の強化と人的資源の開発・活用を模索し、民間セクターによる私立大学の開設や教育事業への参入を認めるようになった。この変化は、コンピューター科学や経営学、IT技術等の技能実践等を重視したカリキュラムの導入を促し、あわせて「クロスボーダー・プログラム」や「トランスナショナル・プログラム」といった多様で柔軟なカリキュラムの展開を可能にした。こうして多様化が進むアジアの大学では、大学間の競争が激化し、結果として大学ランキングや国ごとの拠点化競争を生み、多くの国が知的交流拠点 (center of excellence) やあるいはハブ (hub) を形成することを自身の政策目標として掲げるようになっている (Knight, 2014)。

他方、高等教育の国際化がもたらしたもう1つの側面として国際連携の動きがある。そこでは、プログラム相互の整合性を図るための単位互換や認証評価の問題があるものの、1) 大学などの教育機関の連携、2) 政府間協力による国際連携、3) 地域機構による地域内および地域間協力による連携が模索され始めている。こうした様々なアクターによる国際連携の他にも、連携を支える質保証のネットワークや、単位互換制度の検討が進められており、こうした高等教育の国際連携は、ヨーロッパのEUのように、アジアに地域化 (regionalization) の動きをもたらすことも指摘されている (杉村、2013)。

II　キリスト教のミッションと国際連携

以上概観したように高等教育の国際化に伴い国際競争と連携が進んでいるのに対して、キリスト教系大学の世界の各地での教育実践活動は、現在のように国際化やグローバル化が唱えられるはるか以前から、教育を普及し、人材を育てることによって地域社会の発展を促すことを目指してきた[2]。こうしたキリスト教系大学の国際連携は、個々の大学や政府、あるいは地域機構による高等教育の国際連携に対して、キリスト教に基づく教育理念や人間観・世界観と、それに依拠する教育活動の意義に基づき、そのミッションを伝えるために形成されている[3]。

Ⅱ－1　東南アジアおよび東アジアカトリック大学連盟（ASEACUU）の事例

　「東南アジアおよび東アジアカトリック大学連盟」（The Association of Southeast and East Asian Catholic Colleges and Universities：ASEACUU）は、カトリックに基づく高等教育の展開とカトリック教会との連携を深めることを目的としている。現在の加盟大学・機関数はオーストラリア2大学、インドネシア10大学、日本11大学、韓国5大学、フィリピン34大学、台湾3大学、タイ3大学、カンボジア1大学の8カ国・地域からの69機関（2013年現在）である。ASEACUUの特徴は、加盟大学全体でネットワークを形成し、かつ加盟大学相互間で交換留学プログラムなどを持っている点である。加盟大学間では相互に連鎖するかたちで連携が結ばれており、そこでの教育交流が学生・教職員の流動性を促す仕組みとなっている。

Ⅱ－2　アジア・キリスト教大学協会（ACUCA）

　カトリックとプロテスタントの両方の大学が含まれる「アジア・キリスト教大学協会」（Association of Christian Universities and Colleges in Asia：ACUCA）は、1976年に発足し、現在ではインドネシア、韓国、タイ、台湾、日本、フィリピン、香港の7つの国と地域のキリスト教系大学が加盟している。本協会は、もともと1950年代から始まったアジアにおけるキリスト教系大学の学長会議が端緒であり、1976年12月にアジア・キリスト教高等教育連合理事会（United Board for Christian Higher Education in Asia：UBCHEA）によってキリスト教主義高等機関の相互協力と質の向上を目的として創設された。主に学長や大学運営者を対象とするプログラム、教員交換プログラムや教員交流、加盟大学間の学生短期留学、スチューデント・キャンプなどを行っている。現在の参加加盟大学・機関は中国・香港3大学、インドネシア11大学、日本11大学、韓国10大学、フィリピン10大学、台湾8大学、タイ4大学である。ACUCAでは、相互交流と相互理解促進のため、2年に1回総会と大会を開催するほか、2002年からは学生移動計画をつくり、学生の送り出しや受入れを展開するようになった。この学生移動計画（Student Mobility System：SMS）では英語を教授用語とするプログラムが主で、サマーセッションや通常の授業に受入れを図っている。また学生移動とは別に、加盟大学・機関の代表者が集まって行う大学運営者会議（Management Conference）も開催して

いる。

II-3　アジア・太平洋イエズス会大学連盟（AJCU-AP）

　キリスト教系の教育機関のなかでも、特にカトリック修道会のイエズス会は、イエズス会が設立母体となっている高等教育機関および学校を束ねるネットワーク組織を有している。イエズス会大学および学校連盟（Academics at Jesuit Universities and Schools）[4]には、世界全体で185の高等教育機関が加盟しており[5]、ヨーロッパ（含レバノン）、ラテンアメリカ、中央アメリカ、北アメリカ、南アジアにもそれぞれ地域ごとのイエズス会大学・学校のネットワークが形成されている[6]。イエズス会は伝統的に高等教育に重点を置き、21世紀に希求される高等教育を、「他者のために、他者とともに」（men and women for others, with others）という精神のもとに、世界の平和と社会の公正の希求、社会の中で周辺におかれた人々へのケア、さらに持続可能な環境の構築を目指す知の創造を掲げている。

　カスタニエダ・髙祖編（1993）は、今日的なイエズス会教育の特徴として、「21世紀のための教育は、現在の社会、中でも、国際社会の中で人々に仕える人格の形成を目的とすることである」（3頁、傍点は原文のママ）と述べている。そのためには「第一に、自分自身と世界について真剣に問いかけ、それらを真に理解する能力、第二に、人間的な観点から人々の行動や社会的状況を的確に判断する能力、第三に社会を改善し、すべての人にとってより正しく、住みやすい世界を建設していくプロセスに進んで加わる能力」（同3頁）の涵養が必要であり、それらはまさに人間の知的、情緒的な行動の諸能力を統一しようとする教育であるとしている。イエズス会大学の国際連携は、そうした教育に対するビジョンを共に追求しようとするネットワークである。

　アジア・太平洋地域の組織としては、アジア・太平洋イエズス会大学連盟（Association of Jesuit Colleges and Universities in Asia Pacific：AJCU-AP）がある。このAJCU-APは、より正式には東アジア・オセアニア地区イエズス会大学 Association of Jesuit Colleges and Universities in East Asia and Oceania（AJCU-EAO）としても知られている[7]。東アジア・オセアニア地区には、中国、インドネシア、日本、フィリピン、韓国、台湾に16のイエズス会が設立母体となっている高等教育機関がある。AJCU-APでもイエズス会系大学のイグナチオ的教育方針に基づき、「研究と教育の場（大学）」と「（途上国の）

地域社会への貢献」を融合させることを目的としたサービス・ラーニングプログラムを展開しており、参加学生が「開発」の知識と経験を共有する場として、学術的探求と、地域社会における実践をリンクし、機能するように設計されている。イグナチオ的教育法とは、背景学習、実践・経験、経過観察、行動、評価、という5つの段階による学習を通じて理解を促進するものであり、共通言語を英語とする東アジア地域のカトリック大学から様々な学生が参加する。

III　国際連携の意義と課題
——イエズス会・グローバルリーダーシップ・プログラムの事例

III-1　イエズス会・グローバルリーダーシップ・プログラムの概要

　以上述べたように、アジアにおいては複数のキリスト教のミッションをもつ大学の国際連携がみられるが、それらが通常の国際連携と異なるのは、目的別に協定を結んで交流が展開されている一般の国際連携とは異なり、キリスト教系大学の場合には、あくまでも、もともとキリスト教がもっているミッションを共通の基盤として連携していくことにある。

　こうした典型例の1つとして、イエズス会系の大学を中心とする「グローバルリーダーシップ・プログラム（GLP）」がある。この国際連携プログラムは、上智大学の発案で、韓国の西江大学、フィリピンのアテネオ・デ・マニラ大学、台湾の輔仁大学の協力のもとに4大学間で2008年に開始され、2012年からはインドネシアのサナタダルマ大学も参加し5大学間で運営されているものであり、その特色は、参加大学がいずれもキリスト教ヒューマニズムに基づく大学教育のミッションを共有しており、かつ一般の留学プログラムやスタディーツアーとは異なり、参加者自らが運営に積極的に関わり、共通の課題を中心として活動する学生参加型・能動型の国際交流プログラムであるという点にある。そこでは、国籍の異なる多様な文化的背景をもった学生が一堂に集い、地球規模の課題について合宿形式で国際理解と共生社会実現のための課題と方策を話し合うことで、将来のグローバルなリーダーシップをもった人材育成に資することを企図している。プログラムの運営は、毎年、担当校が持ち回りで行うこととなっており、第1回が上智大学で行われ[8]、その後、韓国の西江大学（2009年、第2回）、フィリピンのアテネオ・デ・マニラ大学（2010年、第3回）、台湾の輔仁大学（2011年、第4回）と続き、その後、2015年までにそれぞれ

第2部　コメントとディスカッション

2回ずつホスト校を務めた。

Ⅲ-2　グローバルリーダーシップ・プログラムの特徴と国際連携の意義

　GLPで最も重要なのは、イエズス会のミッションに基づいてテーマを決め、学生たちが能動的に論議する場を設けるということである。すなわち、「他者のために、他者とともに」というミッションを掲げているイエズス会にとって、様々な文化的背景をもつ多地域の人々が、地球規模の課題としての貧困、環境、教育および、倫理という4つの側面を重視して議論し合うこと、特に次世代を担う若者がそうした議論を通じて問題を共有しあい、政治的・社会的差異を抱えながらも課題解決を目指して共に歩む方策を探ろうとすることは、最も大切な教育の使命の1つであるという点である。

　GLPが提起するもう1つの重要な点は、そうした地球規模の課題解決には、個々の学問・研究分野だけではなく、複数の領域が学際的に取り組む必要があり、本セミナーでは多方面からのアプローチを学生たちが実感するようにプログラムを構成しているという点である。第1回のプログラムでは、「格差問題」というテーマが選ばれ、その後、「異文化コミュニケーション」（2009年、西江大学）、「創造的共存：環境と社会貢献――生物多様性を中心として」（2010年、アテネオ・デ・マニラ大学）、「人格教育」（2011年、輔仁大学）、「復興と再構築（自然災害からの復興：人々はどう立ち向かうか）」（2012年、上智大学）、「技術と人道的価値」（2013年、西江大学）、「社会起業を通じたインクルーシブな社会の建設」（2014年、アテネオ・デ・マニラ大学）といった学融合的テーマが担当校によって選ばれてきた。これらのテーマは、まさに国境を越えて議論し学びあう多角的な議論の場があってこそ学び得るものである。

　こうした学びは、まさにイエズス会の教育が希求してきたものに他ならない。髙祖（1993）は、イエズス会教育使徒職国際委員会が1986年に編集し、ローマのイエズス会本部から発表された「イエズス会の教育の特徴」（The Characteristics of Jesuit Education）に示されているビジョンを、1）世界への肯定的態度と「一人一人への心遣い」、2）自己学習力の育成と教師の役割、3）リーダーの育成と卓越した人間教育の追求、4）現実世界への建設的批判と変革の担い手の育成、5）教育共同体と潜在的カリキュラムへの注目、6）果てしなき刷新と生涯学習の実践、の6つの側面からまとめている。また、カスタニエダ・髙祖（1993）は「イエズス会の学校では質の高い教育が目指されており、

有能な社会人の養成がおこなわれながらも、学ぶ者が学んでいることの人間的な意味について内省し、最も深い意味の真理に接することによって、人類家族の責任のある一員になるように導かれる。教育は自国や企業にただ無条件に盲目的に献身する者をつくりあげるためのものでもなければ、自分だけの将来を保障するための手段となるべきものでもない」(4頁) としている。そのうえで、知的な活動ばかりでなく、国の内外を問わず、いろいろな形で困っている人々に手を差しのべるボランティア活動に従事することの大切さや、自分の生活状況と異なった異文化の多様な背景をもった人びとと触れあうことの意義をあげている[9]。GLPは、まさにその意味で、そうしたイエズス会教育のミッションが核となったプログラムである。

Ⅲ-3　国際連携の課題

　他方、こうした複数大学による国際連携には課題もある。第1にプログラムをどのように運営するかという点である。国際連携による国際共同プログラムは、大きな意義を持つものであるが、実際の連携にあたっては、密接な調整や連絡が求められ、多様な意見をまとめるのもより複雑な過程を経なければならない。イエズス会グローバルリーダーシップ・プログラムの場合も、まず問題となったのは一堂に会しての合宿をどの時期に設定するかというアカデミックカレンダーの問題であった。結果的には8月初旬に東京でのセミナーを開催したものの、フィリピンのアテネオ・デ・マニラ大学だけはどうしても夏期休暇とずれてしまい、学期中ながらも特例としてセミナーへの参加を認めるという措置をとってもらうことでこの日程に確定した経緯がある。また、本プログラムに限らず、一般的に、教授言語をどうするか、またプログラムの質保証と関係して、カリキュラム相互の認証評価や単位認定はどうするかということもよく取り上げられるプログラム構築上の論点である。グローバルリーダーシップ・プログラムの場合、教授言語は英語で行い、当初は単位認定の対象ではなかったが、2013年度から上智大学においては単位が付与されるプログラムとして認められるようになった。

　プログラム運営の問題のほかに、第2の課題として国際連携を維持するうえでのガバナンスの問題がある。前述のとおり、国際連携には様々な担い手があり、それぞれがどのような関係性をもっているかがプログラムの成否に大きく影響することは言うまでもない。グローバルリーダーシップ・プログラムの場

合には、各大学の担当教員および国際交流担当者が中心となって連絡を密にとって準備を進めているが、一般的に国際連携では、それぞれのガバナンスの違いがあり、特に政府間協力による国際連携の場合などは国家間の政治的関係が反映される。国際連携の重要な点は、単に一過性のものとしてではなく、持続可能性をもつ枠組みとして位置づけ、継続的に実施してこそはじめて意義がでるものである。その意味では、プログラムを支える財政上の問題やスタッフの問題も実際のプログラム展開上、十分に考慮すべき点である。いずれにしても、国際連携の公共性と社会的責任をそれぞれの担い手が十分に認識して取り組む必要がある。

ま と め

　本稿では、特に1990年代以降、国際化が進むなかで展開されている高等教育の戦略と国際連携の流れを整理したうえで、キリスト教系大学が従来から展開してきたミッションに基づく国際連携の取り組みに注目し、その特徴を整理した。キリスト教系大学の取り組みは、アジア各国の大学がとってきた高等教育戦略とは異なり、国際化ということが言われるはるか以前から国境を越えて取り組まれてきたものである。特に実際のキリスト教系大学の国際連携をみると、異なる価値観や文化的差異を認め合い、多様性を尊重して社会問題や地域規模の課題を論議するプラットフォームが形成されていることがみてとれる。

　特にイエズス会大学の国際連携で特徴的なのは、そこでの学びが、国境を越え、かつ学問の領域を越える形で分析・検討されるべき地球規模の課題、すなわち貧困や環境、教育、倫理といった論点に重点が置かれている点であろう。こうした観点は、国際的なネットワークがあってはじめて取り組むことができる点であり、あわせて、国際化が進行する中で今後ますますその重要性が高まる教養教育、全人教育といった学際的・学融合的教育が求められるプログラムである。そのことは、スチュワート（2013）が、イエズス会の中等教育に関する国際セミナーにおいて、イエズス会学校の生徒をいかに世界に通用するグローバル世界のリーダーとして育成するかが課題であり、そのためにはイエズス会学校がこれまで築いてきた国際的なネットワークを利用して、様々な国の生徒による共同研究や共同学習、提携校の拡充、協働奉仕プログラム、教科資料の開発の可能性を主張していることとも通じる。

今日ではアジアの大学の国際連携は、単にアジア域内の国際連携にとどまらず、域外との連携や協力のネットワークにも広がりつつある。また国際連携によって移動する対象も、教育の中心にある学生のみならず、プログラムを支える教職員、そして教育機関や制度にもその傾向がみられる。国際化の進展とともに、今後も高等教育にみられる戦略的な国際競争と国際連携は活発化する傾向にあるが、重要な点は、実際にどのような学生を育て、かつそのために彼らにどのようなプログラムを提供し、学びの相互作用を促す基礎を提供することができるかということであろう。そこで求められているものは、イエズス会大学が国際連携を通じてこれまで取り組んできたミッションとそれに基づく教育のあり方そのものに他ならない。グローバル化が進み、高等教育が国際高等教育として新たな可能性をもつようになった今こそ、異なる文化をもつ他者への理解と共感、ならびに多様性の尊重を礎に、知の構築と世界をつなぐネットワークのもとで次世代の育成を担ってきたイエズス会大学の教育は、国際競争の戦略としての高等教育ではなく、新たな国際高等教育の1つのモデルとしてその真価が問われている。

注
1　本稿は、2013年7月に上智大学で行われた日本比較教育学会第49回大会の公開シンポジウム「アジアの大学と国際連携」を基に編纂された同学会紀要『比較教育学研究』第48号の特集所収論文、音好宏・杉村美紀「アジアにおけるキリスト教系大学の国際連携」(東信堂、2014年、104-115頁)の第2節をもとに、共著者である音好宏教授の承諾を得て大幅に加筆修正したものである。
2　人類学者の川田順造(2007)は、「人間集団の移動や接触に伴う文化の変化」が地球規模で起こることを「グローバル化」ととらえ、その第一段階は「15世紀末のコロンブスやガマの時代以降の海の道による拡張の時代に始まった」としており、その意味では、宣教師による教育普及はまさに「第一段階のグローバル化」の時代に展開されたといえる。
3　本稿で述べるアジアにおけるキリスト教系大学の国際連携のほか、日本の国内では「日本カトリック大学連盟」がある。「日本カトリック大学連盟」は、1975年日本国内のカトリック大学11校によって創設され、現在20大学によって組織されている。そして、「大学の基本的な使命は、研究を通して絶えず真理を探究し、かつ社会のために知識を保存・伝達することにあり、カトリック大学はこのような使命を持ちつつ、独自の特徴と目的をもって教育・研究活動を行っていること、そしてその礎には、2000年の歴史に培われた、現在も世界中の人々に共有されているカトリック教会の価値観、倫理観が

あり、共通の建学の理念がある」というビジョンを掲げ、日本におけるカトリック大学間の協力関係を推進し、カトリック教育の使命達成のために活動を行っている。

4　イエズス会大学および学校連盟については http://www.ajus.org/about-us.php を参照（2014年8月10日最終閲覧）。

5　イエズス会の高等教育機関一覧は http://www.sjweb.info/highEdu/directory.cfm に掲載されている（2014年8月10日最終閲覧）。

6　イエズス会の世界全体の教育機関概要については http://www.ajus.org/institutions.php（2014年8月10日最終閲覧）に詳しい。

7　全世界に広がっているイエズス会は、アフリカ、北ラテンアメリカ、南ラテンアメリカ、北ヨーロッパ、西ヨーロッパ、東ヨーロッパ、中央ヨーロッパ、東アジア・太平洋、南アジア、アメリカの10の地区（Assistancy）に分かれている。日本管区は「東アジア・太平洋地域」に属しており、この地域には他に中国管区、韓国管区、フィリピン管区、ベトナム管区、インドネシア管区、オーストラリア管区、マレーシア・シンガポール地区、東ティモール地区、ミャンマー地区、カンボジア地区が含まれる。

8　第1回イエズス会・グローバルリーダーシップ・プログラムの詳細については、上智大学国際学術情報局国際交流センター編『第1回イエズス会東アジア4大学グローバルリーダーシップ・プログラム報告書』（2008年）にまとめられている。本節の内容は、同報告書所収の拙稿「プログラムをふり返って——総括と課題」（81-83頁）より引用した。

9　イエズス会教育を中心とするカトリックの教育に対する使命については、2014年3月にローマのグレゴリアン大学で行われた国際シンポジウム「過去から未来へ——アジアにおけるカトリック教会の使命——上智大学の貢献」（上智大学100周年記念事業）でも論議された。その成果については Pontifical Gregorian University（2014）を参照。

参考文献

Knight, Jane (ed.). (2014). *International Education Hub; Student, Talent, Knowledge Innovation Models*. Springer.

Pontifical Gregorian University. (2014). *Between Past and Future, the Mission of the Catholic Church in Asia: the Contribution of Sophia University on the Occasion of the 100th Anniversary of Sophia University (International Symposium, March 14-15, 2014), Gregoriana* 8. Gregorian & Biblical Press.

イエズス会教育使徒職国際委員会編、髙祖敏明訳（1988）『イエズス会の教育の特徴』中央出版社。

イエズス会社会正義・エコロジー事務局編（2015）『特別文書：イエズス会の大学における正義の促進』イエズス会日本管区（原文は『Promotio Iustitiae』No.116、2014年）。

梅宮直樹（2009）「東南アジア地域における地域的な高等教育の質の保証—その特徴と原動力—」日本比較教育学会編『比較教育学研究』37号、東信堂、90-111頁。

音好宏・杉村美紀（2014）「アジアにおけるキリスト教系大学の国際連携」日本比較教育学会編『比較教育学研究』48号、東信堂、104-115頁。

梶山義夫監訳、イエズス会中等教育推進委員会編（2013）『イエズス会教育の特徴』ドン・

ボスコ社。
カスタニエダ，J.・髙祖敏明編（1993）『イエズス会教育のこころ―世界人をはぐくむネットワーク―』みくに書房。
川田順三（2007）「グローバル化に直面した人類文化―無形文化遺産保護の意義―」（国連大学グローバル・セミナー第 7 回金沢セッション「グローバル化と文化の多様性」基調講演）『文化の三角測量』人文書院、2008 年、97-137 頁所収。
黒田一雄編（2013）『アジアの高等教育ガバナンス』勁草書房、2013 年。
髙祖敏明（1993）「イエズス会の今日的教育理想：最近の『イエズス会の教育の特徴』をてがかりに」カスタニエダ，J.・髙祖敏明編（1993）、前掲書、235-251 頁所収。
杉村美紀・黒田一雄（研究代表）（2009）『アジアにおける地域連携教育フレームワークと大学間連携事例の検証』文部科学省平成 20 年度国際開発協力サポートセンター・プロジェクト報告書。
杉村美紀（2013）「アジアの高等教育における地域連携ネットワークの構造と機能」『上智大学教育学論集』47 号、21-34 頁。
杉本均編『トランスナショナル高等教育の国際比較―留学概念の転換―』東信堂、2014 年。
スチュワート，V.(2013)「世界を教室に（A classroom as wide as the world）」『神学ダイジェスト』114 号（13 年夏季号）、44-51 頁。

第2部　コメントとディスカッション

パネルディスカッション

　各大学からの発表に続いて、サンフランシスコ大学アジア研究科長のアントニー・ウセレル（SJ）教授と上智大学総合人間科学部の杉村美紀教授が司会を務めたパネルディスカッションと質疑応答が行われた。

ウセレル　すべての講演が終了したところで、まず講演してくださった先生方に、発表の中で言い残した点や他の先生方の発表を聞いて考えたことなどを述べていただきたいと思います。その後さらに議論を深めてまいりましょう。

クルス　杉村先生のお話は大学共同体の中での現象としての国際化と、そしてそれがどうアテネオ・デ・マニラに影響するかということを考えさせてくださいました。フィリピン人はとても国際的です。労働力の10％は常に国外に出ていますし、海運に携わる船員の約22％はフィリピン人です。しかし多くの人々が、私たちは島国的な考え方をしていて、フィリピン人気質を行く先々へ持ち込んでいると言います。私たちの大学でさえも、私たちが目を向ける課題とその解決方法はとてもローカルなものばかりです。私たちはグローバル化のもたらす利益と、グローバル化による画一化との狭間にいるわけです。気を付けていないと、グローバル化の力に押し流されて伝統や創立時の理念を失ってしまいかねません。グローバルな大学でありながら伝統も維持するためにはどうすればいいのでしょうか？

　この問題について私は、グローバルな問題に向き合うことでグローバルな大学になることができると思います。ローカルな課題はもちろんとても大切ですが、国境を越える問題に投資し、愛をもって様々な地域を見ることで教育・研究の方法を変えていくのです。グローバルな意識と能力をもち、グローバルな奉仕活動への思いをもった学生を輩出すること。フィリピンの学生であれば、自分たちの国で起こる問題は世界の別の場所でも同様に起きていて、問題とその解決法は人類共通のものであると理解させること。私たちはそんな大学でありたいと思っています。

川村　私は3つの時期に分けて、カトリックあるいはカトリック教育の中のイエズス会、そして上智大学の話をしました。しかし私が一番言いたかったのは、まず宣教師たちは必ず社会の最底辺から宣教を始めたということです。

ところが日本に受け入れられるためにどうしてもしなければいけないことを無視できず、アレッサンドロ・ヴァリニャーノといった人たちが順応ということを言います。そのあとマテオ・リッチが中国でも同じことを言います。そして向かっていく対象が常に変わってしまいます。どちらかというと社会の上層、知識層に働きかけることが重要視されて、一番初めに何をしてきたかは忘れ去られてしまう傾向にあります。それが日本でも16世紀の宣教師時代、19世紀の明治新政府時代、戦後の20世紀と繰り返し行われているということを指摘したかったのです。

そしてカルマノ学長もおっしゃった、社会や伝統を破壊していくということ。カトリックはもう少し頑なに残すべきところを残しながら教育も教会づくりも行うべきだったのではないかという反省のうえに、私は自分の発表をしたつもりです。抵抗を示すときには抵抗を示し、社会に完全には迎合しないポイントもちゃんと示す。社会のパン種といいましょうか、この社会でこう生きていてはだめだという信念のようなものがカトリック教育の中で示されないと、カトリックの意味がないと思いますね。ではそれを私たちの大学はしているかというと、実は時流に乗りすぎて、他の大学がするからそれを追いかけているだけではないか、そんな反省も私は個人的にもっています。カトリック大学として、この世の光ないしはパン種的な面を教育面で実現させていくことを考えないと、今後カトリック大学の未来はないのではないかと思っています。

ジェンドロン カルマノ先生はカトリック大学の分裂的なインパクトについて話されました。今日私は自分の発表の中で、中国のカトリック大学は分裂的インパクトが強すぎて閉鎖しなければならなかったと述べました。私たちの神学部もそうです。後には何も残りませんでしたが、台湾の別の土地で再スタートを切りました。私は、大学の使命はどのように達成できるだろうかと問いかけました。そのことに関して輔仁大学は、アメリカのカトリック大学から学びました。アメリカの多くのプロテスタント大学はキリスト教的特徴を失ってしまっていますが、私たちはその特徴を保っています。約20年前、台湾の教育省は仏教団体による大学創立を認可しました。現在台湾には6つの仏教系大学があり、全生徒は必修科目として仏教を学んでいます。台湾のカトリック大学では、以前はこれができませんでした。第一に、どのような宗教であれ、それを必修科目で教えることは違法でした。ところが後になっ

て政府は、様々な宗教を紹介するという形であれば宗教の授業を開講してよいと通達してきました。数年前にはヴァチカンの特使が台湾の教育省とカトリック高等教育について協議を行い、カトリックの思想や神学を教える授業を開講する許可が与えられました。我が校の学生の95％は非キリスト教徒ですが、カトリックの思想や基本的霊性や信仰を知ることによって新たなものの見方を学ぶのです。それを信仰するかどうかは別の問題で、ただ、人生の哲学の1つとして学ぶことが重要なのです。しかし理事会は、全学でのこのような教育に対してはとても慎重な姿勢をとり続けています。

アディ　申し上げたいことが2つあります。1つは学生たちについて、もう1つはイグナチオ的教授法に関して、です。大学で私は学生センターの責任者をしていますが、学生たちのほとんどはハイテクです。彼らはいろいろな電子機器を使っていて、時には自分たちにしかわからない不完全な言葉使いをしています。そこで私が聞きたいのは、そのような学生に対して、どのようにして思考力と想像力を深めさせるかということです。台湾、韓国そして日本の学生はみなハイテクだと思うので、ここに来た時まずそのような疑問を持ちました。

　2つ目に、教育というものはスピリットに関わるものです。ある時政府は我が大学に助成金を与えようとしました。それは私たちがイグナチオ的教授法を取り入れようとしているからでした。政府は、これは一体どんな教授法だろうかと不思議に思っていたようです。これをイエズス会の学校だけでなく、公立校にも適用することは可能だろうか、と。私たちの大学で、イグナチオ的教授法の責任者はイエズス会員ではありません。そしてその部署では、より一般に開かれた形でこれを示そうとしているので、とても興味深いものとなっています。イエズス会の教育機関であってもそこで働くイエズス会員はあまり多くないので、これは大変なことです。例えば私たちの場合、300人ほどの教職員のうち、イエズス会員は約25人ほどです。

ウセレル　それではいくつか、私のほうから質問を投げかけさせていただきます。カトリック大学の国際協力とその意義について杉村先生がおっしゃったことはとても面白いと思いました。今日は5カ国の現場の状況を伺うことができましたが、これは特に現地に生きることを大事にするカトリックの伝統にとって大切なことです。ですからこれら1つ1つの社会・政治・宗教・文化の状況は異なっています。しかし私はユン先生とクルス先生が初めにおっ

しゃったことを聞いてなるほどと思いました。講演者はそれぞれ、グローバルとローカル双方の現状の違いについて異なった視点からお話しになりました。私たちはグローバル化や国際化についてよく話しますが、しかしこれの真の意味は何でしょうか。宗教をもたない一般の大学が他国との共同のプログラムを行ったり、他国にキャンパスをもったりしていることを考えると、それらは利益をもたらしています。イエズス会のジョイント・ディグリー（共同学位）の課程を行う可能性はあるでしょうか？　上智、西江、輔仁で同時に学位を得る教育課程を作ってはいかがでしょう？　もちろん、組織的なことや法的な手続きは大変複雑なものとなりますが、このようなアイディアが実現すれば利益性もあるうえに革新的だと思いませんか？　中国と日本は島の領有権をめぐって政治問題を抱えており、韓国もそれに関わっています。「私たちは一緒に活動し、密接なネットワークで学生を行き来させることで平和の促進に努力している」ことを示す証拠になるのではないでしょうか。創造的な分裂を巻き起こすトランスナショナルな案を述べてみましたが、いかがでしょうか。

カルマノ　「ダブル・ディグリー」という表現を聞くと、まるで一石二鳥のように聞こえてしまいます。私たちがしているのはそういう話ではありません。3つのイエズス会大学によるジョイント・ディグリー制度においては、そのすべての大学で人格的勉学に励むことが必要だと思います。単位の計算や地方政府による学位の認可については多少の困難がありますが、解決可能です。3つの異なる土地で学位取得に向けて勉強することは、その学位により高い価値を付与するものだと思います。

ウセレル　一石二鳥という意味ではもちろんなく、1つの学位の中に3つの構成要素があるというジョイント・ディグリーを提案したかったのです。

ユン　ウセレル先生のアイディアは素晴らしいと思います。でも、アジア太平洋イエズス会大学連盟（AJCU-AP）で働いていた時、一番機能していない部署がイエズス会大学連合でした。現状はさておき、大学が協力していく必要性は大きいです。とはいえ、より重要なのは、今日教育は需要側の市場であって、供給側の市場ではないということです。つまり私たちは学生のニーズや希望を知らなければなりません。これこそニコラス総長がメキシコでの講演で述べたことです。私たちは若者の考えや望みを理解しなければいけません。それができたなら、提案は実行できると思います。手続き上の問題は

第2部　コメントとディスカッション

解決できるでしょう。

クルス　杉村先生がフィリピンの学事日程がアジアや世界の国々のそれとは合致していないことを指摘してくださいました。来年には、6月から3月という学事日程をもつ国は唯一フィリピンだけになってしまいます。その問題に対処すべく、アテネオ・デ・マニラは2015年に学事日程を8月から5月のものへと移行する予定です。とはいっても、日程が合致することは学生を呼び込んだり他大学とのプログラムを共同で行ったりする助けにはなっても、それだけでは十分ではないということを学事局と確認し合っています。私たちの大学で行うプログラムは、役立つもので、かつ魅力的でなければなりません。それはまた、困難があっても協力して乗り越えていけるよう、私たち自身のみならず、他の人にとっても意義深く、魅力的である必要があります。現時点でイエズス会系の高等教育機関は220校ありますが、国際的協力の度合いはかなり低いままです。この状況は、私たちみんなにとって好ましい教育課程を模索する努力が不足していることから生まれているのではないでしょうか。

ジェンドロン　2つ申し上げたいと思います。私たちの大学では、経営学部が非常に創造的な取り組みを行っています。それは、中国の大学とアメリカのイエズス会大学との提携プログラムです。プログラムはすべて英語で行われている、革新的なプログラムです。卒業する時にはアメリカと中国から2つの学位を得ます。私たちは学位を授与しませんが、中国の大学とイエズス会の大学との間を取りもつ掛け橋の役割を果たすことができます。

　2つ目ですが、香港のリベラルアーツ・カレッジについてです。ヨーロッパ、ラテンアメリカやアメリカのイエズス会大学はこのカレッジに興味を示しています。というのも、卒業生が大学院課程でそれらの学校に進学する可能性が高いからです。ジョイント・ディグリー（共同学位）ではありませんが、関連しています。

アディ　インドネシアの学生に、なぜ韓国に行きたいのかを聞くと、Kポップ、つまり韓国のポップカルチャーを学びたいのだと言います。ではどうして学生はインドネシアに来たいのでしょう？　言葉や文化を学びたいわけではないのです。でも多くの学生が対話、特にイスラム教徒との対話について学びたいのです。ですからこのような学生の需要に対して、2週間や1カ月といった短期のプログラムで応えようとしています。今期、西江大学から4年間の

協力体制構築についての提案がありました。というのは、4年間の協力プログラムについて私たちが韓国政府に提案を出し、誰のどのようなニーズがあるかを知ろうとしていたからです。特定の需要に基づくジョイント・ディグリーを行おうとしています。

杉村 先ほどユン先生がそれぞれの国や場所のコンテクストを重視しなければならないとおっしゃいましたが、もう1つ大変興味深かったのは川村先生が指摘された「歴史に学ぶ」ということです。イエズス会が現在東ティモールに聖イグナチオ学院という教員養成のための大学をつくり始めているのをご存じでしょうか。その学校を偶然見に行かせていただく機会がありました。東ティモールは独立してわずか10年の国です。イエズス会の神父様たちが現地のテトゥーン語を使いながら、まさにこれから国づくりをしていく人々が求めているものを一つずつ積み上げていらっしゃるのを見ました。私はそういう活動はてっきり世界史の中の16世紀の話と思っていたのです。ところが、今地球のある所でそういう活動をしていらっしゃるイエズス会員がおられるというのを目のあたりにした時に、大学の社会的責任とは何なのかということを思いました。川村先生は先ほどカトリックが守るべき伝統を大事にすべきだとおっしゃったのですが、イエズス会の大学が社会的責任として守るべきことは何かということを、日本のコンテクストでも教えていただけますか。

川村 杉村先生とウセレル先生がおっしゃったことは共通の学位ということでまとめられてしまいましたけれども、実はイエズス会の横のつながりをもっと生かせと言っておられるような気がするのです。イエズス会には強い横のネットワークがありまして、それをもっといろいろな場で生かさなければいけないという話に集約できると思います。私たちはディグリーとか結果論ばかり言いますが、誰のためのディグリーかといった時に、それはやはり学生あるいは教職員のためです。彼らが何かを見る、あるいは経験するといった時に、私たちがそれを橋渡しできるという、他の公立学校や企業にはないネットワークがイエズス会にはあります。私はこれはものすごく利用価値があると思います。

ウセレル では私からもう1つ、分裂的かつ刺激的な質問をさせていただきます。「アジアにおけるイエズス会大学の役割」という看板を朝から見ているわけですが、この中で他のどれより一番目立っている単語はアジアです。今

日の話の中にはアジアで大きな地位を占めるインドや南アジアを含めませんでした。東アジア、北アジア、東南アジアについて多く話しました。「アジアのイエズス会大学」というのは果たして存在するのでしょうか？　これらの現実には、共通するものが本当にあるのでしょうか。それとも人為的なものなのでしょうか。少しばかり挑戦的な質問です。私たちは共通点についてたくさん話し合いましたが、共通点があるとしたらそれは何なのでしょう？　それとも、現実はかけ離れていて共通のことについて話すことは困難なのでしょうか？　アジアとはこのコンテクストにおいてどのような意味をもつでしょう？

ジェンドロン　それについて申し上げます。まず、アジア太平洋と書いておくべきだったと思います。イエズス会では東アジアとオセアニアという分け方をしていました。今この呼び方はアジア太平洋と改められています。私たちが話しているのはアジア太平洋のことだと思います。私は6年間中国管区の管区長を務めましたが、その際半年ごとに5日間、オーストラリア、日本、韓国、フィリピン、ミクロネシア、インドネシアなどを含むアジア太平洋地域の管区長たちと会議を行っていました。地域ごとの様相は大きく異なっており、多様性はイエズス会の存在する他のどの地域よりも豊かであると思います。

　1つ例を挙げましょう。今神学院は6校ありますが、そのように多くの神学院を運営する資金はありません。ですから、イエズス会の神学校として1つにまとめられればいいのですが、中国唯一の神学校を閉校するわけにはいきませんから、これは実現不可能です。若いイエズス会員が皆いなくなってしまうのは痛手です。しかし一方で、アジア太平洋で神学を学んでいるイエズス会員の半数はマニラに集中しているのです。これを考えると、協力体制も望めなくはありません。ヨーロッパやラテンアメリカとは違いますが、多様性があります。今お話しした例はイエズス会に特化したものですが、大学についても示唆を与えてくれると思います。

質 疑 応 答

ウセレル 聴衆の皆様からの質問をお受けする前に、講演者の先生同士で質問やコメントをしていただくところから始めたいと思います。

クルス フィリピンのカトリック校やカトリック大学は私学のため、政府の補助金を得ることはほとんどありません。例外があるとすれば、得られた事業利益が必ずその機関に再投入される限りは課税されない税額免除ぐらいです。カトリック大学がどんな困難に直面したかという点に関しては、年齢を重ねた世代は若者世代を理解するのが難しいという側面が挙げられます。したがって、若者に対してより深い理解が寄せられる必要があると思います。私が考えすぎなのかもしれませんが、フィリピンの場合、キリスト教やイスラム教など様々な宗教上の伝統が混在しているということよりも、信仰心を持つか持たないかということの方が問題だと思います。今の若者を見ると、信仰心や宗教を妨げる様な文化の風潮を感じます。ですがそれ以上に、多くの若者はどうやら信仰心を持つための機会があまり与えられていないような気がします。当然のことですが、教会やカトリックの大学などの機関はたくさんありますが、それと同様に重視されていいのは、無信仰にもたくさんの形があるということです。

ジェンドロン 上智大学がどうやってカトリックの使命を維持し、育成しておられるのかを具体的にお聞きしたいと思います。またアテネオ・デ・マニラはエリート大学と伺いましたが、フィリピンにあと4、5校あるイエズス会大学とどのような違いがあるかを教えてください。

川村 非常に難しい問題ですね。日本のカトリック人口は少数派さえ形成できていないのに、カトリック大学が大きな影響力をもってきたというのは事実です。信仰しなくても何らかのカトリック的価値観を少し知りながら生きるということは、やはり大切なことだと思っています。まったく信仰者にならずカトリック教会に入らないという人たちにも大きな力を少しずつ出していますので、それを続けていくしかないと思います。大きな変化、大きな効果はないかもしれませんが、少しずつでもやってきたことを続けるしかないと思います。

髙祖 終戦から今日にいたる上智大学の発展を見てきますと、いくつかの角度からお話しができると思います。1つの大きなポイントは、戦後世界のいろいろな国から優秀なイエズス会員が上智にやって来て日本と世界をつなぐ掛け橋となり、同時に人間的な魅力と、人間との関わりということを非常に大切にしました。それが日本の若い人たちを育てるうえで非常に貢献したということです。これに加えて、上智大学ではキリスト教をベースにした、現在人間学と呼ばれている、哲学・倫理学・宗教学を一緒にした科目を必修科目にしています。人生経験が浅い若者にとっては理解するのが非常に難しいのですが、卒業生の少なからずが、社会に出ていろいろな経験を積んで初めて人間学で教えられたことの価値がわかったと言います。しかし信者になるかどうかは別問題であると川村先生がおっしゃったとおりですが、世界の見方、ものの見方、価値観といった面では大きな影響を与えていると思います。ただこの観点は、グローバリゼーションがどんどん進んでいる時代の中でやはり1つの挑戦を受けていると思います。かつての枠組みでの人間学では対応できない時代になってきています。そうすると現代の世界が抱えている問題に対して、人間学という生きる力、あるいは私たちの人との関わりという点からどこにポイントを置いてこの使命を果たしていくかというのが問われていると思います。ニコラス総長が2008年、イエズス会再来日から100年の時、上智での講演において、イエズス会の大学が抱えている4つのチャレンジを指摘なさいました。その第1は貧困の問題です。つまり生活の安定。平和を築くためにその背後にある貧困をどう解決するかという問題。第2は、持続的な発展を可能にする環境の問題に対してどう関わっていくかということです。そして第3は、特に発展途上国と言われている地域の子どもたちへの教育の問題です。十分な教育を受けることができないと、人とのコミュニケーション能力も十分に育ちません。自分の人生を自分で選び取ることも難しいのです。そのように人間としての役割を果たしていくという意味での教育の重要性です。それから第4は人間の生き方です。これまでの消費主義といいましょうか、資本主義に基づいた大量生産大量消費という生き方から、もっと人間が人間の価値を大切にする、あるいは地球的な規模の価値を大切にするという生き方に変えていくのです。この4つのチャレンジを、上智大学も今のこの時代に重点的な教育と研究のポイント、あるいは社会貢献、国際貢献のポイントとして展開していこうとしております。

ウセレル では、アテネオ・デ・マニラと他のイエズス会大学の違いという点に関して、クルス先生お答えいただけますか。

クルス アテネオ・デ・マニラ大学が興味深い点としては、多様性を重視していることで、そのために全授業料収入のうち15％を初めから奨学金に充てています。これは、大学がリーダーを育成できたとしても、ある特定の社会階級の学生しか教育を受けられなければ、国全体の指導者を育成することはできないと考えているからです。私たちの教育が国全体に良い影響を及ぼしていくようにするうえで、多様性は私たちの優先事項です。

　もし他のイエズス会大学4校のいずれかが代表としてここにいたとしても、各々の大学が自分たちの地域で最も影響力をもっていると主張するでしょうし、私もそれに賛成です。アテネオ・デ・マニラ大学はその名前とは裏腹に、国全体のための大学として機能しています。しかし他の4校は、工学など固有の分野でアテネオ・デ・マニラよりも優れており、明確な強みをもっていますが、設立された地域に奉仕する大学です。例えばアテネオ・デ・サブウァンガは南西地方にありますが、キリスト教徒とイスラム教徒の対話に貢献しています。またダバオやミンダナオ北部のザビエル大学では、その地域の人々がきちんと教育を受けられるように尽くしています。ですから4校とも、国でも教会でもとても重要な役割を果たしています。

杉村 先生方の発表を大変興味深く伺いました。髙祖先生のご指摘にあったとおり、これからの社会のためにどのような教育をするのかということはカトリック大学の大きな使命なのだということを痛感しております。カトリック教育は、今日のグローバル化が始まる以前から世界のネットワークの中で果たされてきた使命をもっているものです。しかし今、これからの教育の中で、果たしていくべきことがあれば指針とさせていただきたいと思います。

ウセレル では、一般の方のための質疑応答を始めたいと思います。

質問1 川村先生に質問です。日本の場合は上智大学、聖心女子大学、清泉女子大学、南山大学などはみな、各修道会のカトリック大学ですけれども、世界のカトリック大学とは違いますね。では、日本においてグレゴリアン大学のような本格的なカトリック大学の可能性はありますか？

川村 先ほど歴史的な説明をしましたが、日本では布教と教育は分けて考えるというかなりはっきりした路線がありました。そこで多分イエズス会の大学、

また1913年につくられた上智大学をカトリック大学と称することはまったくできなかったと思います。カトリック大学とは何かを定義するとき、カトリック信者を教育する大学なのか、カトリック信者がたくさんいる大学なのか、それともカトリック的な素養や世界観を一般の人に知らせることが使命の大学なのかの3つを考えると、上智大学は3つ目だと思います。ごく少数のキリスト者ももちろんいますが、そうでない人々の方を向いている。だからカトリック大学とは言えないのだと思います。異論もあるかと思いますが、歴史的にそのようにやってきたので、日本においてカトリック大学であるということは、グレゴリアン大学のような大学をつくることではないと思います。

ウセレル アジアを越えたディスカッションになってきましたね。カトリック大学とは何なのか、それはどういう意味をもっているのか。これも後ほどお話ししましょう。

質問2 　私は2003年から2007年まで台湾に派遣されていました。あるところから、輔仁大学の神学部では台湾の学生と中国本土からのシスターが一緒に学んでいると聞きました。私の修道会の国際的責任者も中国本土からの学生を経済的に支援することを決定して、台湾のコミュニティがその活動に関わっています。中国本土の学生が台湾の学生と神学を共に学んでいるということに関して、何らかの緊張は起きていますか？

ジェンドロン 台湾の大学はどこでも多かれ少なかれ、中国本土からの学生を受け入れています。輔仁大学の学生2万6,000人のうち200人ほどが中国本土からの学生です。私たちは、中国でトップの大学に入れるような優秀な学生しか受け入れません。結果として、輔仁で彼らはいつもトップクラスにいます。しかし神学部に関してはこの限りではありません。シスターや神学生や司祭たちが学問的に特別であるわけではありませんが、台湾出身の神学部生とうまくやっています。そして一般の神学部生たちのレベルに感心しています。これは、第二ヴァチカン公会議で言われた、一般信徒の信仰を養成するということに関して台湾の教会が発展しつつあることを示しているでしょう。中国には地下教会という問題がありますが、学生たちはひとたび国を離れると、このような問題を気に留めなくなるようで、みな仲良くやっています。互いに話ができるということはいいことで、中国の教会への奉仕だと思います。

ウセレル 台湾が中国本土の学生や労働者を受け入れるようになったのはいつからですか？

ジェンドロン かれこれ3年ほど前からです。まだ厳しく規制されています。台湾政府は中国本土からの学生が学生総数の2〜3％を超えることを望んでいません。それでも徐々に増加しています。神学に関しては、学生の半数が中国本土出身者です。これは特別な状況で、政府と台北のヴァチカン大使が取り決めを交わして、中国の教会の人々の信仰形成という必要性に応えるために受け入れ可能なだけの学生を中国本土から受け入れることにしたからです。

質問3 輔仁大学では中国本土からのシスターや神学生がいるということについて、ジェンドロン先生に伺います。輔仁大学と中国の神学部に何かつながりはあるのですか？ 例えば上海などはどうですか？

ジェンドロン 上海の神学院はもう1年以上前に閉校になりました。上海教区の司教が愛国団体から脱退したため、政府は神学院を閉鎖することで教区を罰したのです。中国の神学院は神学部ではありませんから、認可された学位を授与できるのは私たちだけです。あと香港の聖霊神学院は神学と教義神学の学位を授与できます。中国本土での神学院の発展は非常に遅れています。だから私たちは生徒を受け入れているのです。私たちはポスドクのプログラムも始めようとしています。すでに神学の学位をもつ教授を招聘して、さらに研究を進めてもらうためです。

輔仁大学の状況についていえば、上智大学と似ているのではないかと思います。学生の中のカトリック人口は1％ほどで、教員では5％ほどです。しかし、ヨハネ・パウロ2世の「カトリック大学憲章」の中国語翻訳版を10〜12人の教授のグループで読んでいるのを見たことがあります。教員のうち60人がカトリック大学のミッションについて完全に賛同していました。現実と違ったのは、憲章ではカトリックの教員が全教員の半数を占めるべきだとしていることです。これは到底無理ですが、カトリック高等教育の理想や目標に関して多くの教員が賛同の意を示したことは非常に画期的です。

質問4 ユン先生に質問です。先生のお話の中でも特に世界中の若者に無償で教育の機会を与えるという世界大学についての部分を興味深く拝聴しました。先生の大学では、オンライン教育に関するお話は出ていますか？

第2部　コメントとディスカッション

ユン　MOOC（大規模公開オンライン講座 Massiv Open Online Courses）についてご存じでしょうか。韓国は現在 IT 面でおそらく最先進国で、携帯を使っている人のうち約 80％ がスマートフォンの利用者です。近年、新しい 2 つの学習方法が生まれつつあります。第 1 に、インターネットを介した E ラーニング、そして今やスマートラーニングです。iPad やスマートフォンがあれば、携帯端末からインターネット上の何にでもアクセスすることができます。その意味で西江大学は優れた可能性をもっています。最近、西江大学の学長が新聞の取材に対し、西江大学を MOOC において最も優れた韓国の大学のハブ校にするための非常に興味深い計画を発表しました。これはオンライン講義による学位授与にも道を開く可能性があると思います。オンラインにとどまらず、携帯端末を含むスマートラーニングについても同様です。

質問5　先生方がそれぞれ別のかたちでお話しになったイグナチオ的アイデンティティについて質問します。イエズス会大学はカトリックとそれぞれの国の文化がカトリック・イエズス会大学としてのアイデンティティを形づくり花開かせているものだと、私は思います。カトリックのアイデンティティと入り混じった文化の要素、特にカトリックのアイデンティティに溶け込んだ教育の要素が、大学の特色をどう生み出したかを教えてください。

　また、組織にイグナチオ的アイデンティティを根付かせる際には、大学はどのように自らを顧み、イグナチオ的アイデンティティを創造し、組織内で具体化していくのか教えてください。

クルス　カトリック国であるフィリピンに答えを限定して申し上げます。フィリピンにはカトリック信者が数多くいますが、信仰が地域的で、ピュアで、閉鎖的で、古風なものだったとしても驚きません。若者のカトリック信仰のあり方は他宗教との対話に開かれているでしょう。ですから私たちはカトリックでありながら、そのカトリック・アイデンティティは他の宗教の尊重と対話の促進という現代的必要性に合わせて明確に表されていきます。若者がそのようなカトリック信者として育ってくれたらとてもうれしいことです。

ユン　カトリックのアイデンティティと他の文化的要素によって形成された別のアイデンティティとがうまく融合した韓国の事例を思いつかないのですが、カトリック信者だった非常に有名な小説家の言葉をご紹介します。彼は「私の頭はカトリック、私の血は仏教、私の心は儒教でできている」と言い

ました。私は韓国のカトリック・アイデンティティは私たちの文化的背景やアイデンティティと深く関連していると思います。でも川村先生がおっしゃったとおり、カトリックの宗教と文化は18世紀の韓国社会ではとても分裂的な要素でした。というのはカトリックは先祖崇拝を否定していますが、当時の政府はこれを社会の安定を脅かすものだとみていたからです。後になって、カトリックと政府間のいさかいはなくなりましたが、私は韓国のカトリック・アイデンティティを大変誇りに思っています、韓国は宗教的に多様な国で、イスラム教や多くの他の宗教が存在しています。でも韓国ではどんな宗教にも共通項があるので、宗教間の大きないさかいという話はまったく聞きません。外からであれ中からであれ、同じ文化的要素を共有しているのです。これは韓国のカトリック・アイデンティティに固有な点だと思います。

　私も所属している大学理事会では現在、大学のキャンパス・ミニストリーと協力して、教職員や卒業生を含めた人々がイエズス会・カトリックの教育哲学に触れる機会を増やすための取り組みを行っています。例えばジョージタウン大学に倣って、イグナチオに関する講義を行うイエズス会ウィークをもつ予定です。DVDで会の歴史を学び、イエズス会員と学生たちが自由に会話することができるようにします。また学院とともに、新入教職員を対象にしたワークショップも行っています。このワークショップは大体2～3泊の宿泊研修形式で行われます。これを通して、大学に新しく入った人が、なぜイエズス会が若者の教育のために韓国に派遣され、またどうして会の教育哲学が200年以上の歴史を越えて現在でも大切なものなのかを理解するための助けとなることができます。

　面白いことに、学院にイエズス会の教育哲学やアイデンティティを紹介するパンフレットやDVDがありません。だから今パンフレットとDVDを作成中で、これは学内と卒業生に配られる予定です。

　最後になりますが、現在西江大学の学長は一般信徒です。これは基礎的な部分において、イエズス会教育への最低限の理解が得られるために学長はカトリックでなければならないことになっているからです。でもこれではイエズス会的カトリック・アイデンティティを保っていくのに不十分なので、理事長、学長、私と二人の副学長は毎月定例会議を行っています。これは相互理解を図るのにまことに良い方法です。学長はまた、理事長とイエズス会韓国管区の管区長とも定期的に会って重要な事項を決定したり軌道修正を行っ

ています。その会話の中心にあるのはどうすればイエズス会教育哲学を活性化させることができるかということです。このように、会話と対話はとても大切です。

アディ　ご質問にあった、一般信徒・組織と学生のためのイエズス会的アイデンティティについてお答えします。私たちはイグナチオ的教授法を5年前に取り入れ始めました。それをカリキュラムのみならず課外活動にも、そしてコア・カリキュラムにも反映させたのです。これは私たちの3つの教育目標、つまり能力（competent）、良心（conscience）、あわれみの心（compassion）をはっきりと示すためです。面白いのは、私たちがこのプログラムの適用を小さな教員のグループから始め、指標を使ってこれら3つの要素を測定してみたことです。学期の終わりに教員と学生で反省会を開き、シンポジウムを行って進捗の状況やイグナチオ的教授法の適用における困難などを話し合います。このようなシンポジウムは、ゆっくりとではありますが継続してイグナチオ的教授法を定着させるための試みです。まだ5年しか経っていませんが、イエズス会員やカトリック信者の教員だけでなく、カトリック信者でない方たちもそれを適用し、理解し、さらには「学生が良心とあわれみの心について成長していることを、どうすれば測定することができるだろうか？」という困難な課題に直面することができているのです。

Preface

Coordinator: **Sali Augustine SJ**
⟨Sophia University⟩

"Go to every part of the world, and proclaim the gospel to the whole creation" (Mk. 16:15). This mission of Jesus to his disciples found in the Gospel of Mark has been the origin and source of all evangelization and the Christian spirit of education for the last 2000 years. After Jesus was taken up into heaven, "they went out to proclaim their message far and wide, ……and the Lord worked with them and confirmed their words by the miracles that followed" (Mk.16:19-20). The gospel is "good news" for the salvation of all. Recognizing this "good news" as a sign in our times, the Society of Jesus (Jesuits) took education as a form of proclaiming the gospel, aiming at a "formation of the complete person" through holistic education.

The Catholic Church since Vatican Council II has been trying to recognize diversity of religion, culture etc., and still promote education based on Christian values, even in non-Christian regions like Asia. This means educating people with the message and values of Christ, especially to become men and women for those who are vulnerable and in need of help. This is the educational philosophy the Church is calling us to live as best we can. Jesus proclaimed, "I am the way and the truth and the life." (John 14:6) and called us to repent. Even in this world full of competition and struggle for economic profit and consumption, education based on the values of Christ is relevant. It is important to have appropriate leaders in this world full of different values. However, it is also time to re-confirm the identity and role of Catholic education, in a context where education itself has been conceived as a field of business. Therefore, taking the centenary year of Sophia University as an opportunity, we are happy to share with you the content of this international symposium, in which the Jesuit universities in Asia try to evaluate themselves.

Analyzing the past and present context of the Ateneo de Manila University in the Philippines, Dr. Jose Cruz looked into the role of Catholic education in the Philippines. He noted that "education in the Philippines and the significant role that the Church has played in it has a long and many-stranded history. Suffice it to say that, particularly in the early centuries but even now, the Church participates in the development of society through its work in instruction and scholarship."

Looking into various academic "ventures" of the Chinese Province, especially the history of Fu Jen Catholic University of Taiwan, Dr. Louis Gendron is concerned that although the "Jesuits have been major contributors to the re-establishment of Fu Jen Catholic University in Taiwan, the Society's presence on campus has been dwindling". But he notes that "there is still hope of keeping some Ignatian spirit on campus" that the St. Robert Bellarmin Fu Jen Faculty of Theology, which is an independent and autonomous faculty, is the only Catholic faculty of theology in Taiwan and continues to be a major priority of the Society. He also stated that despite decreasing vocations, collective management and the struggles of Chinese history, the institutions are "relying minimally on Jesuits and mostly on professors and staff well trained in the Jesuit tradition of higher education."

Dr. Shinzo Kawamura divided the history of Japanese mission schools from the Meiji Era (1868~1912) into three periods to analyze the history of Sophia University's 100 years. Trying to understand what is going to be the future of Catholic education in Japan, he then pointed out three major changes of approach in education during these years. The first period of Catholic education was interested in the salvation of souls at the grass-roots level "separated from social concerns". The second period made an effort to "follow society closely" while keeping its distance from nationalistic prejudice. Finally in postwar Japan, Catholic education has tried to be "inside society" in an effort to keep its own identity in a changing world.

Introducing the efforts of Sanata Dharma University in Indonesia, in inter-religious dialogue as part of education in the context of its multi-ethnic-religious and multi-cultural reality, Dr. Kuntoro Adi emphasized the special characteristics of its Catholic identity. He observed that it is important for Catholic universities to reflect and practice programs that bring opportunities to have interfaith dialogues as part of education to make peaceful co-existence possible.

Korea is seized by 'education fever'. Dr. Benedict Jung took the case of Sogang University, which has contributed to Korean society since the 1960s, to analyze especially the socio-political and cultural tasks of Catholic universities in Korea. He focused on two modern Jesuit axioms, "men and women for others" and "the service of faith and promotion of justice" in our education that "become the litmus test that identifies a school as Catholic and Jesuit." He confirms that "the mission of Sogang is an offspring of this Jesuit philosophy of education that forms the whole person with traditions flowing from Catholic, Jesuit, Korean tenors to commit themselves to human development and the world".

Considering these contextual analyses of Jesuit universities in Asia, and foreseeing the fact that present globalization will continue to affect Asia further, Sophia University vice president Dr. Miki Sugimura presented some of the projects these universities are engaged in, to face the challenges. Affirming that "the education of the universities of the Society of Jesus has been devoted to bringing up the next generation by constructing knowledge and the networks that link the world", she emphasized the importance of international cooperation through Jesuit and Catholic networks to be activated to achieve our educational goals in today's context.

Education starts with the action of 'conveying'. True conveying is what helps people to live their life fully, brightly and joyfully. Only then can one truly be a 'person for others'. In the context of our global society we need to ask, in order fully to follow the words of Jesus, "go and proclaim the gospel" to all, if there is still 'meaning in that mission' today. It was indeed a fruitful effort to look into the mission of Jesuit higher education in Asia, in a multifaceted approach, on the occasion of the 100th anniversary of Sophia University.

It is with the idea and guidance of Prof. Toshiaki Koso(chancellor of Sophia corporation) together with the support of Prof. Tadashi Takizawa (then President of Sophia University) that made the symposium and this publication a reality. Finally let me thank all the speakers, the commentator Dr. Michael Calmano from Nanzan University, Dr. Antoni Ucerler and Dr. Miki Sugimura who chaired the sessions and Ms. Marina Sakai who worked on translations, as well as all those who participated in the symposium and those who worked on this publication.

Contents

Preface   Sali Augustine SJ ⋯⋯ 123

Introduction:
Sophia International Symposium — The Role of Jesuit Universities in Asia
                                                                      Toshiaki Koso SJ ⋯⋯ 129

Part 1   Report and Prospects of Five Universities in Asia

Jesuit Education in the Philippines:
   Ateneo de Manila University
                                                                    Jose M. Cruz SJ ⋯⋯ 134

Catholic Identity and Catholic Education in Modern Japan since 1868
                                                                Shinzo Kawamura SJ ⋯⋯ 144

Higher Education in the Chinese Province of the Society of Jesus:
   Abrupt Ending, New Start, Renewed Visage of Mission
                                                             Louis Gendron SJ ⋯⋯ 176

Jesuit Education of the Whole Person in Sanata Dharma University
                                                              C. Kuntoro Adi SJ ⋯⋯ 184

Catholic Education in Korea:
   A History of Responses to Challenges Since 1960
                                          Benedict Kang-Yup Jung SJ ⋯⋯ 194

Part 2 Comments and Discussion

Comments   Michael Calmano SVD ······ 220

International Cooperation of Higher Education in Asia
　and the Role of the Jesuit Universities
                                                Miki Sugimura ······ 225

Panel Discussion ·· 238

Q & A Session ··· 245

　　Writers List ··· 253

Introduction

Sophia International Symposium
The Role of Jesuit Universities in Asia

Toshiaki Koso SJ
〈Chancellor, Sophia School Corporation〉

This is a report of the symposium on the role of Jesuit Universities in Asia held on December 7, 2013 as one of the events to mark the centennial year of Sophia University in 2013. On November 1, Raffaele Cardinal Farina, special envoy of His Holiness Pope Francis, participated in a ceremony in the presence of the Emperor and Empress of Japan in the Tokyo International Forum. The message was "Sophia − Bringing the World Together," which sums up the history of the first century of Sophia as well as its mission for the 21st. The symposium aimed at giving life to the role of Jesuit universities in Asia. This report should put into the hands of all those involved in this vital apostolate the means of giving it more life with deeper understanding. We pray that it will help to bear fruit in bringing the world one step closer together in one better human family.

Sophia University has its roots in the middle of the 16th century when the Jesuit missionary, Francis Xavier, wanted to create a college in the capital of Japan. It took 350 years because of persecutions and the banning of Christianity. But in the 20th century Pope Pius X sent an envoy to explore the possibility of a Catholic university in Japan. The envoy reported back that the prospects were good if the university were truly Catholic, that is open to the world. With this, the dream of Francis Xavier began to take shape. The Pope entrusted to the Jesuits the founding of a college which they wholeheartedly accepted. In 1908 the Jesuits sent to Japan three people, a German expert on Chinese and Indian philosophy, the French chancellor of the French Academy in Shanghai, and an Englishman working in the Buffalo Mission in the United States. With the cooperation of Japanese priests and professors, study groups began introducing the cultures and thought of Western Europe, India, China and the United States to

Japanese people and the Japanese culture to the Europeans. The wisdom (Sophia) in this bringing of the world together marked the birth of Sophia in the spring of 1913.

After World War II, Sophia University became free to offer education and research based on the Catholic spirit, in order to share the sufferings of all human beings and to be of service to the welfare and creative progress of the world in accordance with its educational policy. Over the years it has devoted itself to contributing to society, to the world, to education and to research. In this turbulent world and even in this country, with less than one percent of its population Catholic, it has managed through thick and thin to enable people to grow with all the wealth of the Catholic spirit. Thanks to the support of Catholics around the world and many other people of good will, the university has now been able to celebrate its centenary.

This symposium celebrates our gratitude for the past and the present, but aims to brighten the future, especially of Asia.

Our Catholic universities around the world are connected through the International Federation of Catholic Universities and under it in Asia the Association of Southeast and East Asian Catholic Colleges and Universities (ASEACCU). Sophia University also belongs to the Association of Jesuit Universities–Asia Pacific (AJCU-AP). These networks give life to Sophia's international mission to bring the world together.

The Asian Jesuit network has given rise to the annual Service Learning Program and the Global Leadership Program in which our students work together with those of Sogang University of Korea, Fu Jen University of Taiwan, Ateneo de Manila University of the Philippines and Sanata Dharma University of Indonesia.

The five universities from different countries in East Asia reporting at this symposium on "The Role of Jesuit Universities in Asia" were supported by comments of Dr. Michael Calmano, the president of ASEACCU who is very familiar with this region.

The reports come from five universities set up at different times in different contexts around Southeast and East Asia. Whereas the Catholic population of the Philippines is over 80%, that of the other four countries is a small minority, especially in Indonesia, Taiwan and Japan. These reports may help us to understand the differences and similarities of the roles, challenges, approaches and evaluations of Jesuit universities over the years, especially contrasting the Philippines with countries with few Catholics.

Jesuit universities in the late 20th century all aimed at educating "Men and Women for Others, with Others." Now let this report of the symposium, which reflected on the future of our universities, find concrete ways to deal with the growing globalization of the 21st century. These five Asian universities must use their connections to work together to meet the challenge. It is my hope that Sophia's international symposium and this report on it will help all those who are involved, to reflect on the mission of education in Asia.

Part 1

Report and Prospects of Five Universities in Asia

Jesuit Education in the Philippines
Ateneo de Manila University

Jose M. Cruz SJ
〈Ateneo de Manila University〉

Education in the Philippines, from the mid-16th through the mid-19th century, was carried out by the Catholic Church. From 1863, when the Spanish colonial government enacted legislation assigning greater responsibility for education to the State, through 1946, when the United States of America recognized Philippine independence, the Spanish, American, and Japanese governments administered education in the country. From 1946, when the Philippines reclaimed independence, to current times, the Philippine government has had that responsibility. Nonetheless, Church-related organizations and initiatives, as they have since the 16th century, continue to participate in a very significant way. Of the four highest-ranking universities in the country today, three are administered by religious groups.

Since the 16th century, education mainly in the form of primary schools comprised a large and critical component of missionary activity.[1] By the 17th century, the predominantly catechetical character of education gave way to broader concern for development of the communities. Colleges were established; and soon universities.[2] Two years after the spaniards arrived in the Philippines, the bishop of Manila recommended to the king the opening of a Jesuit school in the capital city. Approval came after a considerable wait.[3]

In 1592, eleven years after their arrival in the Philippines, the Jesuits opened in Tigbauan, Iloilo in the Visaya islands a primary school where reading, writing, singing and playing musical instruments were taught. Its primary purpose was catechetical.[4]

A similar school soon opened on the island of Cebu. This eventually became the College of San Ildefonso, where reading, writing, counting and religion were taught.[5] The students where Filipino, Chinese and Spanish boys. The Jesuits later opened primary schools in four parishes east of Cebu on the islands of Leyte and Samar.

Meanwhile in Luzon three primary schools were established. By the first decade of the 17th century, the Jesuits had several schools in the archipelago of which one was in Manila. The school in Manila, the result of the bishop's earlier intervention, had opened in 1595. It was a school of secondary instruction.[6] Similarly, the College of San Jose, opened in 1601.

Slow but steady growth in the establishment of schools took place in the last decades of the 17th century and the first decades of the 18th. In a letter to a European friend, the Austrian Jesuit Andreas Mancker said that in the Visayas, where the Jesuits were active, a school for boys and another for girls were typical features of a Jesuit parish.[7] The Jesuit historian Pedro Murillo Velarde wrote that, in 1616-1716, a Jesuit parish would typically have schools for boys and girls up to the age of fourteen. In 1743, Jesuits were serving 134 towns mostly located in the Visayas.

In 1752, the colonial government directed that the salary of school-teachers be taken from public funds. Between 1752 and 1863, the template for primary schools had the teacher salaries come from the government; but the supervision of the school and the provision of venue and equipment were the responsibility of the local parish. Due to fluctuations in government resources up to and even after 1863, however, the burden of operating the schools was de facto borne mostly by the parishes.

Observers of the first decade of 19th century Philippine society noted that as a rule towns had primary schools of rudimentary character. Those in the third through sixth decades also reported that schools were widely present, although these often had low attendance in their classes. Deficiencies notwithstanding, there were occasionally exuberant assessments such as that by the Frenchman Jean-Baptiste Mallat, who, after three trips to the islands, claimed that "everywhere one finds primary schools which are supported by the people; . . . nearly all of the Tagalogs know how to read and write."[8]

It is warranted to say with caution that, by the mid-19th century, about 600 towns and villages had a primary school where religion, reading, writing, counting and singing were taught. The French traveller Jean-Baptiste Mallat offered the view that "the education of the *indio* is far from being retarded when compared with that of the common people of Europe."[9]

The wide distribution of primary schools was due to the policy of religious orders to establish schools wherever it was feasible. Religious orders other than the Jesuits also established schools. In 1611, the Dominicans founded a college which later became the royal and pontifical University of Santo Tomas. In 1640, a school for Spanish boys established under the direction of the Dominicans later became the College of San Juan de Letran. Boarding schools for Spanish girls were opened in Manila by nuns: Santa Potenciana in 1591 and Santa Isabel in 1632.[10]

In the mid-19th century, when the Jesuits returned after their expulsion, there were numerous schools in various parts of the country, some with a long history and a few with distinction.

The growth of Ateneo de Manila University

1859-1959

The school was established quite by accident, or, as some of us deeply believe, by providence.

In 1767, some 227 years after the founding of the Society of Jesus, King Charles III of Spain decreed the expulsion of the Jesuits from all Spanish dominions. As a result the Jesuits in the Philippines were arrested and their property was confiscated.

In 1773, Pope Clement XIV suppressed the Society of Jesus throughout the world. His action would be followed by restorations and other suppressions.

In 1880, the Society of Jesus was once again legalized in the Spanish empire. In 1852, after one of the restorations, Queen Isabela II asked the Spanish Jesuits to return to the Philippines to resume the evangelization of Mindanao and Sulu.

On February 4, 1859, six priests and four brothers under the leadership of Father Jose Cuevas set sail from Cadiz. They landed in Manila on 14 April.

Soon after the Jesuits' arrival, the city council of Manila requested that they take charge of the Escuela Pia, a primary school for boys subsidized by the government. Father Cuevas at first refused. The civil governor however managed to prevail on him after taking responsibility for explaining to the home government Father Cuevas's non-compliance with the instructions to go to Mindanao.

On December 10, 1859, the schoolmaster formally handed over the Escuela Pia to the new Jesuit faculty. The school took the new name Escuela Municipal, municipal school.[11]

In 1862, the city council of Manila suggested that it upgrade itself to include secondary instruction. The idea went into effect in 1865. Soon after, some technical courses such as commerce, surveying, and industrial mechanics were set up. It was at this time that the school was renamed Ateneo Municipal de Manila.

Although the school was established primarily for Spanish boys, the Jesuits allowed Filipinos to attend the school. By the end of the 19th century, nine-tenths of the student body was natives and *mestizos*.

In 1865, two Jesuit scholastics of the Ateneo Municipal de Manila, Francisco Colina and Jaime Nonell, published in a local paper their observations on a typhoon which had recently passed near the city. Using meteorological instruments they had assembled, they showed how the approach and trajectory of typhoons could be forecast, thus saving lives and property. The business community, quick to see the usefulness of the technology, arranged for the purchase of a universal meteorograph, a continuously recording instrument designed by the Italian Jesuit Father Angelo Sechi.[12]

When the meteorograph arrived, it was assembled and operated by another Jesuit scholastic interested in scientific work, Federico Faura. A meteorological observatory, simply called Manila Observatory, was set up. In 1879, the observatory issued its first typhoon warning.

In 1884, the Spanish government made the observatory a state institution with a network of subsidiary stations throughout the archipelago. A seismic station was added to it in 1886, a magnetic section in 1887, and an astronomical section in 1899.

The degree of Bachelor of Arts was first granted in 1870 to ten students who completed a five-year program consisting of high school and college components. The degree later required six years; and in 1921, eight years. The division between high school and college was not as distinct as it is currently.[13]

In 1898, the United States took over the Philippine colony from Spain.

The American authorities retained the Manila Observatory as a government institution, but withdrew the government subsidy from the school. As a consequence, the Ateneo Municipal de Manila became the private school Ateneo de Manila, with the adjective "Municipal" dropped from its name.

In 1908, the Ateneo de Manila was authorized to confer the four-year degree of Bachelor of Arts and certificates in commerce, stenography, electrical engineering and topographic measurement.

English gradually replaced Spanish as the medium of instruction. Adaptations were made to the American public school system, without sacrificing the basic objectives and methods of Jesuit education.

By 1914, the school had three departments: a department of elementary education; a college department comprising six years of humanistic and scientific studies; and a department of applied studies with courses in commerce, surveying, mechanics and electricity. There were electives in painting, music, stenography, typewriting, and gymnastics.

It became increasingly clear that the changed social milieu demanded more than a mere reorganization of studies; it demanded American teachers. In 1921, Jesuits from the Maryland-New York Province were assigned to the Ateneo de Manila. Under American administration, the B.A. course was lengthened to four years, organized athletics were introduced, and greater stress was placed on extra-curricular activities, particularly those with a social orientation. Among the latter were the Chesterton Evidence Guild and the Catholic Radio Hour, which through lectures, debates, discussions and a radio program, sought to propose Catholic solutions to contemporary problems.

On August 13, 1932, a fire destroyed the school buildings and the school had to relocate from within the city walls to a site outside.

Despite the fire, the Ateneo de Manila showed resilience and vitality. In response to repeated requests by sugar planters in the Visayas, the course in sugar technology offered since 1925 was expanded into a separate department of industrial technology. Soon the law school, the school of commerce and the graduate school were established.

The Ateneo de Manila was well on its way to becoming a university when the Second World War intervened. The Ateneo students and alumni who fought for the motherland are held up as venerable heroes.

July 1945, with the war over, the high school classes resumed at a borrowed site. The following year the school moved to temporary structures built over the ruins of the original buildings outside the walled city.

In 1952, except for the law school and the graduate school, the Ateneo de Manila moved to its present main campus at Loyola Heights in Quezon City.

■ 1959-2013

On the occasion of its 100th year in December 1959, the Ateneo de Manila was conferred university status.

Keenly aware of its beginnings as a public school, the university has always seen itself as existing for a social purpose. It reminds students that the national hero Jose Rizal is an alumnus.

In the 1960s and 70s, when socially-committed citizens called for radical changes in society, many Ateneo students and faculty members involved themselves in nationalist movements that sought justice for the dispossessed; greater appreciation of local culture; and, in the university administration, increased leadership roles for Filipinos. In the 1970s and 80s, Ateneo students, faculty and alumni involved themselves deeply in the campaign against the Martial Law regime of Ferdinand Marcos. A major policy shift in those years allowed women to enroll in the college. In recent decades, the university has articulated its sense of mission and identity in terms of closing two gaps: the gap between the rich and the poor in Philippine society and the gap between itself and universities overseas with greater capacities and resources.

This consciousness is evident in the establishment of the Ateneo School of Medicine and Public Health.

Today there are some 12,000 students in 8 faculties: Humanities, Social Sciences, undergraduate Management, Science and Engineering, Law, Business, Government, and Medicine and Public Heath.

Because health is so important in life, through the years there had been suggestions to open a school of medicine. The idea consistently met with strong resistance. Administrators were of the opinion that the country already had too many schools of medicine; another one would be redundant.

The resistance gave way to enthusiastic support, however, when the proposal was made about establishing a school to train a special kind of doctor. The graduates were to be outstanding clinicians with mastery of clinical skills and compassion to care for the health needs of the individual; dynamic leaders with the expertise to bring systems and resources together to enable the clinicians to practice their craft; and finally, social catalysts who would solve the systemic problems of ill health and poverty and make quality health care available to all.

Opened in 2007, it sees itself as taking a leadership role in redefining health, and how health is accessed and delivered in a developing country, even as it produces excellent clinicians. Interestingly, the students in this program graduate with two degrees: an MD and an MBA.

Aside from the School of Medicine and Public Health, there are many policies and decisions illustrative of the Ateneo's sense of mission and identity, such as that which automatically sets aside 15% of tuition revenue for scholarships.

■ 2013 and Beyond

In which direction is the university headed; on which concerns and frontiers does it wish to place its focus and energies?

A point of reference is the remarks of Fr. Adolfo Nicolás, Superior General of the Society of Jesus, on the challenges to Jesuit higher education today. He notes three distinct but related challenges: a) promoting depth of thought and imagination; b) rediscovering and implementing "universality" in the Jesuit higher education sector; and c) renewing the Jesuit commitment to learned ministry.[14]

The other point of reference is the university's strategic plan centered on three thrusts: a) mission and identity; b) nation building; and c) environment and development.

In his address to Jesuit universities in 2010, Father Nicolás identified the increasing interconnectedness of the world as the new context for understanding the world and the Jesuit mission in higher education.

He encouraged Jesuit universities to foster in their students the desire, skill, and conviction to engage the real, and indeed to enter the real at its depth. The starting point is always that which can be experienced most immediately through the senses. But students must be led to what is beyond, namely, the hidden presence and action of God in that which is seen, heard, touched, smelt, and felt. An encounter with the real at its depth and with the God active in the real carries with it the powerful possibility of profound change in the person of the students.

In reference to this, Father Nicolás asked Jesuit universities: "How many of those who leave our institutions do so with both professional competence and the experience of having, in some way during their time with us, a depth of engagement with reality that transforms them at their deepest core? What more do Jesuit universities need to do to ensure that we are not simply populating the world with bright and skilled superficialities?"

For the Ateneo de Manila University, that question is both a challenge and an indictment. For there have been many times when we did not achieve the goal, and as many times when we went about doing our work without being fully mindful of the goal of our endeavors, namely, depth in the Ignatian sense.

This is not to say that there have not been structures designed precisely to allow students to grow in knowledge and in their person. Among these would be the strong liberal arts program and an accompanying four-year non-academic formation program that every undergraduate student undergoes, regardless of major.

In the current Ateneo strategic plan, strengthening Ignatian spiritual formation is one of the ten goals. By this we mean highlighting Ignatian spirituality as the motive force that animates the life of the mind, the dialogue held with those of other traditions, the care of those in need, and the stewardship of creation. It is no less than the formation of the whole person.

In addition to the promotion of depth of thought and imagination, Father Nicolás asked Jesuit universities to seek to insert themselves into society, not just to train professionals, but in order to become a cultural force advocating and promoting truth, virtue, development, and peace in society. He sees universities as a social project.

In the Ateneo strategic plan, nation-building is a major thrust. By this we mean that the university contributes to social transformation by being a change catalyst, strategic thinker and culture shaper. As change catalyst, it promotes the mobilization and convergence of the forces dedicated to social change. As strategic thinker, it attends to the higher-level thinking required by the complex, culture-bound, non-linear mechanisms and systems that perpetuate poverty and other social ills. And as culture shaper, it generates renewed understanding of and love for country.

The environment and development are another thrust in the university strategic plan. It addresses the challenge of developing methodologies to assess and manage the risks posed by development models that promote the use of environmental resources in conventional ways; drafting blueprints for an alternative sustainable development; and applying the blueprints locally on campus. We have recently established the Ateneo Institute for Sustainability.

Father Nicolás further suggested that if we are to be true to our Ignatian heritage, research in our universities must always ultimately be conceived of in terms of "learned ministry." This means that, even as we require that research be rigorous, we also direct it towards the service of humanity and the Kingdom of God.

Father Nicolás recognized the emergence of "knowledge societies" in which the development of persons, cultures, and societies is tremendously dependent on access to knowledge in order to grow. Globalization has created new inequalities in terms of access to knowledge and its benefits. He asked Jesuit universities to counter the inequality of knowledge distribution and so to identify the people for whom they generate knowledge and who will have access to it.

The Ateneo strategic plan does make reference to this divide, but still has to invest on the enormous and complex task ahead.

Father Nicolás ended his reflection on Jesuit universities by asking Jesuits the question: "If Ignatius and his first companions were to start the Society of Jesus again today, would they still take on universities as a ministry of the Society?"

The answer, Father Nicolás suggested, might be found by asking the related question: "What are the needs of the Church and our world, where are we needed most, and where and how can we serve best?"

In the same vein, he asked yet another question: What kind of universities would we run, with what emphasis and what directions, if we were re-founding the Society of Jesus in today's world?

As an institution, the Ateneo de Manila University still has to grapple more strenuously with the question of mission and identity. It has some resources and the great resolve to discern what it means to be a Jesuit university in our time.

Education in the Philippines and the significant role that the Church has played in it have a long and many-stranded history. Suffice it to say that, particularly in the early centuries but even now, the Church participates in the development of society through its work in instruction and scholarship. The Ateneo de Manila University, from its beginnings as a school in 1859, exemplifies one strand of that history.

The Ateneo de Manila University exercises an influence beyond its relatively small size of 12,000 students and its young age of 54 years. It counts among its alumni the current president of the country, chief justice of the Supreme Court, speaker of the lower house of Congress, archbishop of Manila, and hundreds of top leaders in industry, government, non-governmental organizations, and various other fields.

This accomplishment understandably brings great pride and joy. Nonetheless, we ask ourselves constantly how we can remain a truly Jesuit and Catholic university.

Notes

1. Among the standard surveys on education in the Philippines are Encarnacion Alzona, *A History of Education in the Philippines 1565-1930*, Quezon City: University of the Philippines Press, 1932, and Evergisto Bazaco OP, *History of Education in the Philippines*, Manila: University of Santo Tomas Press, 1939.
2. John N. Schumacher SJ, *Readings in Philippine Church History*, Quezon City: Loyola School of Theology, Ateneo de Manila University, 1979, pp. 141-152.
3. Thomas B. Cannon SJ, "History of the Jesuits in the Philippines," *The Woodstock Letters* 65, no 3.
4. Henry Frederick Fox, "Primary Education in the Philippines, 1565-1886," *Philippine Studies* 13, no 2, 1965, 207-231.
5. Horacio de la Costa SJ, *Readings in Philippine History*, Manila: Bookmark, 1965, p. 75.
6. William Charles Repetti SJ, *The Beginning of Jesuit Education in the Philippines*, Manila: Manila Observatory, 1940.
7. Fox, p. 222.
8. Jean Mallat, *Les Philippines*, Paris: A. Bertrand, 1846, II.
9. Ibid, p. 246.
10. See Fidel Villaroel OP, *A History of the University of Santo Tomas: Four Centuries of Higher Education in the Philipines, 1611-2011*, Manila: University of Santo Tomas Publishing House, 2012.
11. Jose Arcilla SJ, "The Escuela Pia, Forerunner of the Ateneo de Manila," *Philippine Studies* 31, no 1, 1983, 58-74. In addition to schools for the youth, the Jesuits also established a school to train teachers. See James J. Meany, "Escuela Normal de Maestros," *Philippine Studies* 30, no 4, and Arcilla, Jose S. SJ, "La Escuela Normal de Maestros de Instruccion Primaria, 1885-1905," *Philippine Studies* 36, no 1, 1988, 16-35.
12. John N. Schumacher, "One Hundred Years of Jesuit Scientists: The Manila Observatory 1865-1965," *Philippine Studies* 13, no 2, 1965, 258-286.
13. James J. Meany, "Ateneo," *Philippine Studies* 4, no 2, 1956, 167-171. This section includes a discussion regarding the tension between the Liberal Arts and specialization in an academic field.
14. Adolfo Nicolás SJ, "Challenges to Jesuit Higher Education Today" remarks made for the conference "Networking Jesuit Higher Education: Shaping the Future for a Humane, Just Sustainable Globe" held in Mexico City on April 23, 2010.

Catholic Identity and Catholic Education in Modern Japan since 1868

Shinzo Kawamura SJ
〈Sophia University〉

Introduction

The history of the Catholic Church in Japan dates back to the missionary activities of the Jesuits, activities that commenced in the 16th century with the endeavors of Francis Xavier. This history, which covers no more than a hundred years, found its way in time into the hearts of Catholics scattered the world over, thanks largely to letters and reports dispatched by those missionaries to the various nations of Europe. These subsequently ignited within Catholics a deep passion for the missions, though that was also an era when Christianity experienced a ban imposed by the Tokugawa government. The tyranny and oppression and persecution that followed lasted for over 250 years until the 19th century, when a new missionary era was ushered in.

In the following pages I attempt a historical reconstruction of the identity and education of the Catholic Church in Japan following the opening of the nation in the wake of the Meiji era, when Japan joined the ranks of the early modern nations.

Mode of Enquiry

I will describe the Catholic Church and its education utilizing the format employed by Robert T. O'Gorman, in his analysis of American society and its related contexts.[1] O'Gorman, whose expertise lies in Religious Education, divides the history of Catholics in the USA from 1790 to the present into three stages, and proceeds to analyze them after having configured each stage in terms of the following format.

The first stage, which lasted from 1790-1920, was a time when the Church was opposed to the nation's culture. It was a period when Catholics were victimized by WASPs and consequently encountered persecution and bigotry, a time when they were

The Format of Robert T. O'Gorman

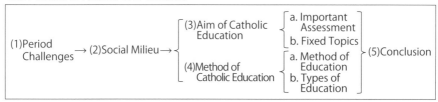

coerced into leading ghetto-like existences. The second stage was from 1920-1960, a period when the Catholic Church entered the mainstream of the nation's culture. This may be viewed, as a time when the exertion of Catholic influence on American society grew more pronounced. During the third stage, which extends from 1960 to the present, the Catholic Church is viewed as permeating American culture like leaven. Specifically it is an era where the Church serves to prop up the nation's culture from within, and issues timely and prophetic forecasts and warnings. This demarcation of periods applies to each of the following:

1) With reference to the challenges of the periods, I shall seek to enquire and discover what it was that impelled a re-questioning or re-framing of Catholic identity.

2) With reference to the social setting, I shall strive to uncover the cultural, economic, political, and social environment that lay behind those challenges, and which influenced the educational aims and methodologies of the times.

3) In seeking to ascertain the ends of Catholic education, I shall pinpoint the values that were underscored. In other words, in the social milieu of those times, what is it that the Church strove to point out in its efforts to face up to relevant issues? It was on the basis of these values that the Church's tasks were chosen and instituted, and carried out to maintain the Catholic identity of those times. This however asks the question, what were the issues of the Catholic Church that were in need of solution.

4) What were the means employed? What were the educational policies adopted and actualized, in order to solve the problems of those times? What were the concrete forms, methods, and content of Catholic education that were used as academic structures, in order to realize those policies?

O'Gorman's analysis consists to the very end in an investigation of the history of the USA. Even so, each question deftly integrates afresh issues that ought to be raised and responded to, whichever area of the world we may happen to be in. It is for this reason that I seek to clarify the Catholic Church's response to this secular age in conformity with this format. It is necessary to consider the Catholic Church within Japanese society. O'Gorman's format helps explain the events of modern Catholic history in Japan: the relationship between the Catholic Church and Japan during the period of the Meiji Restoration, the transformation witnessed at that time in Catholic identity, and an overall assessment of the course of action adopted by the Catholic Church during that period.

Three Periods in the Catholic History of Modern Japan

The history of the Catholic Church in Japan, from the time of the conclusion of the Kanagawa Treaty of Peace and Amity in 1854, which led to the opening of the nation in the Edo period, until today can be divided into three stages, each having its specific characteristics.

Period 1, (1854-1890)	Divorced from Japanese society	A period of grass-root effort for personal salvation
Period 2, (1890-1945)	Inching towards Japanese society	A period of life amidst ultra-nationalism and prejudice
Period 3, (1945-present)	Within Japanese society	A period of developing individual status

Period 1 witnessed in 1844 the final phase of the Edo government. Fr. Theodore-Augustin Forcade of the Society of Foreign Missions of Paris arrived in Ryukyu just prior to the reopening of Japan, when people were endeavoring to enter the country. In 1854, when the American Commodore Perry set foot in Uraga, the Edo government concluded the Kanagawa Treaty of Peace and Amity, Japan ended its 250-year-old policy of seclusion, and opened its doors to the world. In 1859, the Ansei Five-Power Treaties were concluded, and Nagasaki, Yokohama, and other ports were opened to foreign trade. Missionaries belonging to the Society of Foreign Missions of Paris entered each of these ports. Prior to this, however, in 1858 the Franco-Japanese Treaty of Amity and Commerce was concluded, and in accordance with this, freedom of religious belief was permitted in areas wherein French citizens resided. From then on Japanese Catholics of the Meiji period became the exclusive monopoly of priests of the Society of Foreign Missions of Paris. During this period of the re-opening of the Catholic Church in Japan, Catholics found themselves with a separate identity from society at large, so the Church had to try to make new contact with Japanese society.

Period 2 commenced in 1890. It was a time when the aims and objectives of missionary efforts that had been accepted and adhered to all along underwent a revision. When viewed from the perspective of current Catholic history, this year could be considered a watershed, but from the standpoint of Japanese society, however, it was a time when the unequal treaties concluded at the time of the opening of the nation were revised, the Meiji Imperial Constitution came into effect, and Japan began to acquire the structure of an early modern nation. Moreover, it was a time when the Meiji government's stress on national prosperity and military strength steadily gathered impetus, and this in time led to Japan's victory in the Sino-Japanese and Russo-Japanese wars of 1894 and 1905. When viewed from the position of the Catholic Church, though, it was a time of fumbling and groping, for this was when the Church tried to apply to the nation of Japan in concrete terms the doctrines and ideologies of the First Vatican Council, which had been held from 1869 to 1870. This Council adopted resolutions affirming the dominance of Rome and the clergy, and sought to impose their rule on the Church in all countries all over the world. In period 1 the Emperor was allotted the primary place within the nation and Shinto was declared the national religion. This could be viewed as an indication of the extremely serious clashes that were going to occur between the nation of Japan and Catholicism in the 1930s.

Period 3 came after 1945 and the defeat of Japan in World War II, ending imperial government and national religious Shinto. Japanese society at that time found a new value in the Catholic Church. Starting with the USA, the allied powers in their occupation and Cold War structures embraced the creation of a democratic Japan. For Japanese Catholics, with foreigners at their nucleus, the waves of democratization and internationalization that followed served as tailwinds, a truly favorable development for their situation. The tendency for Japanese society to accept Christians showed a marked increase, and the influx of vast numbers of foreign missionaries and religious served to invigorate the Church, causing a remarkable transformation of both the Catholic Church and Catholic education.

Today the Catholic population in Japan amounts to roughly 0.3 percent of the nation's population, or around 400,000 people. Generally, less than one percent of a population is a small minority. Yet, when viewed from the standpoint of the qualitative influence exerted, the contribution of Japanese Catholics towards education by means of their schools is neither trivial nor peripheral. In other words, regardless of the fact that Japanese Catholics have not yet shown a noticeable increase in their numbers, yet the influence their doctrine and ideology have exerted upon the average Japanese citizen cannot by any means be ignored or overlooked. The average Japanese may not be too inclined to adopt Catholicism as their religion by baptism, but they hold in high esteem the system adopted by Catholic educational institutions for having turned out high-level graduates. The enquiry into each of these periods, will proceed on the basis of O'Gorman's format.[2]

I Analysis of Period 1 (1854-1890):
An Offspring of the Illegal Christian Faith
—Personal Salvation in a Hostile Ambience and Development of a Community of Believers

I-1 Challenges of Period 1 from a Characteristic Epoch
Continuation and Increase of the Christian View or View of the False Creed

A vital issue to be borne in mind here is the fact that from the year 1549 onwards, after about a hundred years of missionary activity, the Catholic Church of Japan experienced an era of expulsion, persecution, and forced concealment, and the Church that emerged after the Meiji restoration was heir to this situation.

As a mission territory of the Jesuits, and later of other religious orders such as the Franciscans, Dominicans, Augustinians and so on, the so-called Christian century of Japan involving a multitude of religious congregations, could at its height boast of having in excess of 500,000 adherents. In fact, around the time of its prohibition, the Catholic Church of Japan was in a position to carve out a history wherein the names of over 40,000 martyrs would be engraved.

Since the Edo government had branded Christianity as an evil religion for 250 years, the average Japanese had come to view it as a false creed, a religion difficult for them to accept. Accordingly, at the time of the Meiji restoration, when Japan made a fresh start in the world as an early modern nation, Christianity found itself in a position where it was forced to begin not merely from zero, but from something less than that. In fact, one might say that ridding the Japanese people of the scorn, contempt, and repulsion they felt towards Christianity, was for the Catholic Church the principal concern of those days.

The prejudice and derision directed against Christianity were not just issues to be traced back to archaic memories linked to the Christian period of the remote past. Indeed, the Meiji government, too, believed it judicious to manifest such an image. Although the harassment of Christianity as an evil faith had ended, yet feelings of hostility towards it remained unabated, and were even known to increase. Prior to this, around the end of the Edo period, feelings of anxiety began to arise within the country with reference to Buddhism and folk religions, and as a result, criticism of Buddhism appeared in swift succession among groups such as the Mitogaku (水戸学) and Fukkoshinto (復古神道) or Shinto revivalism. Mention was often made of the divinity of Japan as a nation, nationalistic Shinto became widespread, and efforts to unite the hearts of the populace through Shinto rituals increased. The Meiji government inherited this situation. The roundup and deportation of the Christians of Urakami in Nagasaki, the Urakami Yonban Kuzure (浦上四番崩れ), the last and biggest of the crackdowns on the Christians of Urakami Village, is clear evidence that the Meiji government in effect did virtually nothing to change the direction that had been taken by the Edo government. Also, the Five Public Notices of 1868 (五榜の掲示), displayed for the public by the Meiji government, extended the injunctions against Christianity.[3] However in 1873, under pressure from the countries of Europe and the USA, which insisted on freedom of worship being an essential requisite for nations desiring to enter the ranks of the early modern states, the Meiji government decisively ordered the removal of the notices that had been displayed by the Edo government. In so doing, the Meiji government did indeed appear to adopt the posture of permitting freedom of worship, yet, their readiness to actively endorse an increase in the number of Christians, was yet to come.

I-2　A Characteristic Social Milieu in Period 1
A National Policy centered on the Emperor and Shinto

Japan was now witnessing a situation where the influx of cultural elements from Europe and the USA seemed virtually uncontrollable, a situation the Meiji government had to confront. They assumed the posture of welcoming these elements but stripped them of their links to Christianity. Soon, they realized that despite every effort, they would never be able to stem the impact that Christianity would exert over the entire nation. They hence realized the need of cultivating a system of faith among the people that was capable of facing up to Christianity on the ideological level, and it was this that ushered in the nation's Religious Policy based on Shinto.

In 1872, the Meiji government, counting on the evangelical power of Buddhism, started a movement of defense against Christianity, whereby three religions, that is Shinto, Confucianism, and Buddhism, would engage in joint proselytizing. Christianity was brushed aside as something private, owing to its having been banned by the Edo government. They saw previously the danger that Christianity could prove a serious threat to their plans of constructing a new Japan with the Emperor and the Shinto religion at its core. This was an open and transparent instance of the conflict that arose between Christianity and National Shinto, a religion that served as a base for the sovereignty of the Emperor, whom they envisioned as the public religious leader of the modern state of Japan. This tense relationship that existed between the two to persisted until 1945, though with periodic vicissitudes. That is to say, the new Meiji government adopted National Shinto as a base for their nation-building program and imposed this as a national policy, with efforts to eject all foreign elements, both spiritual and doctrinal, that had been imported into Japan by Christianity. Viewed from this angle, this exessive stress on Shinto indicates that the Meiji government was aware of the latent pressure that the Christian faith was liable to wield over the masses, as well as the obstacles it was likely to raise with regard to the creation the new democratic order.

I-3 The Objectives of Catholic Education in Period 1

Active Participation towards Personal Salvation and the Nurturing of Believers from the Lowermost Strata of Society

In the early days of the Meiji era, the Catholic Church showed little concern with leading Japanese society.[4] A distinct feature of the Church of that period was the fact that unlike the Protestants, who began their evangelical work at about the same time as Catholics, the Catholic Church did not display any commitment towards the newly born society of Japan. In fact, this divergence from Protestants, who sought by means of their high school education to convert leading members of the younger generation to

Christianity, was rather obvious. In that period, the Catholic Church and missionaries associated with the Paris Foreign Missions Society, the spiritual guides of that time, valued greatly the private salvation of souls. This in turn paved the way for their involvement in primary school education linked to charitable works, and the cultivation of groups of Catholic believers, comprising both individuals and families.

During the mid-19th century, after the trauma of the French Revolution, the Pope in Rome had become the standard-bearer for the Catholics of Europe, hardening their attitude against Liberalism and Modernism. The Syllabus of Errors, issued by Pope Pius IX in 1864, condemned modernist propositions. The Pope himself and the Holy See led the Catholic Church through a period of agonized, militant confrontation with modernist society.[5] Priests, religious, and ordinary Catholic believers manifested this same attitude in their everyday lives. Rather than engage in social reform, Catholics oriented themselves towards saving the souls of their neighbors, paying greater heed to personal and internally oriented faith-related activities. Missionaries of the Paris Foreign Missions Society in particular, who had been involved in carrying out evangelical works within the country ever since its opening, manifested a fixation that was typical of the times. Since, at the time of the Revolution, the Catholic Church of France had faced a crisis that bordered on almost total annihilation, there was a tendency to make a total divorce between the Sacred and the Profane. Catholics were suspicious of current social movements such as Secularism, Rationalism, and Liberalism, and hence they shut themselves out of society. This happened to be the general tendency at that time within the Catholic Church of Europe, and the Catholic Church of Japan in the Meiji Period was in every respect reliant upon the Church of France.

For Catholic believers, the most vital activity was the redemption of those they saw before them, the 'salvation of souls.' Hence, their activity in the early stages of the Meiji era was for the most part oriented towards humanitarian works (works that were relatively fixed). Catholic education of Period 1 catered to orphaned infants and children, problems associated with the primary school level. It was for this reason that missionaries, starting with the Paris Foreign Missions Society, scarcely ever turned their minds to issues linked to middle or high school education.

The Catholic Church has always had deeply rooted within its doctrine the injunction to love one's neighbor, realized in the performance of various works of mercy. The last judgment as found in chapter 25 of the Gospel of Mathew described the righteous individual as one who accepts as his neighbor the least (that is to say poorest) person. This indeed is the spiritual cornerstone of traditional Catholic morality. Throughout the middle ages of Europe, the generous and compassionate sanctuary and security afforded to lepers, travelers, and orphans, was hailed as a quintessential attribute of Christianity. After the thirteenth century however, groups of Catholic believers, referred to as confraternities, became the principal proponents of such activities. Activities like these flourished even in Japan owing to efforts of groups such as the Misericordia, and in religious doctrine in the Christian period (what is commonly referred to as Dochirina Kirishitan) the seven works of mercy are commented upon with profound deference. To feed the hungry, to give drink to the thirsty, to grant shelter to travelers, to clothe the naked, to visit the sick, to visit and console those in prison. It was such acts of mercy and kindness (opera misericordiae) that were revered and held in high esteem as the principal constituents of Catholicism, and such a tradition has never ceased to constitute the sum and substance of Catholic works of compassion and mercy. In the Church of France in particular, which had reached a virtual nadir owing to the violence and barbarism witnessed and experienced at the time of the revolution, such a spirit continued to maintain itself, and it was manifested chiefly in the various congregations of Catholic nuns that were formed in the 19th century. Hence, irrespective of whether these people eventually entered Japan and worked as missionaries or not, their specific objective was not the establishment of Catholic mission schools. Rather, their target was nothing more than the salvation of the souls of the most wretched and despised of God's people, namely orphans, lepers, and other suffering people whom they encountered when Japan opened its doors to the outside world.

I-4　The Methodology of Catholic Education in Period 1
Primary Education linked to Philanthropic Activities

It is well known that Blessed Mother Teresa, who worked along with her religious sisters in the city of Kolkata in India, had a deep aversion to people labeling her activity 'social work'. Regardless of their religious beliefs, she would kindly pick up those who had collapsed on the roadside and lovingly minister to them until they died. "As long as there are people before us who are in need of our assistance, we should assist them." In saying so, Mother Teresa probably felt that what she advised was nothing exceptional, but merely something obvious for a Christian.

Catholic Identity and Catholic Education in Modern Japan since 1868

In the early stages of the Meiji period, the average Japanese was poor. On surveying the manifold Catholic activities undertaken in Japan in those days, we notice that those standing out rather markedly are activities resonant of the Misericordia of the sixteenth century, regardless of whether they were engaged in by missionaries of the Society of Foreign Missions of Paris or Japanese ladies who worked with and assisted them. They were activities akin to those later undertaken by Mother Teresa. When we speak of the early days of the Meiji era, most people are inclined to recall the efforts made by Japan to join the ranks of early modern nations, for it was a time when the minds of the Japanese were wholly engaged in this. Yet, the fact remains that in every area of the nation in those days plagues and pestilence were rampant, and multitudes of the destitute daily made their way to the towns. In the city of Nagasaki for instance, up until the middle of the Meiji period, people suffered from epidemics like typhoid, smallpox, cholera, and dysentery, all of which were heightened and spread by poverty, while the situation in Yokohama was about the same.

The missionaries of the Society of Foreign Missions of Paris were based in the settlements for foreigners, yet they traveled around and worked in all areas (up to 40km) permitted by the government. As the so-called 'walking priests,' they left behind indelible footprints in the newly born nation of early modern Japan, which had just seen the light of day in an ambience of destitution and pain. If we consider just the Catholics, French priests founded the Seieikai (聖嬰会), a home for orphans and neglected children in 1872 at the Oura Catholic Church in Nagasaki and in the same year in Yokohama L'Institut des Soeurs de l'Enfant Jesus established the Jinjido (仁慈堂). In Nagasaki Iwanaga Maki also set up the Urakami orphanage set up in 1874. Many other such institutions existed besides. Indeed, with no exception, they were all institutions catering either to orphans or those who had nobody to care for them.

Of all these individuals, perhaps the most outstanding would be two women, Sr. Yamakami Kaku (山上カク) of Yokohama and Iwanaga Maki (岩永マキ) of Nagasaki. Sr. Yamakami Kaku was one of the earliest members of the L'Institut des Soeurs de l'Enfant Jesus. She served as assistant to Sister Matilde, who on the invitation of Fr. Petitjean, Fr. Girard, and other first-generation missionaries of the Society of Foreign Missions of Paris, arrived eventually in Yokohama. Sr. Matilde established in the Yamanote Sanbanchi, Yokohama Jinjido, an institution that could accommodate a vast number of orphaned children. This was the first orphanage established in the city of

Yokohama, and Sr. Yamakami who served as subordinate to Sr. Matilde, walked the length and breadth of the city visiting the sick and the poor, and gathering abandoned children. If ever she came across a child with no family register, she promptly listed the child's name in her own, and in course of time she sent the child back into the world bearing her own surname. She prepared traditional Chinese medicines, and if ever she came across people suffering from leprosy, she would instantly shelter them in huts located within her convent and provide them with food and drink. During her lifetime she enabled 568 individuals to receive baptism, and the orphan children whom she cared for numbered around 3,600 in all. In 1897, Jinjido of Yamate had grown to shelter 482 orphans. The citizens of Yokohama referred to it as the Amadera orphanage, and they were very familiar with the institution. When the law governing private schools promulgated in May 1902 made all enterprises involved in providing relief to orphans regular primary schools, Jinjido was renamed Sumire Jogakkou (菫女学校). It suffered massive damage at the time of the great Kanto earthquake. In 1924, it fell under the government category of an endowed school, and with this the history of Jinjido, which had lasted for nearly half a century, eventually came to an end.

The Catholic woman named Iwanaga Maki replicated in the city of Nagasaki the work done by Sr. Yamakami of Yokohama. After the Urakami Yonban Kuzure, the final assault on the Christians of Urakami village in Nagasaki, Ms. Iwanaga, was exiled to the penal colony of Tsurushima in the feudal domain of Okayama. When she was allowed to return to Nagasaki, she received the guidance of Fr. Marc-Marie de Rotz of the Society of Foreign Missions of Paris, and thereupon began working for the education of little children in Motohara. The city of Nagasaki in those days was habitually assailed by typhoons and epidemics, and this in turn gave rise to vast numbers of orphans. On the advice of Fr. De Rotz, a Catholic gentleman named Takagi Sen-emon (高木仙衛門) volunteered to donate his house and the entire property to the Juujikai (十字会 Society of the Cross), a religious group of women (popularly known as Onnabeya) started under the leadership of Ms. Iwanaga. Even though members the Society of the Cross do not take the three vows of religious, they nevertheless abide by the same spirit. A fact that certainly influenced them into choosing this path was the tradition of the Nagasaki Misericordia, whose members had worked in the city of Nagasaki in the 16th century.

The year 1877 heralded the second phase in the works of women's Catholic religious congregations linked with France, when the Congregation des Soeurs de l'Enfant-Jesus de Chauffailles began the Kobe Joshi Kyoikuin (Kobe Women's Educational Institute), the Osaka Youikuin (大阪養育院 Osaka Orphanage, which opened in 1877), and other works, all of which were institutes catering to children and infants. In 1878, the Congregation des Soeurs de St. Paul de Chartres landed in Hakodate, and instituted the Sei Paurokai Akatsuki no Hoshien (Garden of the Morning Star of St. Paul's Congregation).Today, nearly all the well known Catholic women's religious congregations engaged in middle and high school education in Japan began by offering services to infants and little children.

The Catholic Church in the early Meiji period did indeed have an interest in starting schools, but their interest was confined mainly to those institutions that would enable the care and upbringing of little children and infants, specifically primary schools. In fact, women of the caliber of Sr. Yamakami and Ms. Iwanaga, who were renowned for their intrepid activity, were certainly never involved in any social enterprises such as schools. On the contrary, their sole concern lay in serving, according to the wishes of Christ, those in society who ranked among lowest of the low, those they witnessed right before their eyes. Yet, such a trend too came to an end, since primary schools as public institutions fell under the supervision of the government.

Around this time, Catholic education endured a serious alteration. Congregations of women religious did indeed make every effort to continue with their primary schools, yet, an impression arose among the Japanese that Catholic schools were establishments

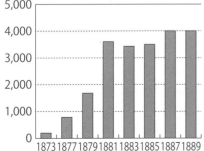

Catholic Primary Schools
—Overall Number of Students

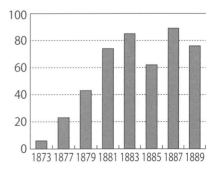

The Number of Catholic Primary Schools

bearing close links to institutions catering to the poverty-stricken and infants. Accordingly, middle and upper-class Japanese families tended to steer clear of Catholic schools, and as a result, the number of newcomers seeking entrance into the schools began to drop. The fall in numbers was eventually compensated for at the primary level, but still from 1880 onwards, the numbers of both students and schools began to register a decline, and statistics reveal that this situation persisted for quite a long time.[6] Even after 1889, the number of Catholic schools and students did not manifest an increase. (Primary schools throughout the nation in 1873 numbered 24,000, and in 1889 too the number was roughly the same). The table above includes not just the numbers for primary schools, but also for orphanages and foundling homes. Until the passage of the law for primary schools in 1885, the demarcation of areas was rather vague.

The idea the average Japanese had about Catholic schools being associated with the impoverished sections of society was not limited to primary schools alone. Yet the stance adopted by the Church, that its principal concern should be directed towards the salvation of the person standing before it, was not restricted merely to orphans. It also included people of other classes and categories. In the initial stages of the Meiji era, it was not the principal policy of the missionaries of the Society of Foreign Missions of Paris to merely erect religious centers and assemble crowds of Japanese within them. On the contrary, they trudged to the very limits of areas permitted to them by the Meiji government, and imbued the spirit of the faith within all whom they encountered. These missionaries persevered with activities such as these until about the middle of the Meiji era, and with the support and assistance of catechists whom they chose and nurtured among the common folk, they finally put down firm roots within the nation of Japan in the form of Home Churches. It was in this way that Japan's pioneer hospital for victims of Hansen's disease that was started in 1889 by Fr. Germain-Leger Testevuide was sustained, as also the Shinto Kyoudoutai (community or believers of Hachioji) and other similar institutions.

In this period, the distinctive trait of the Catholic Church was the fact that while it was unquestionably in touch with the marginalized ranks who constituted the lowest echelons of the nation, yet, it had scarce if any contact with the society that had brought them forth into the world, and this in the opinion of some could perhaps be described as the ghettoizing of the Church. Nonetheless, the option to strive for the salvation of souls has been the Church's time-honored choice, and that in itself is something one could be justly proud of. However, occasions later arose when a change in this option gave rise to a relative change within the Church, but that is a topic that will be dealt with in the following pages.

II Reflections on Period 2 (1890-1945): Initiating Contact with Society

In the latter half of the 1880s, owing to labels such as 'false creed', 'illegal creed' and others that had been affixed to it by Japanese society, the public image presented by the Catholic Church had effectively reached the pits and, besides, public repugnance at its association with the lowest ranks of society continued unabated, thereby making it an undesirable entity for the common man. In that situation, the year 1890 proved a watershed, both for Japanese society and the Catholic Church, owing to the fact that several issues that had begun at the start of the Meiji period underwent a radical transformation and moved to occupy new commanding positions.

II-1 Challenges from the Characteristic Age of Period 2
The Imperial Rescript on Education and the Education Ministry [Directive 12]

The Meiji government pursued the policy of Europeanization until 1887 and this in a way proved a benefit to Christianity. At the same time, however, Inoue Kaoru, who happened to be a campaigner for this policy, continued to negotiate a reconsideration of the 'unequal' treaties. However, when these negotiations eventually ended in a stalemate, an ambiance of ultra-nationalism was observed to gradually pervade Japanese society, and an anti-Christian upsurge was seen to steadily gather momentum.

In 1889, the Meiji Imperial Constitution was promulgated and, according to its directives, freedom of religion was permitted within the country, though under certain conditions. Shrine Shinto was given a superior level of sacrosanctity, and it was revered as transcending all other creeds. The dictates of the Imperial Rescript on Education that were endorsed in 1890 established the relationship between the Emperor and subjects on the basis of education, and rendering devoted service to the Emperor was declared to be the fundamental way of life for the common man. In other words, the reign of the Emperor over the nation of Japan was transformed into a phenomenon that was stable and undeviating. More than education, it was the so-called pseudo-religions that the document appeared to be concerned with. According to the statistics of 1887, 93 Catholic schools catered to around 4,780 students, and needless to say, they were all either primary or middle schools. After the promulgation of this rescript in 1889, however, the number of Catholic schools manifested a drastic decline in numbers, so much so that on scrutinizing the statistics of 1909, we find that the Catholic schools in the nation had decreased to a mere 26.

What perhaps constituted the most critical challenge for Catholic School education was Directive 12 of the Imperial Rescript, which was enforced by the Ministry of Education. In 1899, owing to the issue of the Treaty Revision, residential settlements for foreign nationals were abolished and foreigners were permitted to live in the same areas as other Japanese. The Ministry of Education at that time, being noticeably alarmed at the possibility of these foreigners disseminating Christian ideas among the common people, promulgated, in consequence, an ordinance entitled Directive 12. According to this ordinance, regardless of whether schools were private or public, the holding of religious ceremonies or the conducting of religious instruction within their premises was forbidden. All schools that decided to persist with such activities were threatened with deprivation of the ministry's sanction and forfeiture of their rights as educational institutions. Since this in effect meant that students belonging to such institutions would no longer be entitled to privileges such as pursuing their further studies in high schools, temporary exemption from military service, the right to sit for examinations qualifying them for government service and so on, there were consequently no candidates prepared to enter schools where religion was taught as part of the curriculum. The measure was no less than an effort to terminate the religious influence exerted by Christian schools, and proved to be a severe blow to both Catholic and Protestant institutions.

II-2 Characteristic Social Environment of Period 2
Within the Threshold of the Creation of a Relationship of Equality between Ultra-nationalism and the Great Powers of Europe and the USA

In the social milieu of Period 2, the government, which was keenly committed to building a nation focused on Shrine Shinto and the Emperor, made aggressive efforts towards realizing this objective. However, it was also a period when Japanese society wholeheartedly embraced as a priority its favorable reception as an early modern nation by the great powers of Europe and the USA. In other words, it could be described as a time when, while a forceful tendency towards ultra-nationalism persisted within the country, the need was felt at the same time to display appeasement towards the great powers. The Catholic Church fell a victim to this two-faced mentality of the Meiji government, and decided upon a position of religious neutrality. In 1889, the Society of Mary opened in Tokyo the Akenohoshi Gakuen (暁の星学園) or Ecole de l'Etoile du Matin, Japan's first Catholic School for boys, just prior to the implementation of the ultra-nationalistic policy of the Ministry of Education. However, a total number of 5,520 students enrolled. To increase the number of students enrolled, various small-scale primary schools were streamlined to form large-scale institutions. In other words, for better or for worse, the attitude of religious neutrality adopted by the Catholic Schools did produce some results.

Changes on the side of the Catholic Church: Regularizing the Ideologies of the First Vatican Council

During this period, the principal transformations that arose within the Catholic Church were engendered not so much by factors arising from within, as factors that had been imported from outside. The resolutions implemented by the First Vatican Council that was held from 1869 to 1870 reinforced even more the anti-liberal and anti-modernist stance adopted by the Church, as well as the urge to centralize all authority around the Pope in Rome and the Catholic clergy. Church officials everywhere strove to disseminate these ideas among the faithful scattered all over the world.

In obedience to the Vatican Council resolutions, in June 1879, the Congregation for the Propagation of the Faith in Rome issued orders that regional synods were to be organized in each mission territory. This was no more than a method of transferring in thoroughness the centralization of the Church of Rome to its diverse regional Churches. On the reception of these directives, the Catholic Church of Japan organized in March 1890 a regional synod at the Urakami Cathedral in Nagasaki. The Catholics of the Korean Peninsula and Japan conducted it together, and three Bishops from Japan and a Bishop's representative from Korea attended the synod with seven Japanese missionaries, who joined in the synod as theological advisors. In 1893, the Congregation for the Propagation of Faith officially sanctioned their resolutions all written in Latin, and in the same year those resolutions were published in Hong Kong.[7] They are as follows:

Chapter 1 : Priests and Theologians (De Clero et Seminariis)
Chapter 2 : Religious (De Religiosis et Sanctimonialibus)
Chapter 3 : Catechists (De Catechistis)
Chapter 4 : Christian believers (De Christianis)
Chapter 5 : Catechumens (De Catechumenis)
Chapter 6 : Books (De Libris)
Chapter 7 : Schools and Orphanages (De Scholis et Orphanotrophiis)
Chapter 8 : Propagation of the Faith and its means (De Mediis ad fidem propaganda)
Chapter 9 : The state of Church Property and other related matters (De bonis Ecclesiae temporalibus).

(9 chapters in all)

A glance at the proposals approved by the Nagasaki synod will reveal both the degree to which the Catholic Church had grown apart from Japanese society at that time, as well as the level of self-righteousness it had come to acquire in its transactions with the world at large. Among the issues emphasized by the synod were an exclusionist and confrontational attitude towards modern society, as well as obedience on the part of the faithful towards the Pope and his agents, the bishops and priests. That is to say, the mood of antipathy of the Church towards society that had all along been confined within the nations of Europe was now being extended to include the entire world. By the use of minute rules and regulations, the Catholic Church throughout the world had become standardized.

In the Catholic Church of Japan, even prior to the Nagasaki synod, it was the Japanese faithful rather than foreign missionaries who occupied positions of advantage in society, and among the believers were some who offered their residences in order to conduct assemblies of either the faithful or other seekers of truth, or to arrange prayer meetings. It was thus that a grassroots community of believers was born, and it was by making regular visits to these spontaneously formed communities that missionaries mainly fulfilled their tasks. However, after the conclusion of the Nagasaki synod, the Catholic hierarchy based in church institutions and offices assumed primary importance, and so the grassroots Church that had existed in the earlier part of the Meiji era had no choice but to alter its structure.

The most noticeable change this brought about within the Catholic Church was revealed in the numbers who opted to receive baptism. Since after the synod, preparation for the reception of baptism was stressed, and since such preparation involved a great investment of time, the number of adult baptisms drastically declined. Statistics reveal clearly that the number of converts per missionary dwindled at an alarming rate, as shown in the following table.[8]

The Nagasaki synod revised the course of the Catholic Church in Japan. Using the residences of Catholic believers for religious activities in place of a church was strictly forbidden, and the baptized were all required to attend Holy Mass without fail. The Church of Japan was converted into a rigidly uniform, western-style Church, the faithful under the guidance of instructors were told to dutifully adhere to Church rules, in times of trial they learned to endure their miseries with perseverance and fortitude, and in course of time they were transformed into a docile and obedient people.

Number of Buptism per priest

1874～1880	40～60 Persons (National Average)
1887	37.3 Persons
1888	34.4 Persons
1890	24.4 Persons
1891	20.7 Persons
1898	9.9 Persons

II-3 The Target and Method of Catholic Education in Period 2

Catholic Education: A Shift towards a Critical view of the Middle and Upper Classes of Japanese Society

The Catholic Church of Japan, in response to the shift in the course chosen by the government as well as that chosen by the worldwide Church, manifested a marked transformation in its attitude to education. Since the impact of the Nagasaki Catholic synod extended to the realm of education as well, Catholic schools (particularly primary schools) had no choice but to rid themselves of the features of religious schools and adopt a neutral position. Additionally, in accordance with pointers that the Church received from Rome, they were called upon to pursue an even more vital alteration in their course. Their chief concerns at this time were that their institutions should change sufficiently in order to enter the categories of middle and high schools, and also that they should begin serving the elite of Japan's society, that is, to educate the sons and daughters of respectable families.

Gyosei Gakuen (暁星学園) or Ecole de l'Etoile du Matin that was founded in 1889 (by the Society of Mary), did not directly engage in the teaching of religion, but rather busied itself in offering its students a neutral education. The spread of Christianity was something entrusted to priests of the Society of Foreign Missions of Paris. That is to say, secular education and religious propagation, or instructing the children of the general public and providing them with knowledge of Catholic doctrine, were clearly distinguished.

The Catholic Church of the 1890s initially chose as its target those who constituted the lower ranks of society, and that was also the time when the so-called 'walking priests' fulfilled their roles. From that point onwards however its focus gradually expanded to embrace first the intellectuals, then the middle classes, and later also the upper classes, all with the object of gaining converts to Christianity. This was also their prime concern in their choice of a course to follow with regard to education. On this issue, they felt a need to adopt as models the Protestant institutions, which from the early stages of the Meiji era had steadfastly sustained links with society, while at the same time being fully engrossed in the education of youth. Even so, one cannot deny that the Catholic Church did indeed in certain ways succeed in steering its way through diverse stages, namely from focusing on the service of the destitute and education of children of the primary and middle school level, to making an absolute commitment towards higher education.

With reference to the Meiji government, too, the situation now was such that chances of the Catholic Church being allowed to engage in higher education had grown relatively high, and this was due to the fact that in the aftermath of the Russo-Japanese war, circumstances for the bolstering of ties with the nations of Europe had become propitious for Japan. Any power the Catholic Church had so far possessed was due to its links with France, and that was only at the grassroots level. Nevertheless, it was also true that the Meiji government was now actively seeking to establish a liaison with the Catholic Church using alternate means, and the upshot of this was that the government eventually welcomed as special envoy His Eminence Cardinal O'Connell and his delegation and accorded them an audience with the Meiji Emperor. Cardinal O'Connell thereupon enquired into the standing of Japanese Catholics and probed chances of establishing tertiary educational facilities in Japan, and having done so, he reported back to His Holiness Pope Pius X. It was following this that the Jesuit oriental scholar Fr. Joseph Dahlmann, on the occasion of his visit to Japan in 1903, began to ponder the prospect of starting tertiary academic institutes in Tokyo, and in this context he later directly met the Pope and underscored that possibility.

The arrival in Japan of the Society of Jesus and the Religious of the Sacred Heart in 1908 were events that sparked off a major alteration in the history of Japanese Catholic education. The Society of Jesus was sent to Japan to establish a university, while in the case of the Religious of the Sacred Heart it was for the founding of an institute of tertiary education for girls. In 1913, the Society of Jesus founded Sophia University, which was the first Catholic University of Japan, while in 1915 the Religious of the Sacred Heart started the Sacred Heart Professional Training College. According to Japanese law, when it came to the issue of higher education, only government universities were granted the required sanction to function as universities. Hence, Sophia University had no choice but to commence as a professional college, and although religious education was banned, yet governmental sanction was obtained due to the fact that the teaching of ethics was permissible. That is to say, Christian universities had no choice but to somehow or other grope their way through to success by emphasizing subjects such as law, foreign languages, or other professional subjects.

This was also a time when the efforts of Catholic intellectuals who sought to exert an impact on Japan's society were stimulated, and here the exploits of Fr. Iwashita Soichi（岩下壮一）in particular are worthy of note. Fr. Iwashita was an employee of Tokyo Imperial University, but wherever he taught he began and directed research groups on Catholicism in those institutions. He also worked as editor or chief journalist for Catholic newspapers (such as the Katorikku Shinbun) and magazines (such as Koe 声), and endeavored by various means to present Catholicism to the intelligentsia of Japan. Credit goes to him for the fact that in the 1920s and 1930s Catholic thinkers such as Yoshimitsu Yoshihiko（吉満義雄）and others rose to prominence.

Yet, the 1930s were a time when nationalism reached a peak in Japan and a mood of anti-Catholicism was observed to be on the rise. This was symbolized in an incident that started in the early 1930s and implicated two Catholic institutions, namely Sophia University and the Ecole de l'Etoile du Matin, the "Yasukuni Shrine Incident" （靖国神社参拝事件）. This was an incident that nearly led to the termination of the university, and resulted a most traumatic situation, that lasted until the end of the Second World War in 1945. The point at issue was whether it was lawful for a Catholic believer to perform an act of reverance at a Shinto Shrine or not. This involved the added issue as to whether such acts constituted worship of Shinto deities, or were merely customs, that is, outward signs of respect for one's ancestors, or expressions of loyalty to the nation. In September 1932, Archbishop Jean-Baptiste Chambon (MEP) of the Tokyo Archdiocese sent a letter to the Education Minister Mr. Ichiro Hatoyama, requesting him to confirm that the act of reverance required at Shinto Shrines had merely a patriotic and not a religious significance. On their reception of this letter, officials of the Ministry of Education replied to the Archbishop stating that since the demand for Shrine veneration was made from the standpoint of education, the salutation performed was an act of loyalty and patriotism. This resolved the issue. Catholic institutions were now free to send students of all classes to Shrines where they performed the required act of salutation, purely however as a sign of loyalty and patriotism and with no religious significance whatsoever.

The Anti-Communist link

However, it was a fact that during this period there persisted within the Catholic Church an unwavering resolve to stick to its own beliefs and to meet head-on the pressure exerted by the government. This was due to the acute anti-communist stance that the Church had come to adopt. The ultra-nationalistic Japanese government and the Catholic Church of those days had this point in common, an aversion to Communism, and due to this, the stance adopted by the Church had grown rather ambiguous. In 1934, the Congregation for the Propagation of the Faith acknowledged the foundation of the state of Manchukuo. There were fears that the Soviet Union was plotting to head south, and the Vatican hoped that this was something the nation of Manchukuo could thwart. The likely threat of Communism was voiced in explicit terms in the papal encyclical *Divini Redemptoris*. This anti-communist link between the government of Japan and the Catholic Church may have been something the Church was helpless to avoid, since it was driven into a corner and was totally incapable of opposing the course adopted by the government.

In the early days of the Meiji era, the Catholic Church had initially granted priority to the salvation of souls, and by engaging in works of mercy it continued to proceed

Catholic Identity and Catholic Education in Modern Japan since 1868

along its chosen path. On entering Period 2, however, it began to focus on the intelligentsia and people with links to the middle and upper classes of society, and finally through the founding of Sophia University by the Society of Jesus and a professional college by the Religious of the Sacred Heart, the Church in all earnestness began to venture into the field of higher education. However as stated earlier, in the tide of nationalism and bureaucracy that swept the nation and the financial distress following the Great Kanto earthquake, the Catholic Church time and again found itself a victim of intimidation and harassment. Indeed, had the Second World War continued another ten years it is unclear whether Sophia University would have continued to exist at all.

III Reflections on Period 3:
Creating an individual slot in Society

On August 15, 1945, the Japanese public heard for the first time the living voice of the Emperor, proclaiming the acceptance of the Potsdam Declaration. Initially they were unable to comprehend the fact that it was a statement of the nation's surrender, yet they gathered from the words of the Emperor that the lengthy and protracted fighting had eventually come to an end. The written agreement that was entitled the 'Japanese Instrument of Surrender' was signed aboard the American battleship USS Missouri, and following this, the unconditional surrender of Japan, the vanquished nation was integrated into the occupation policy of the Supreme Commander of the Allied Powers. National Shinto, loyalty to the Emperor, and similar values which earlier had constituted models for the general public, were shattered, and the common man was spiritually flung into a deeply forlorn state. The people had an intense need for spiritual solace, and their future, in fact, was genuinely and effectively consigned to the military headquarters of General Douglas MacArthur, the Supreme Commander of the Allied Powers. With this, the structure which since Period 1 had served as the basis for the enmity between the Catholic Church and the Modern State of Japan, and which itself was grounded on the sovereignty of the Emperor as public religious head of National Shinto, to all intents and purposes came to an end.

What was MacArthur's attitude with regard to the Catholic Church and Catholic education? There is a thought-provoking record available that provides an answer to that question. On November 10, 1947, Fr. Edmund Walsh SJ, an American Jesuit and founder of the Georgetown University School of Foreign Service, arrived in Tokyo, sent by his Superior General on a tour of inspection of postwar Japan. As a scholar he was noted for his research both on anti-Soviet policies and Communist States, and besides, at the Nuremberg Trials, he was known to have probed the truth behind the religious persecution carried out by the Nazis. General MacArthur waited in eagerness to meet Fr. Walsh, and on the day after his arrival he received him kindly and arranged a conference for him at the General Headquarters. According to the diary of Fr. Walsh, General MacArthur thereupon made the following statement:

> The People are receptive and ready for a spiritual religion. They are in essence a mystic people...What is now done here can make history in these parts for the next thousand years.[9]

MacArthur considered himself a Protestant, and it is reported that he also had relatively strong links to Freemasons. However, it would be fair to recall that it was an era when the Cold War structure between East and West was growing ever more pronounced, and in Japan in particular the upsurge of Communism was evoking ever more concern. Even though MacArthur was not a Catholic, yet one reason why he relied so much on Catholics was perhaps the fact that he felt the revival of Japan depended on in its serving as a bulwark against Communism. MacArthur perhaps sought to nurture within Japan's people a reverence for religions based on spirituality. During the period of the occupation, under the eye of General Headquarters, the Catholic Church (like the Protestant groups) received massive amounts of aid from nations around the world. That aid and the newly erected Cold War structure of those days, within the nations of the western camp, served to bolster the significance of Christianity.

MacArthur told the Jesuits through Fr. Walsh how he trusted that they would help to build up Catholic education into a key element in the reconstruction of Japan. In February 1948, Fr. Walsh convened a meeting of Jesuits in their university residence to plan the course of Catholic education in the country.

III-1 Challenges of Period 3 from a Characteristic Epoch
A Defeated Nation: A Third level Consciousness and Anti-Foreign Complex

One may perhaps say that the most crucial challenge of this period, lay in the consciousness of a nation that had just experienced defeat. As a people who had lost all they possessed, the thoughts of the Japanese were focused not so much on erecting a new nation, as in living with the trauma they had just undergone. To quite an extent, their minds were ruled by an anti-foreign complex, which was sparked off by the treatment meted out to them as a third-world nation, and an occupied people. This was aggravated by the fact that while being occupied they were prevented from forging direct links on their own with foreign nations, and there appeared to be no means whereby they could rid themselves of such emotions and anticipate something new. While duly embracing democratic freedom, secularism, and other such concepts that had entered Japan along with the Americans, they nevertheless awaited an occasion where they could reclaim their pride as a nation, and we may perhaps say that here, both Catholic believers and institutions, were called upon to indicate a road that would lead to a change in this mindset.

As an outcome of their defeat, the Japanese began a process never before witnessed in their history, and that was a re-appraisal of their values. Their traditional values were observed to have failed, and new ones like democracy, democratic freedom, and others had been imported into the country by the victors in the war, namely the Americans. The end result of all this was that between these new values and the old ones that they were obliged by tradition to retain the pathetic figure of the common man was visible, running hither and thither in a mood of total bafflement. Needless to say, though, not everything ushered into the country by the Americans could be classed as Christian or was grounded in Catholic values. Materialism, pragmatism, naturalism, Deweyism in education and so on entered Japan at one stroke along with sub-cultural elements, and soon set about permeating the nation's society.

III-2 A Characteristic Social Environment in Period 3

In the aftermath of defeat in the war, as the nation began to show signs of recovery, the leaning towards American-style secularism and materialism began to manifest a corresponding growth, pervading all facets of Japan's society. This was a key phenomenon of those days, and the munitions boom and financial advancement that ensued from the 1953 upheaval in the Korean Peninsula, triggered off the nation's high economic growth.

From 1955 to 1974, during a space of 20 years, Japan underwent an unprecedented social transformation. This is referred to as the period of high economic growth, and yet, the fact of the matter is that the Japanese of this period experienced a deviation in their consciousness, what we refer to as the consciousness of the "relatively disadvantaged." This term denotes the consciousness of those members of Japan's society who failed to benefit from the nation's high economic growth. They mainly constituted the middle class and comprised those involved in cottage and petty industries, owners of medium and small enterprises, and those often viewed as minorities. It is said that such people, when in need of comfort sought to obtain it not from the Catholic Church, but rather from the newly formed religions of Japan.[10]

Within the Catholic Church, too, a fresh era soon dawned. In 1963, the Church encountered its most significant postwar landmark, and that was the Second Vatican Council, which lasted until 1965. The Council, bearing in mind the concept of Aggiornamento or 'bringing up to date,' revised the earlier priest-centered and Vatican-centered mode of thought, and proposed the creation of a Church that was more amenable to society. The Church saw that it had a choice before it. Should it persist in shutting its doors to the world as it had done so far? Was it willing to reject the posture of defiance it had adopted all along towards non-Catholics and search for ways and means whereby all might live together in mutual harmony and respect? These were some of the trials posed by the Council to the Church, and the Church duly responded to them. Its attitude to other creeds and sects did undergo a change (confer the Ecumenical Movement), and ties of brotherhood with non-Catholics gained importance. Some have expressed the view that the reason for this change is the fact that the Church had ultimately come to see that isolation and smugness did not bode well for its future. The fact that it was an institution positioned midway between the mutually opposing Eastern and Western camps, and the fact that it placed such a high premium on spirituality made it clear to the Church that, if it truly desired to survive and continue, it had no choice but to opt for this road. As one might expect, this change had far-reaching consequences in Japan, with reference both to the Catholic Church and to Catholic education.

III-3 The Target of Catholic Education in Period 3
Developing Influential Human Resources in Society

Directly after World War II, starting with MacArthur, the General Headquarters embarked on a reform of the education system. In accordance with the new 6-3-3 system that was launched, secondary school education underwent a substantial alteration. The Society of Jesus that administered Sophia University had founded Rokko High School in pre-war days, and now they established two new high schools. During this period, due to the wave of democratization that had been ushered in from America, the type of education adopted by Americans was in vogue, and since opportunities for interaction with foreigners too had risen, from the very start select aspirants assembled for entrance into schools administered by the Society of Jesus, such as Eiko High School (founded in 1947), and Hiroshima High School (founded in 1956). Even Sophia University recovered suitably to welcome 640 candidates, who assembled like candles flickering in the wind, making the institution all primed to begin its postwar years.

These schools had on their staff several foreign people, and they succeeded in imparting to all an image that was emblematic of democratic Japan. That is to say, prospects were high that institutions like these would eradicate all negative feelings that were seen to ceaselessly persist within the minds of the Japanese. Apart from the desire that the Japanese accept them with feelings of love, there existed another principle, which guided the Jesuits who were involved in the management of these institutions. It was an aspiration that had lingered latent in their hearts ever since their immersion in middle and high school education in Period 2, but now it gained a fresh chance to bloom, and that was the nurturing of human resources capable of exerting a forceful impact on society. On the occasion of the Jesuit regional meeting of February 1947, Fr. Hans Hellweg spelt out this point in the following thought-provoking terms.

> If the Society of Jesus in Japan were to attain a high evaluation in the field of education, the Catholic Church too will be correspondingly assessed. In this context, the primary task before the Jesuits in the field of high school education is not to guide vast numbers of our students to the reception of baptism, but rather to enable them to attain an ever higher level of knowledge and transmit it to the world.[11]

Fr. Hellweg continued as follows.

Rather than run an average school with a large number of mediocre students, having a school where the intellectual level of the students gets ever higher would be a service to the Church, even if the numbers were few.[12]

This statement appears to manifest a re-confirmation of the course adopted by our Catholic schools in Period 2, when terms like 'School' and 'Religion' were clearly elucidated. When we say that our schools need to attain a high evaluation in the field of education, do we mean they should merely turn out vast numbers of graduates who will become future leaders in society? The phrase 'attaining an ever higher level' perhaps means the quality of education offered by these schools should rank among the best in the country. For a purpose like this, there is no need for our institutions to persist in clinging on to their appellation of Catholic schools, because we will realize soon enough that all we need to do is to select our students from the vast numbers of aspirants who come flocking to us and educate them in a consistent manner. Hence, fears have arisen among some that even if our schools were to abandon their character as religious institutions, they would still continue to forge ahead as normal but high-ranking schools. In the postwar American-style democratic educational ambience that pervaded the nation of Japan, Catholic schools felt the need to employ large numbers of foreigners. Those foreigners were seemingly in a position of advantage, as the group that could best bring this about.

What this amounts to saying is that the conversion of our Catholic mission schools into elite institutions is not to be viewed as any form of a compromise, and yet, the fact remains that there is no guarantee at all that running elite schools will raise the rating of the Catholic Church as a whole, as Fr. Hellweg desired. On the contrary, those now entering the Church owing to their having received a Catholic education are a minority, since most Japanese tend to make a distinction between Catholic schools and Catholic education. Many of the parents of children attending Catholic schools have the same attitude, namely that they would like their sons and daughters to attend Catholic schools, but they would prefer that they do not receive baptism. In other words, their choice of a Catholic school for their children was not made on account of their high esteem for Christianity, but rather, because they felt that if their children graduated from Catholic schools, they would find themselves in a more advantageous position in society.

III-4 The Method of Catholic Education in Period 3
Dispatching Numerous Foreign Teachers: The Possibility of Developing Global Human Resources through Enriching Language Education

In the aftermath of World War II, Christianity, with regard to both Catholics and Protestants, experienced rapid growth. In fact in the 1950s, the number of Catholics alone who accepted baptism soared to over 10,000 per year. This sudden rise was reinforced by the arrival of large numbers of religious congregations at the end of the war, and as a consequence a sizeable investment made its way into the country, both in economic as well as manpower terms. Money needed to erect large numbers of churches, kindergartens and so on was almost entirely obtained from abroad, and the number of foreign Catholic priests exceeded their Japanese counterparts to such an extent, that in the 1950s there were six times more foreign priests in the country than Japanese. It was only in the latter half of the 1980s that Japanese priests began to outnumber foreigners.

In the postwar setting of liberalism, democratization, and reform of the educational system, the number of aspirants, students, and graduates of Catholic schools displayed a startling increase. Sophia University, which in 1948 could boast of having received only 674 students, was transformed 20 years later into an impressive academic institution with a 1,500 percent rise in student numbers, and this progress was spurred on even more in 1957, when admission was opened to women. Above all, the fact that, by steadily focusing on foreign language education, the university had succeeded in turning out graduates capable of serving in a global milieu was esteemed highly, and besides, teaching small numbers of students in classes produced exceptional results. In the postwar generation of baby boomers, universities adopting a small class system were viewed as having a special charm, and gifted female students endowed with an aptitude for languages flocked to the university in hordes. In other words, the transformation of Sophia into a top-ranking university had begun.

A key factor behind this incredible growth of the university lay in the character-building (cura personalis) education, provided by the foreign missionaries. In the Japan of those days, securing a teaching position in a university for a foreign professor was an overly cumbersome task, and yet, the Society of Jesus, utilizing its vast global network, managed to amass within the university professors not just from English-speaking nations but from diverse other nations as well, and in this way they fulfilled a primary need of the times, which was to rid the country of its anti-foreign bias and create an ideal educational setting. A roughly similar situation prevailed in other Jesuit educational institutions as well, besides those run by other religious congregations. At an exchange rate of 360 yen to a dollar, foreign travel was hard for the Japanese who had become financially weakened by their defeat in the war, and so the possibility that they could remain within their own country and yet obtain the benefits of interaction with foreigners proved a great boost to their expectations.

I now wish to statistically review the scale of the role played by foreign missionaries in the pedagogical endeavors of the Society of Jesus, whose members have constituted the core of the university since the end of the Second World War. From 1908 to 1945, during the space of close to 40 years, the number of foreign Jesuits who set foot in Japan was 140, but between 1947 and 1949, which is a brief two years, 71 Jesuits entered Japan. From 1950 to 1965, 218 Jesuits entered Japan, and these were primarily involved in education. When we consider the fact that from 1966 to 1999, which covers a period of 30 years, the number that entered Japan had declined to 60, the 218 who entered during the 15 years spanning 1950 to 1965 does indeed appear to be large. In this context, the period from 1958 onwards, when Fr. Pedro Arrupe began to serve as the Jesuit Provincial of Japan, is truly distinctive. Fr. Arrupe, who later became Superior General of the Jesuits to unify the entire order, traversed the world recruiting missionaries for Japan, and the fact that in institutions like Sophia University, Eiko Gakuen,

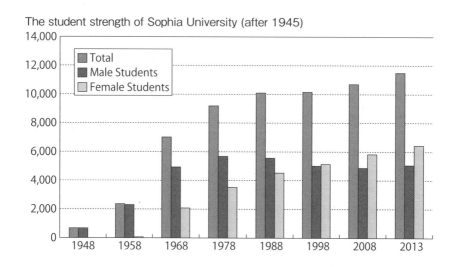

Hiroshima Gakuin and others the number of Jesuits working as teachers showed a significant increase was clearly an outcome of his efforts. By working as language teachers, the vast majority of these Jesuits offered the Japanese youth (who at the time had few if any chances of going abroad) the means to gain both expertise in foreign languages and knowledge of foreign nations, as though they were physically present within the nations themselves. The fact that Sophia as a university succeeded in ascending to the level of being rated a preeminent institution was almost wholly due to the education it offered with regard to foreign languages, and its globally oriented teaching programs. Today, graduates who were recipients of this education are scattered far and wide, responding to the diverse needs of society.

Mission middle and high schools also received numerous foreign staff, and were able to responded to the tide of the times and attained the prestige of exalted institutions. The consistency that marked the education provided with reference to languages and etiquette by foreign nuns evoked hopes among people that there would soon blow into the country an ambience of freshness and efficacy, which the nation had so far never known. In course of time, though, several of these schools ceased to receive aid from abroad. The number of nuns and male missionaries coming to Japan dropped drastically, and the spirit of responding to the needs of the times also appeared to have been lost. Nevertheless however, these institutions continue to draw students of high quality and persist in their roles as portals to well-known universities.

Catholic Schools and universities never pressed the religious program crucial in the eyes both of MacArthur and of the Jesuit authorities. For them, reacting to the needs of the times and capturing the hearts of Japan's people did not by any means supersede in importance the road to be chosen and methodology to be adopted by their institutions with reference to education. All the same, it must not be forgotten that it was on account of the sympathetic and meticulous *cura personalis* or character-building that was provided by dedicated priests and nuns, that so many of our graduates have been drawn to the Catholic faith.

Conclusion

To conclude, I wish to place before you certain intricate issues that have arisen from this historical survey.

First of all, the salvation of souls, which was the chief aim in the education offered by the Catholic Church in the early ages of the Meiji era, underwent a change. Sad to say, the aim of education was altered to focus instead on an ever-growing increase in social effectiveness. Of course, the Church later did indeed seek to modify and adjust things so as not to reject the original aim completely, still, how are we to judge the results of having made that change? Even assuming such a choice was unavoidable in those days, yet cannot the Church now review the issue and study the chances of reinstating the salvation of souls in its current style of education?

Second, around 1890, intellectuals of the middle and upper classes were targets of Catholic education. What has been the result of that choice? Also, how are we to understand the term 'result' that is used here? What would higher or tertiary education mean for a Catholic?

Third, after World War II, when Japanese society was all inclined towards ridding itself of its anti-foreign complex and learning about foreign nations, the Catholic Church built a place for itself in the field of education by focusing on the teaching of foreign languages, with the assistance of foreign professors. Yet, from the 1960s to the 1970s, Sophia University had offered an education which was global and oriented to small numbers of students, and which did indeed turn out to be a success. Now, however, the situation has changed, since other schools offer similar advantages. Hence, what is it that today constitutes the greatest contribution of Catholic Schools to Japanese society? Also, in the period of high economic growth that followed the end of the War, the Catholic Church failed to respond to the needs of the lonely and depressed, and hence many of those people approached the newly formed religions for consolation. How would a Catholic today react to this?

Fourth, how much success has Catholic education had so far with reference to early modern Japan? What is it in Catholic education that early modern Japan needed? What is it in Catholic education that early modern Japan felt it did not need?

These issues have all arisen as the outcome of historical research, and so they are worth pondering and discussing.

Notes

1 Robert T. O'Gorman, *Catholic Identity and Catholic Education in the United States Since 1790, A Monograph on the History of Catholic Education in the United States,* Catholic Education Fu-

tures Project, 1987.
2 See also, Toshiaki Koso, "Americano Catholic kyokaino yukue", *katorikku kyouikukenkyuu*, 1992, No. 9, pp. 71-88.
3 Chiharu Miyoshi, "meiji ikouno katorikku kyoukaino rekishi", in *Hyakunenno kioku: iezusukai sairainichi kara isseiki*, ed. Japanese Province, Nansousha, 2008, pp. 23-40.
4 Gen Aoyama, "meijikini okeru nihonno katorikku kyoukai" in *kirisutokyoshi vol. 9.11*, ed. Sophia University chuseishisokenkyuujo, heibonsha, 1997.
5 Pius iX, "Syllabus" (1864) in *katorikku kyokai bunshoshiryoshu*, Denzinger-Schonmetzer, translated by Hama kangoro, enderude shoten, pp. 441-447.
6 Roger Aubert, *History of Christianity*, translated-supervised by Sophia University Institute of Medival Thought, Chapter 11 (written by Gen Aoyama) Heibonsha, 1997, p. 414.
7 *Acta et Decreta primae synodi regionalis Japoniae et Coreae. Nagasaki Habitae A.D. 1890.* Hong Kong: Typis Societatis Missionum ad Exteros, 1893.
8 Roger Aubert, ibid. p. 417.
9 Shinzo Kawamura, "20 seiki nihon iezusukaishi: sairainichizenshikara sengo", in *Hyakunenno kioku: iezusukai sairainichi kara isseiki*, ed. Japanese Province, Nansousha, 2008, p. 89.
10 Chiharu Miyoshi, ibid. p. 38.
11 Shinzo Kawamura, ibid. p. 92.
12 Ibid. pp. 92-93.

References

O'Gorman Robert T. (1987), *Catholic Identity and Catholic Education in the United States Since 1790, A Monograph on the History of Catholic Education in the United States*, Catholic Education Futures Project.

Koso Toshiaki (1992), "Americano Catholic kyokaino yukue", *katorikku kyouikukenkyuu*.

Miyoshi Chiharu (2008), "meiji ikouno katorikku kyoukaino rekishi", in *Hyakunenno kioku: iezusukai sairainichi kara isseiki*, ed. Japanese Province, Nansousha.

Aoyama Gen (1997), "meijikini okeru nihonno katorikku kyoukai" in *kirisutokyoshi* vol. 9.11, ed. Sophia University chuseishisokenkyuujo, heibonsha.

Aubert Roger (1997), *History of Christianity*, translated-supervised by Sophia University Institute of Medival Thought, Chapter 11 (written by Gen Aoyama) Heibonsha.

Kawamura Shinzo (2008), "20 seiki nihon iezusukaishi: sairainichizenshikara sengo", in *Hyakunenno kioku: iezusukai sairainichi kara isseiki*, ed. Japanese Province, Nansousha.

Higher Education in the Chinese Province of the Society of Jesus
Abrupt Ending, New Start, Renewed Visage of Mission

Louis Gendron SJ
⟨Fu Jen University⟩

I Fu Jen Catholic University

I-1 Abrupt End of an Era, Start all over again on a New Base

Fu Jen Catholic University was founded in Beijing in 1925 and was run by the Benedictines. Later, because of economic difficulties, the Society of the Divine Word took over the university until 1950, when it was confiscated by the communist government.

By 1955, Fu Jen alumni who had moved to Taiwan began proposing to re-establish the university in Taiwan. The idea was well received by the Church authorities in Rome and in 1959 Archbishop Yu Pin was appointed President of Fu Jen University in Taiwan. The archbishop had grandiose plans and wanted to quick-start the university with the help of the diocesan clergy and of seven religious congregations, including the Society of Jesus.

Since 1923, the Society of Jesus had been running an Institute of Higher Education in Tianjin specializing in engineering and commerce, which came to an abrupt end when it was taken over by the communist government in 1951. Archbishop Yu Pin asked the Jesuits to open the Colleges of Commerce and Engineering in Fu Jen. (Jesuits had also established Aurora University in Shanghai in 1903. It was abruptly ended when taken over by the communist government in 1952.)

In the late 1950s, several Jesuits were already teaching in national universities in Taiwan and they were not especially interested in joining the re-establishment of Fu Jen. However, major superiors opted for collaboration. In the end, only the Jesuits, the Society of the Divine Word, Holy Spirit Sisters, and the diocesan clergy involved themselves fully in building up Fu Jen University.

After a laborious and complicated search for suitable land, a campus was bought in 1962 and the Jesuits ended up taking responsibility for putting up the College of Law and later the College of Management. Jesuits had to pay one-third of all expenses: buying of the land, putting up buildings for their own colleges, and paying salaries. From that day and for more than 30 years, the university was run like three semi-autonomous colleges sharing one campus. The President of the university and his staff had to rely on subsidies provided by the three so-called "sections." The most powerful administrators were the three "Regents" (kind of autonomous vice-presidents): one SVD, one Diocesan priest and one Jesuit.

The complicated internal structure of Fu Jen University (three schools in one) was functioning quite well, with some kind of competition between them. But the Ministry of Education was never very happy with such an arrangement. Some professors were critical of the situation and complained of a lack of efficiency. At the level of the Board of Trustees, there were some basic misunderstandings. The Jesuits and the Divine Word Fathers understood the university as a collaboration of three equal parties (bishops, SVD and SJ), while the bishops understood the university as being their own, with the religious providing an important service. Eventually, in the late 1990s, a decision was made by the Board of Trustees to unify the three Sections, under one President with full administrative powers, while the three groups (Diocesan, SVD and SJ) would continue to make a contribution in their own Section. In other words, the founding groups lost their administrative power while being invited to collaborate with the central administration and while also keeping some spiritual and moral influence in their original Sections.

I-2 Active Promotion of the Mission

In the 1980s, the SVD and the Jesuits had become aware of the importance of actively promoting their particular vision of education (Catholic + SVD, or Catholic + Jesuit) if the university was to keep and increase its sense of mission. Catholic universities in the USA and other parts of the world were already making similar efforts. The diminishing number of religious and priests on campus and the very small number of Catholic professors, staff and students made it necessary to find all kinds of ways to formulate more clearly the mission of the university and to help professors/staff/student leaders identify with the mission. A remarkable effort was made in Fu Jen, first in the

Section run by the SVD and later in the Jesuit Section. An Office for Jesuit Mission was put together, gifted staff was hired, budgets were approved and series of activities were organized over a number of years, with positive results in the general atmosphere of the Section and among a number of professors and staff members. All this happened while deep structural changes were considered and eventually enacted towards the unification of the university under the president and the transfer of administrative power from the heads of Sections to the central administration of the university. Some of the good initiatives that were initiated in one Section were eventually promoted successfully in the whole university; this was the case of service-learning, which was created in the Jesuit section and later became popular in all the colleges.[1] But other good initiatives that had been successful at the Section level had to be discontinued or lost their appeal when proposed at the university level. The religious orders felt that they had lost a good part of their ability to really make a difference on campus, including in the colleges that they had traditionally been in charge of.

I-3　Educational Mission Transferred to Lay Leadership

Another difficulty met by the Society of Jesus was a progressive diminishment in the number of qualified Jesuits working on campus, because of a lack of local vocations and a lack of interest of foreign Jesuits to come to Taiwan and contribute to higher education (while there has always been a strong interest for Mainland China). We were then faced with a difficult discernment: Should the Society of Jesus dissociate itself from being a corporate member of Fu Jen University? The discernment is still going on today.

Let me share the proposal that is presently under consideration by the Chinese Province:

> Keep the institutional presence of the Society in the university (Board of Trustees, Delegate, Mission Office, etc.) for at least 10 more years (while possibly closing the campus community after a few years). At the same time, increase the actual presence of the Fu Jen Faculty of Theology of St. Robert Bellarmine on campus through signed agreements. This should be possible without missioning new Jesuits to the Fu Jen University campus. A well-planned effort should be made to provide for the ongoing formation of Ignatian apostolic partners on campus (people

well aware of the values and methods of Jesuit Education) and to make sure that the personnel of the Jesuit Mission Office has a well-thought and workable plan for implementing effectively its mission statement and to periodically renew the plan in line with environmental changes. This may require additional funding and the recruitment of consultants. Professors and staff members who are already active members of Ignatian-inspired communities are to be contacted and invited to work together to implement Jesuit values on campus. The goal is that after ten years a solid structure and excellent personnel resources will have been installed so that the Jesuit and Ignatian educational values will continue to inspire many people at the university, even if the Society would no more to be institutionally present on campus.

Fu Jen University is a Catholic university and not a Jesuit university, although in the past one Section of the university was clearly under Jesuit leadership. This is not the case anymore, although there is still a Jesuit Mission Office with some moral leadership in a few colleges: College of Law, College of Management, and College of Social Sciences and to a certain degree College of Medicine. The Society of Jesus has clearly felt important limitations in its capacity to create in Fu Jen University a space for Jesuit Higher Education.

II   The larger context:
The Chinese Province of the Society of Jesus and Higher Education

II-1   Abrupt End to School of Theology in China, Transfer to New Base

The Society has been running the ecclesiastical Faculty of Theology of St. Robert Bellarmine since 1929. It was started in Shanghai (China) and functioned until 1952 when it was forced by the political environment to abruptly close its doors and move away from China to the Philippines (Baguio). At that time the faculty was only for Jesuit scholastics and priests and had two cycles (no doctoral program). In 1967 the Faculty moved to Taiwan on a campus adjacent to Fu Jen Catholic University and opened its doors to any qualified students. It established an Institute of Religious Studies for those students who did not have previous studies of philosophy. Then it began providing also the third cycle of studies, leading to the Doctorate in Theology or in Religious

Studies. The Faculty has now over 200 full-time students, including about half from Mainland China. In 2012, it was renamed "Fu Jen Faculty of Theology of St. Robert Bellarmine." Although independent from Fu Jen University, it has a collaborative agreement with Fu Jen University. The agreement covers a great number of areas. Since the university does not have a faculty of theology, our faculty is trying in some way to bring a theological presence to the university.

Professors at the Faculty of Theology belong to different religious congregations, to the diocesan clergy, and several are lay professors. The Society has the leadership of the Faculty. We provide also a program in Spirituality with special emphasis on Ignatian spirituality. The Society is keen to keep this apostolate and continue to view it as an apostolic priority of the Chinese Province. It is also making an effort to have a positive impact on Fu Jen University.

II-2 Re-starting in China, in a Small Way

Another Jesuit institution of Higher Education under the Chinese Province of the Society of Jesus is "The Beijing Center." This is an autonomous teaching and research institution, with a Board of Trustees. It is a small operation, with about 100 undergraduate students who spend one or two semesters in residence, taking courses that are accredited by a Jesuit university (Loyola University Chicago). It serves mostly American students from Jesuit and other Catholic universities and it has a reputation for excellence. The Beijing Center was founded fifteen years ago and is located on the campus of the University of International Business and Economics. Several Jesuits from different provinces of the Society are on the faculty of The Beijing Center. It provides an excellent introduction to and knowledge of China (and Chinese language) for foreign students and is a way of perpetuating in a small way the heritage of Matteo Ricci and other Jesuit missionaries to China. In China, especially in Beijing and Shanghai, there are many other centers caring for foreign students. The Beijing Center has tried hard, has been creative and has mostly succeeded in providing the best formation for foreign students who are willing to spend one semester or one year in China.

II-3 A New Type of Jesuit College, in Hong Kong, for China

Another important academic "venture" of the Chinese Province over the last few years has been the project to establish a Jesuit Liberal Arts College in Hong Kong. The civil administration of Hong Kong had been planning to make Hong Kong an important hub of higher education in the Far East. The University of Hong Kong is considered the best Chinese university in the world. Several other public universities in Hong Kong are also of excellent quality. The Hong Kong government decided to promote the establishment of other private, self-funded universities, including residential colleges. Jesuits in Hong Kong, together with alumni of Jesuit high schools in Hong Kong, had been developing parallel thinking over the last few years: Why not establish a Jesuit Liberal College in this Chinese territory? Such a Jesuit Liberal Arts residential college would care not only for Hong Kong students (one-third), but also for Mainland Chinese students (one-third) and Asian students (one-third). In Hong Kong, the Society would have the required political and academic freedom to offer a real program in Liberal Arts, and to prepare future leaders for China, Hong Kong and other Asia Pacific countries.

This project has been very well received by the international web of Jesuit universities and many Jesuit and lay professors from Jesuit universities have shown great interest. Experts from several Jesuit universities got together with a team based in Hong Kong and devised a detailed program for the Liberal Arts College. In September of 2012, the Hong Kong government ("Hong Kong Council for Accreditation of Academic & Vocational Qualifications") gave official accreditation to the new College, upon recommendation by an international panel of experts who studied the project and who met formally with the preparatory team (Institutional Review was held on 25-27 June 2012). In January of 2013, the Board of Trustees met for the first time; the Board is composed of fifteen Jesuit experts from a number of foreign Jesuit universities and ten Hong Kong experts and social leaders.

The Hong Kong government, already three years ago, had publicly announced that a public piece of land ("Queen's Hill") had been earmarked to become the campus of a private residential college and would be given to the group best qualified to establish the college. Around ten different groups started preparations to claim the land and waited for the government to publish an announcement. In the meantime, Hong Kong elected a new head of government who seems to have other priorities. Until now, no announcement has been made. As a consequence, the project for a Jesuit Liberal Arts College has not been able to move ahead as planned. The preparatory team has been thinking of other options. It is now considering buying a plot of land to start building a campus. Under this new plan, the College would start more slowly, it would take fewer students at the beginning and it would have the freedom of growing at its own pace, which would not be possible if a land grant (Queen's Hill) was made to the Society. This Liberal Arts College would be very much in the Jesuit tradition, although most professors and administrators would not belong to the Society of Jesus.

III Concluding Remarks:
Historical Evolution of the Jesuit Educational Mission in China

The Chinese Province of the Society of Jesus has been involved in higher education, first in Mainland China since the beginning of the 20th Century, and then in Taiwan beginning in the 1960s. Jesuits have been major contributors to the re-establishment of Fu Jen Catholic University in Taiwan. However, the Society's presence on campus has been dwindling. There is still hope of keeping some Ignatian spirit on campus. The Fu Jen Faculty of Theology of St. Robert Bellarmine, which is an independent and autonomous faculty, is the only Catholic faculty of theology in Taiwan and has been and continues to be a major priority of the Society. In recent years it has been developing, especially with the recruitment of students from Mainland China (there are no degree-granting faculties of theology in China). The faculty is also having some impact on the campus of Fu Jen University.

Fifteen years ago, a small but energetic center was established in Beijing, providing foreign students with a solid introduction to Chinese culture and Chinese language with also a Chinese approach to their academic major. The Beijing Center cares mostly for undergraduate students and fulfills part of their 4-year college curriculum.

Currently, the Chinese Province is trying to establish a College of Liberal Arts in Hong Kong, to serve not only Hong Kong but also Mainland students. This will clearly be a Jesuit institution, but of a new variety, relying minimally on Jesuits and mostly on professors and staff well-trained in the Jesuit tradition of higher education.

Note
1   In fact, the impact of service-learning is not limited to the Fu Jen campus. The Jesuit section at Fu Jen first implemented the service-learning program in the 1990s, and its success has inspired

many other universities to participate in developing this particular pedagogy. By 2007, the Ministry of Education officially launched an initiative to encourage all universities in Taiwan to promote service-learning.

Jesuit Education of the Whole Person in Sanata Dharma University

C. Kuntoro Adi SJ
〈Sanata Dharma University〉

Introduction

On January 2010, the presidents of U.S. Jesuit colleges and universities offered a consensus statement that explained the defining character and apostolic rationale of Jesuit colleges and universities (AJCU, 2010). They also addressed a set of key relationships that are important to engage positively in the Jesuit apostolic ministry. They stated that being "Catholic Jesuit Universities" is the defining character that makes the institutions uniquely what they are. Their significance is founded on the fact that they are universities with all the important dimensions of what universities are. Through the exercise of an intellectual apostolate, the mission is the formation and education of students to develop a good influence on their lives, society, professions and service.

As *Jesuit* universities, we carry over the Ignatian legacy and the distinct character of Jesuit education. St. Ignatius, with his charism and his Spiritual Exercises, inspires what we do and how we educate students to seek God in all things, promote discernment, and "engage the world through a careful analysis of context, in dialogue with experience, evaluated through reflection, for the sake of action, and with openness to evaluation" (General Congregation of Jesuits 35).

Each of our universities has its own way of deepening and applying this Catholic Jesuit character through what it does. Let me highlight some important characteristics derived from these identities by: 1. looking at the context where the university lives, namely Indonesia, 2. looking at the Christian Humanist characteristics of our education ministry, 3. looking at the education of the whole person through Jesuit education, 4.

looking at contemporary challenges and issues, especially interreligious dialogue in a multi-ethnic, multi-culture and multi-religious context such as Indonesia.

I The Indonesian Context—Sanata Dharma University

The Indonesia Central Bureau of Statistics (BPS) noted in 2010 that the population of Indonesia was 237.6 million, with 58% living in the island of Java. It is projected to surpass the USA and become the world's most populous country after China and India by the year 2043.

Indonesia has a richness and diversity of races, cultures and languages spread throughout the country. The diversity is also reflected in the religious and sociological composition of the population. Islam is the largest religious group. 88.1% of the Indonesia population are Muslims, 6.1% Protestants, 3.2% Catholics, 1.8% Hindus, 0.6% Buddhists and 0.2% "others", including traditional-indigenous believers (BPS, 2010).

This cultural diversity is rooted in its history. Throughout the first millennium the influence of Indian cultures brought a Hindu-Buddhist cultural blend that initiated the emergence of important political empires. At the beginning of the 14th century, Islam spread through trade and later on through Muslim rulers. The process of Islamic expansion that lasted until the end of 19th century was also part of the Indonesian movement against the Dutch that had colonized Indonesia since the beginning of the 17th century (Muller, 1999).

The Catholic Church in Indonesia is quite young. Only in the middle of the 19th century did the Netherlands allow any missionary activities in Indonesia. Jesuits from the Netherlands first began to work on the islands of Flores and Timor, and since the beginning of the 20th century they have concentrated mainly in Java.

Indonesia's independence in 1945 marked a new era for the Church. In that year, there were only 700,000 Catholics and 100,000 of them were in Java. Today there are about 6.89 million Catholics constituting 2.91% of Indonesia's population. Muller (1999) observed that this astonishing growth reflects the strong attraction of the Catholic Church, especially when the Church adopted a much more Indonesian character. Indonesian bishops almost exclusively represent the leadership of the dioceses today. The number of Indonesian priests, nuns and brothers is continuously increasing and has almost completely replaced foreign missionary workers. Lay-people have also played an important role in the Church, and the Indonesian Church has had a long tradition of providing services to people, especially in the areas of health and education.

Although Sanata Dharma became a university in April 1993, its history dates back to 1955, when the Jesuits decided to establish a teacher-training institute. The name "Sanata Dharma" means gift of service. This gift of loving service is devoted to the nation and the Church.

To meet the demands and needs of modern society and to keep up with the progress of science and technology, in April 1993 Sanata Dharma became a university. While maintaining the teacher training program in the School of Teacher Training and Education, the university has opened new departments. Currently Sanata Dharma runs seven schools or departments with twenty three undergraduate programs, three graduate programs, two professional programs and some language courses (Tatang, 2006).

II Christian humanism

II-1 The term

The terms "humanism" and the "humanities" derive from the Italian Renaissance of the 15th century and its promotion of works of literature—called the *studia humanitatis*—as the basis for the educational curriculum (O'Malley, 2000). That literature consisted of Greek and Latin works of poetry, oratory, drama, and history, which, when properly taught, were believed to produce an upright, articulate, noble and socially committed person, which Erasmus would later specify with the word *pietas*—maturity of character. Such a goal required students to do serious study of good literature. Through such study they would acquire an eloquent style of speaking and, just as important, be inspired by the examples of the virtuous behavior they would encounter in the best authors. They would acquire a practical prudence in public life, and a wisdom that would enable them to influence others. Therefore, the goal of education was to produce leaders.

It is interesting to note that the humanist movement in the Italian Renaissance had at least one important characteristic: it was Christian. This means, for instance, that the way it developed particular aspects of the discipline of rhetoric combined with Christian doctrine and theology, resulting in the new theme of human dignity.

II-2 Some defining characteristics of Renaissance Humanism

Modras (2004) underlined some important characteristics of Rennaissance Humanism as follows.

1) Classicism

The humanist movement cultivated Greek and Latin classics. Those classical literatures were believed to generate clarity of form and taste for literary elegance and neatness

2) Educating the whole person

The term of *studia humanitatis*, implied that an education in classical literature served to form a particular desirable kind of human being—a person developed as far as possible in virtue. They believed that good literature produced good, well-rounded, whole persons.

3) An active life of civic virtue

To achieve a full measure of *humanitas* required a person to develop cognitive as well as practical skills. The ideal product of a humanist education was someone whose oratory was admired not only for its qualities but also for its ability to shape public opinion, and in that way fulfill the civic duties of a citizen.

4) Individualism within community

People living in a Renaissance culture nourished a strong sense of membership in a community. One's identity and responsibility were still determined by corporate ties to family and class. However, there was also a new sense of being an individual who was able to express feelings and opinions.

5) Human dignity and freedom

Renaissance culture saw human persons as the only free creatures in nature. They are blessed with the privilege and the responsibility of shaping their destinies. To be human is to face a moral choice: to lead a virtuous or depraved life.

6) The unity and universality of truth

The humanists believed in a harmony of faith and reason, philosophy and theology. Thomas Aquinas offered useful guidelines: "God, who is the author of all truth, ensures a unity of truth." This principle gave rise to the Renaissance idea that truth is where you find it.

III Ministering to the whole person

The *studia humanitatis* formed the central discipline acquired in Jesuit schools and colleges. As mentioned before, the word *humanitas* related to both the process and the studies that developed moral goodness, devotion to truth, and a disposition to act for the civic good.

Education, like other Jesuit ministries, is to address the whole person—character and morals, as well as cognitive faculties.

There is no Jesuit theory of education, but there are principles in Ignatian spirituality and Jesuit practice that suggest a characteristic point of view toward education. They are recorded in three important documents: Ratio Studiorum (1599), The Characteristics of Jesuit Education (1986) and Ignatian Pedagogy (1993).

a) Ratio Studiorum, 1599

Ratio Studiorum is a collection of job descriptions for everybody involved within the process of education in the Jesuit system. There are four important areas discussed in the document, namely, administration, curriculum, method and discipline.

The Ratio is concerned with doing a job in the most effective way possible without very clearly mentioning the philosophy of education that might make the job worth doing in the first place.

Therefore, over the last three decades, a Ratio for the new millennium has been developed. This did not occur as an intentional attempt to revise the Ratio Studiorum of 1599. It happened rather as the result of a series of responses to the urgent need expressed by educators, lay and religious persons in Jesuit schools, colleges and universities as they faced the new challenges in the comtext of a rapidly changing world (Duminuco, 2000).

b) The Characteristics of Jesuit Education, 1986

The characteristics of Jesuit education are derived from reflection upon the world vision of Ignatius, applying it to education in the light of the needs of men and women today. It serves as the contemporary identity document of Jesuit education.

The document lists the characteristics of Jesuit education, gives a common vision and a common sense of purpose, and provides a standard against which Jesuit schools measure themselves.

The document proved to be helpful in clarifying the nature and mission of Jesuit schools. However, the question is: "In order to realize the goals, to make principles take life, how can we make the characteristics real in the daily interaction between teacher and student, so that we can move from theory into practice, from rhetoric into reality?" (Duminuco, 2000).

c) Ignatian Pedagogy: A Practical Approach, 1993

Ignatian Pedagogy offers practical guidelines in moving from theory into practice. This document underlines the interaction between vision and method in any meaningful pedagogy—the way teachers accompany learners in their growth and development.

What is the goal? The goal is to form men and women for others (Arrupe, 1974); people who are well-rounded, intellectually competent, open to growth, religious, loving, and committed to doing justice in generous service to the people of God (Kolvenbach, 1986), men and women of competence, conscience and compassionate commitment (Kolvenbach, 1993).

Ignatian Pedagogy strives to go beyond academic excellence. It is a collaborative process between and among teachers and students which fosters personal and cooperative study, discovery and creativity, and reflection to promote life-long learning and action in service to others. Ignatian Pedagogy is, therefore, a way in which teachers accompany learners. It is a process that takes into consideration the importance of context, experience, reflection, action and evaluation. It is a continuous and repeated cycle of learning and growth.

The Characteristics of Jesuit Education and Ignatian Pedagogy, taken together can be seen as a comprehensive document. Fr. Kolvenbach (1986) stressed that they are not definitive or final, for that would be very difficult or impossible. Rather, it is an instrument which gives a single perspective, a goal and a way to achieve it.

IV Contemporary challenges and issues

IV-1 Promoting depth of thought and imagination

Fr. Adolfo Nicolás, current Superior General of the Society of Jesus, during the Conference of Worldwide Jesuit Higher Education in Mexico City, April 2010, observed the existence of what he called the globalization of superficiality. It affects profoundly the thousands of young people entrusted to us in our institutions. The globalization of superficiality (superficiality of thought, vision, dreams, relationships, convictions) challenges us to promote in creative new ways the depth of thought and imagination that are distinguishing marks of the Catholic (Ignatian) tradition.

Depth of thought and imagination has a concern for a profound involvement with the real, a refusal to let go until one finds the substance. It is a deep analysis for the sake of integration around what are essential: God, Christ, the Gospel.

What is the depth of the education we provide? The questions of Fr. Adolfo Nicolás on the occasion of the 150th Anniversary of Jesuit Education in the Philippines (2009) are relevant: How deeply do we respond to our students' needs? How do we respond to their deepest hunger for meaning and purpose? How deeply do we invite them to see and to think? How deeply do we form their inner persons, their commitments and convictions, their faith and their strength? Are we able to produce people who can "decide from inside"—people of discernment?

In (Jesuit) education, as Fr. Nicolás pointed out, the depth of learning and imagination includes and integrates intellectual rigor with reflection on the experience of reality to work toward building a more faith-filled, humane, just, sustainable world.

IV-2   Re-discovering Universality

The new realities of globalization bring us a sense of common belonging and responsibility. A more universal perspective, which allows us to see beyond our narrow concerns, is needed in our world. The great challenges of the world, as Fr. Nicolás mentioned, cannot be responded to by one region or by one university alone. They require the breadth of vision and spirit that overcomes little sectarianisms so we can work with each other. The challenge for Catholic higher education is how to be a more universal education in the sense of breadth of belonging and wideness of concern and responsibility.

> "If our universities can deepen formation and intellectual work, and make more collaborative and universal our work together, our universities will truly serve the Church's mission of integral human development..." (Nicolás, 2009)

IV-3   Interreligious dialogue initiatives: Indonesian context

Interreligious dialogue is one of the main concerns of Jesuits and their apostolate. This concern as expressed in the Jesuit General Congregations (GC 32, 34, 35) properly corresponds to the challenge of the Church in Asia to develop a contextual theology in relationship to the ways of dialogue: dialogue of experience, dialogue of life, dialogue of action and dialogue of theological exchange (Prakosa, 2011).

In response to the above-mentioned concerns, the Jesuit Conference of Asia Pacific has set up a program called the Asia Theological Encounter Program (ATEP).

The objectives of the ATEP program—as described by Fr. Heru Prakosa—are: to answer the call of the 35th General Congregation for building bridges of understanding and dialogue, to respond the challenges of the Catholic Church in the Asian context to encounter the problem of poverty, religious pluralism and cultures, to stimulate the students (Jesuit Scholastics) to reflect upon and to develop a contextual theology.

The content of the program is the faith paradigm, the Qur'an, Qur'anic commentaries, Hadith, history of Islam (in Asia, in Indonesia), Islamic Law, Islamic Theology, Philosophy and Mysticism; and Muslim—Christian Dialogue.

The dynamics of the program are divided into four interrelated methodical steps. It starts with the social reality experienced in a group and moves towards particular action to answer a particular problem. The dynamic takes place by means of social analysis and reflection of social theology (Muller, 1999). This method is not really new. Many Jesuits have a long tradition to employ what they called the Ignatian Pedagogy paradigm with the pattern of "context—experience—reflection—action—evaluation."

In this approach, the first stage (experience) aims at recognizing and experiencing the social situation and problems through participative observation. An important activity in this stage is an immersion—a firsthand experience of living and working with the Muslim community. The experience wishes to bring participants to be touched by the joys and hopes as well as the sorrows and worries of the community.

The second stage (academic analysis) places the experience in a broader social context. In this stage, the experiences of the first stage are analyzed critically using an inter-disciplinary approach (sociology, economics, cultural anthropology—especially those related to Muslims in Indonesia).

The third stage (reflection) is doing contextual-theological reflection upon the result of the social analysis. In this stage, the product of social analysis is confronted with the messages of the Scripture and other Christian traditions, including the Church's doctrines on dialogue. In other words, the social reality is understood in the light of the Gospel.

The fourth stage is action. It is the realization of faith in facing social problems analyzed and reflected on previously. This action shows that what one believes in has real impact on everyday life.

Observing the 2011 and 2012 ATEP programs, the director of the program, Fr. Heru Prakosa, SJ, said that the week spent living and immersed in a *Pesantren* was a very valuable experience. The participants could verify and perhaps falsify what they had received from the class and the books related to Islam. During the following reflection stage, for example, the participants accompanied by Fr. Kieser, SJ, a Jesuit teaching theology in the Theology Department of Sanata Dharma University, reflected on their experiences with Muslims and their understanding of Islam from the perspective of Christian Theology and Ignatian Spirituality.

The program offers valuable insights and different perspectives, and helps participants understand better the places where they live and work.

Conclusion

A Jesuit education that focuses students to study the best of human culture, relates this to their spiritual growth and experience of God, uses their knowledge for the common good, and shows them as citizens of a global culture concerned about the well-being of all its people is certainly relevant to the needs of our own time.

References

Arrupe, Pedro, SJ. (1974). *Men For Others*, Washington, D.C.: J.S.E.A.

Association of Jesuit Colleges and Universities (AJCU). (2010). *The Jesuit, Catholic Mission of U.S. Jesuit Colleges and Universities*.

Duminuco, Vincent J. (ed)., (2000). *The Jesuit Ratio Studiorum: 400th Anniversary Perspectives*. New York: Fordham University Press.

Kolvenbach, P.H., SJ. (1986). *The Characteristics of Jesuit Education*. Rome: Jesuit Curia.

Modras, Ronald. (2000). *Ignatian Humanism: A Dynamic Spirituality for the 21st Century*. Chicago: Loyola Press.

Muller, Banawiratma, SJ. (1999). "Contextual Social Theology — An Indonesian Model," *East*

Asian Pastoral Review.

Nicolás, Adolfo, SJ. (July 13, 2009). *Challenges and Issues in Jesuit Education.* On the Occasion of the 150th Anniversary of Jesuit Education in the Philippines, Ateneo de Manila University.

Nicolás, Adolfo, SJ. (April 23, 2010). *Challenges to Jesuit Higher Education Today.* Remarks for "Networking Jesuit Higher Education: Shaping the Future for a Humane, Just, Sustainable Globe," Mexico City.

O'Malley, John W., SJ. (2000). "From the 1599 Ratio Studiorum to the Present: A Humanistic Tradition?", in Duminuco Vincent J. (ed). *The Jesuit Ratio Studiorum: 400th Anniversary Perspectives.* New York: Fordham University Press.

Prakosa, Heru, SJ. (1993). "Building Interreligious Dialogue as Survivors in Line with Local Wisdom" *Ignatian Pedagogy: A Practical Approach.* Rome: Jesuit Curia.

Prakosa, Heru, SJ. (2011). *ATEP: Asia Theological Encounter Program — A Report.*

Tatang, Iskarna. (2006). *Sanata Dharma Prospectus.* Yogyakarta.

Catholic Education in Korea
A History of Responses to Challenges Since 1960

Benedict Kang-Yup Jung SJ
〈Sogang University〉

Education's purpose is to replace an empty mind with an open one.
——Malcolm Forbes

I Introduction

Since the 1960s, Korea's "compressed modernity" with economic and social development has drawn the acute interest of the world (Chang, 1999). The development is said to be indebted to Koreans' almost religious zeal for education and a careful establishment of the educational system by the government. While it is certainly true that "education fever" was a fundamental ingredient of the economic and political development in Korea, the Korean education phenomenon failed to address a series of problems as reasons and results of the education fever. Meanwhile, the strong engagement of the government in education left little room for religiously-affiliated schools, including Catholic schools, to differentiate themselves from other public schools.

This paper focuses on how Catholic education in Korea interacted with social, political and cultural challenges since 1960 when Sogang University was founded. In the following section, the social and economic contexts in which Catholic education in Korea was situated will be examined. It will sequentially identify several challenges to Korean education and Catholic education. I will next outline the measures that the Catholic Church and its educational institutions adopted in order to meet the challenges, mainly social and educational. Finally, several suggestions for discussion will be presented with a view to drawing out a collective intelligence to mitigate the educational issues and to amplify the educational commitment of the Catholic Church.

II Social and Educational Development and Challenges

II-1 Development and Characteristics of Korean Education

One of the attributes of Korean educational development is *the inseparable connection between education and economic growth*. As to the strong positive correlation between economic development and the role of education, with the latter being the catalyst for the former, Korea has been of keen interest to economists and educators (Chung, 2010; Y. H. Kim, 2010; Lee, Jung, & Kim, 2006; OECD, 2001; Seth, 2002, 2005). Since 1960, based on the human resources development policy, the Korean government coordinated its educational strategies with industrialization policy in order to meet the specific needs of labor forces at each stage of development.[1]

This cooperative correspondence between education and industrialization policy produced another characteristic of Korean education development called "sequential bottom-up approach." Rapid industrialization and the resulting demand for a skilled labor force brought about a successive expansion of access to education from elementary to higher education. This approach was able to supply a relevant and necessary work force according to the economic development stage designed by the government. However, the rapid sequential expansion of educational opportunity was also propelled by Koreans' enormous passion for education.

Koreans' fervor for education cannot be matched anywhere else in the world. The passion for education—called "education fever" (Seth, 2002), i.e., an obsession with schooling—has deep roots in the Confucian perception of education. It is seen as a true vehicle that helps people to become mature and perfect, and through which people are equipped with the necessary skills to govern a country. Korea's education fever (敎育熱) has been a primary factor of Korea's educational development, while also producing a negative repercussion. It is not surprising to hear how much suffering is incurred because of such high expectations regarding children from parents due to education fever.

Finally, it is clear that Korean students and their parents fall victims to the *obsession with the entrance examination for universities* as soon as they begin kindergarten. All energy and strategy are spent converging on the entrance examination. Each year in November, the whole country stands still on the day of the exam. Even airplanes are grounded during the listening test for it is the most important day in most South Koreans' lives. The test scores that students receive from this single set of multiple-choice tests is said to determine their future in such a way that they will "enhance or maintain social status by earning prestigious degrees" (Seth, 2005, p. 24). This brutal preoccupation with the entrance examination has created negative social ripple effects such as excessive private education expenditures (shadow education), social disharmony between the rich and the poor (polarization), the promotion of an academic attainment-oriented society (credentialism), and "an examination hell" for college entrants.

II-2   Challenges and Social Environments

Against this backdrop, several issues that the Korean education system faces have become tasks for the government to address. In addition, some particular issues pertinent to private and religiously-affiliated schools, like Catholic educational institutions, will be discussed.

A   General Challenges of Korean Education

a)   Shadow Education

It is greatly ironic to see that education fever or education obsession has been a double-edged sword. The primary factor for economic development was Koreans' ferocious education fever which resulted in *shadow education*. This shadow education escalated private spending on education and led to the demise of confidence in the regular classroom education system.[2]

According to Statistics Korea (2013), in 2012 the total expenditure for shadow education for students from primary to high school reached about 19 billion USD, which accounted for about 1.6% of the GDP. The average monthly expenditure per student was about 236,000 won [210 USD], and about 69.4% of the total student population participated in shadow education.[3] This data shows that Korean parents are making heavy use of shadow education for their children. A large part of household income is allotted to private education at the cost of other areas such as housing, retirement, or entertainment.[4]

b)   Globalization and the Advent of the Knowledge-based Society

Globalization was a painful wake-up call to the Korean education system and brought two challenges with it: "to support the nation's competitiveness in international markets and ... to realign the educational system to meet the challenges of human resource development" (Lee, Kim, Kim, & Kim, 2006, p. 66). Traditionally engulfed by a harsh regimen of endless cramming and rote memorization, the advent of the knowledge-based society forced the Korean education system to become more aware of the education system and context which makes students creative and proactive.

c) School Collapse

In the U.S., "school failure" is the situation where schools fail to create social equality and fail to help students achieve high academic performance. However, "school collapse" in Korea is a different situation, where students have low respect for teachers, lack of discipline and less interest in class. Associated with the shadow education problem or intensive private learning, school collapse became a hot potato for frustrated teachers who regard handling students in the classroom as "a battlefield." In this respect, learning in the classroom is dysfunctional. Three factors make students lose interest in classroom learning: "the limitations of schooling in not effectively coping with the new era of information technology and a consumption-oriented culture, ... the clash between generations and between youth culture and school culture, ... [and] recent unsuccessful education policies resulting in a deterioration of teachers' authority and teachers' control over students" (M. Kim, 2003, p. 143).

Deep dissatisfaction with the public education system has led many parents to send their children to foreign countries from the primary to tertiary levels of education. The number of students studying abroad from primary school to high school is on the decline, especially after 2008, in the wake of the global recession, while the number of tertiary level students continues to grow. In 2011, approximately 165,000 Korean students at the tertiary level and about 16,500 students from primary to high schools were studying abroad. The number of students at the tertiary level is on the increase while

Table 1   Number of Korean students studying abroad

	2006	2007	2008	2009	2010	2011
Primary school	13,814	12,341	12,531	8,369	8,794	7,447
Middle school	9,246	9,201	8,888	5,723	5,870	5,468
High school	6,451	6,126	5,930	4,026	4,077	3,570
University	113,735	123,965	127,000	151,566	152,852	164,169

Chart 1 Expenditures for study abroad

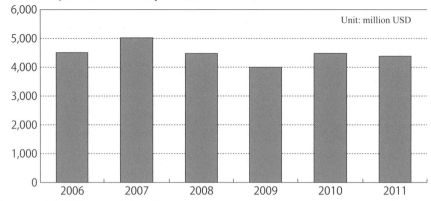

Source: e- 나라지표 [e-country indicator]
http://www.index.go.kr/egams/stts/jsp/potal/stts/PO_STTS_IdxMain.jsp?idx_cd=1534

the number of students before the tertiary level has been decreasing (Table 1)[5]. The total amount spent to study abroad for all students was almost over 4 billion USD every year and in 2011 it was almost 4.4 billion USD (Chart 1).

d) Polarization of Society and Education

A recent educational, social and political challenge has been how to reduce or resolve the educational gap. The education gap was said to begin due to the education reform passed in May 31, 1995, which was propelled by neo-liberal approaches to education and by the Asian financial crisis of 1997.

e) Multiculturalization

Until recently, Korea has been a largely homogenous country ethnically and linguistically, which allowed the government to adopt and implement a national common curriculum with ease and efficiency (Y.H. Kim, 2006, p. 354). However, massive numbers of international marriages, one out of ten, and a big influx of immigrant workers began to change the demographic picture of Korea. In 1995, the number of foreigners was approximately 270,000 and in 2005, 750,000. In 2009, the number reached 1.1 million which accounted for about 2.2% of the whole population. At this rate, by 2050, the number of foreigners will be 4 million which will account for 10% of the whole population (Park, 2009, p. 20). Given the high tendency of ostracization of students from international marriages, the issue at stake is how multicultural education can help children from international marriages and foreigners become integrated into this traditionally homogenous society.

f) Demographic Change and Restructuring Universities

Korea has experienced the greatest decline in fertility rate over 50 years among OECD countries and has the highest participation rate in private education in Asia (Anderson & Kohler, 2012). This high correlation between the low fertility rate and the high private education expenditure illustrates parents' strong desire to make their children successful and competitive by raising no more than one or two. The low fertility rate began to take a heavy toll on the Korean education system and society, particularly colleges and universities. As a result of this decrease in birth rate, from 2018, the government anticipates that the number of high school graduates will go below the overall university quota. This bleak picture caused by demographic change has led the Ministry of Education to decide to implement a regulation through which all universities should consider how to respond to the government's plan to reduce the quota and reshuffle the system of universities from 2015 (K.H. Lee, 2013, November 12).[6]

B Particular Challenges to Catholic Schools

Catholic schools have the dual role of providing education, both religious and academic, not only "as a privileged means of promoting the formation of the whole man" but also as "part of the saving mission of the Church" (The Catholic School, 1977, #8-9). However, there is a fine line between the general picture of the Korean education system and the reality of Catholic schools. Copious research has dedicated numerous pages to an understanding of the particular challenges and issues that Catholic education has faced (Han, 2007; see also B. C. Ahn, 1998; Kang, 1999; The Federation of Catholic Educational Foundation, 1999, 2007).

a) Examination-centered Education

The obsession with the university entrance examination leaves Catholic schools with no option but to hop on the bandwagon of fierce competition to help as many students as possible succeed in securing a seat at prestigious universities. Even though Catholic schools acknowledge that the skewed view of education giving priority to memorization over creativity and examination-centered education over whole-person education should be revised, pressure from parents and students cannot be ignored. As long as the school climate in Korea is engulfed in *arrivisme* and credentialism, it is hard for Catholic schools to pursue the formation of holistic beings.

b) The Government's Educational Policy: One Size Fits All

Given the dual function of Catholic schools, public responsibility and ecclesial role, supervision of the government as a public educational institution is understandable. However, the ecclesial responsibility and function is easily sidelined by the government's policy, which endangers the mission of Catholic education. In addition to the uniformity of the national curriculum and the governmental authorization of textbooks, a series of education reforms which ventured into curbing education fever also resulted in reducing the autonomy of Catholic schools in terms of their rights to select students.[7]

The equalization policy and the revised private school laws highlighted the public role rather than the autonomy of private schools, which diluted the autonomy and distinctiveness of private schools, as well as the mission of each private school. Private schools cannot recruit new students appropriate to the founding philosophy of a Catholic school and have restrictions on the distinct curriculum reflecting the founding philosophy.

c) Financial Crunches and Identity Crisis

Another tool to control private schools is subsidies. Caused by the equalization policy, the issue of financial independence or sustainability for private institutions surfaced in a stark manner. The government deprived private schools of the right to determine tuition by forcing them to levy the same tuition. Since 1971 and 1979 respectively, the government began to give subsidies to private middle schools and high schools so that all students of public or private schools would have equal opportunities. The subsidies are to make up for financial deficits that are incurred by private schools. In 2006, subsidies for private schools were about 3.5 billion USD and accounted for 73.7% and 44.3% of the annual budget of middle and high schools, respectively. It made private schools pseudo- or quasi-public schools without distinct characteristics and diversity since the government takes the helm (The Ministry of Education, 2007).

d) Curbs on Religious Education

In 1992, the government introduced "certification of religion teachers" so that religious education was incorporated into the regular curriculum as an elective. This seemed to be a remarkable measure in that the government ruminated on the special position and autonomy of private schools. However, the government's intervention into religious education persists. After the legalization and institutionalization of religious education, different manners of interventions and control were put in place: supervision of the training and certification of religion teachers as well as the content and selection of religion textbooks. The government's control of religious education looms large in that Catholic schools suffer from "a necessity for systemic supplementation for the curriculum, lack of teaching resources, shortage of competent teachers, increasing level of disappointment of teachers, [and] budget issues" (Han, 2007, p. 40).

e) Lack of Collaborative Work Within the Church

The most significant *raison d'etre* which represents the identity of private schools resides in its founding philosophy and this is supposed to assure "the right of school choice" by students and "the organization of curriculum and right of student recruiting" by schools. In response to a host of intervening schemes of the government, Catholic schools and the Catholic Church did not present a collaborative and timely measures.

It was only in 1986 that the Association of Catholic Education Corporations was established, which in 2005 became the Federation of Catholic Educational Foundation (Catholic 學校法人聯合會), in order to enhance cooperative partnership among Catholic educational institutions. The Catholic Bishops' Conference of Korea (CBCK) began to engage in education much more actively since 2006, when amendments to the Private School Act gave rise to controversy.

III Catholic Education and Responses

III-1 Status of Catholic Education

The Catholic Church made a considerable contribution to the history of Korean education. In 1865, St. Joseph's Seminary, the first of the modern schools, was established in Baeron, in eastern Korea, and in 1911, Benedictines opened Sungshin Teachers' College, the first teachers' college (The Federation of Catholic Educational Foundation, 2007).

Data referring to 1963 shows statistics of the Korean education system: total, private and Catholic. In terms of the number of schools, Catholic schools from kindergarten, primary school, middle school, high school and university, represented 15.4%, 0.2%, 2.8%, 4.5% and 8.6% of the national total, respectively. The number of students enrolled in Catholic kindergartens accounted for 20.7% of the national total and at the university level it was 2.0%. The number of Catholic schools represented 15.6%, 17.4%, 6.9%, 10.4% and 14.7% of private schools, respectively (Table 2).

Almost 50 years later in 2012, the number of kindergartens, high schools and universities increased (213, 38, and 10, respectively) while those of primary and middle schools decreased (6 and 28, respectively). The number of students increased overall at each level except middle schools, which saw a decrease from 18,377 to 15,915. An increase in the number of students in kindergartens and universities is noticeable. The former increased from 3,858 to 22,903 (493%) and the latter grew from 2,192 to 43,450 (1,880%) (Table 3). However, it is also worth noting that between 1963 and 2012 the proportions of the number of the Catholic schools and their student numbers all decreased in comparison to the total numbers of the schools and the students and those of private schools.

III-2 Response of the Catholic Church

Two general characteristics made it difficult for Catholic educational institutions to implement Catholic education. One is the education system controlled by the government, which does not allow the autonomy and uniqueness of Catholic schools and the other is a prevalent ethos in society that focuses on learning regular subjects with a focus on the university entrance exam, in which regular subjects take definite priority over religious education (Kang, 1999). Catholic schools find it difficult to provide students and parents with persuasive rationales for extracurricular subjects that help them to have a whole-person education. Catholic schools became pseudo-public schools by losing their uniqueness due to uniform tuition, education policy of regulation and control, curricula control and limits to schools' rights to choose students. Meanwhile, Catholic education became more dependent and lost the ability and will to run schools based on the educational philosophy of the Catholic Church. In this context, recalling the 29th Superior General of the Society of Jesus Fr. Kolvenbach's (2001) statement about society's effort to, "educate 'the whole person' intellectually and professionally,

Table 2 Statistics of Korean Education in 1963

	Total # of Schools			Total # of Students		
	Sum	Public	Private	Sum	Public	Private
Kindergarten	363	4	359	18,668	246	18,422
Primary	4,835	4,789	46	4,421,541	4,407,977	13,564
Middle	1,114	662	452	665,760	387,080	278,680
High	669	381	288	365,020	208,493	156,527
University	58	24	34	109,063	35,370	73,693
College	36	3	33	14,423	577	13,846
	Catholic Schools	C. Schools Ratio vs. Total	C. Schools Ratio vs. Private	Catholic Students	C. Student Ratio vs. Total	C. Student Ratio vs. Private
Kindergarten	56	15.4%	15.6%	3,858	20.7%	20.9%
Primary	8	0.2%	17.4%	2,598	0.1%	19.2%
Middle	31	2.8%	6.9%	18,377	2.8%	6.6%
High	30	4.5%	10.4%	11,133	3.0%	7.1%
University	5	8.6%	14.7%	2,192	2.0%	3.0%
College	No data			No data		

Table 3 Statistics of Korean Education in 2012

	Total # of Schools			Total # of Students		
	Sum	Public	Private	Sum	Public	Private
Kindergarten	8,538	4,525	4,013	613,749	127,347	486,402
Primary	5,895	5,819	76	2,951,995	2,909,999	41,996
Middle	3,162	2,517	645	1,849,094	1,519,004	330,090
High	2,303	1,356	947	1,920,087	1,072,986	847,101
University	199	43	156	2,122,747	477,960	1,644,787
College	142	9	133	769,888	16,792	753,096
	Catholic Schools	C. Schools Ratio vs. Total	C. Schools Ratio vs. Private	Catholic Students	C. Student Ratio vs. Total	C. Student Ratio vs. Private
Kindergarten	213	2.5%	5.3%	22,903	3.7%	4.7%
Primary	6	0.1%	7.9%	3,674	0.1%	8.7%
Middle	28	0.9%	4.3%	15,915	0.9%	4.8%
High	38	1.7%	4.0%	32,280	1.7%	3.8%
University	10	5.0%	6.4%	43,450	2.0%	2.6%
College	1	0.7%	0.8%	1,864	0.2%	0.2%

Sources: Korean Educational Development Institute: http://cesi.kedi.re.kr
Catholic Bishops' Conference of Korea: http://cbck.or.kr

psychologically, morally, and spiritually" (p. 23), it seems that creating the whole person is almost an illusion.

Though slow but humble, the Catholic Church and Catholic institutions began to question their identity and reflect on how to create students equipped with gospel values and implement a range of systematic responses to the challenges. The effectiveness of these responses still remains questionable. Responses of four different players can be identified: Catholic educators, the CBCK, the Committee on Education under the CBCK, and Sogang University.

A Catholic Educators

a) The Federation of Catholic Educational Foundation (http://www.cascfe.or.kr/cascfe/)

On October 11, 1986, chairs of the board of trustees of Catholic educational institutions gathered at Sogang University to discuss issues that the institutions were facing and agreed on communal actions by fostering partnerships so that the mission of the institutions based on gospel values should be protected and fulfilled. On December 6 of the same year, they created the Association of Catholic Educational Corporations, the title of which in 2005 was changed into the Federation of Catholic Educational Foundation (Catholic 學校法人聯合會). The purpose of the federation is "to discuss current issues that Catholic educational institutions under the dioceses and religious orders are facing, to foster cooperative partnerships among them and to implement the Catholic education mission collaboratively." The federation is composed of several bishops, priests, and sisters, though no lay people sit on the board. The federation is engaged in several undertakings in close collaboration with the Committee on Education under the CBCK.

b) Association of Catholic Educators

In 2010, the Association of Catholic Educators was formally established at the end of the 2nd Catholic Educators Conference at Sogang University. The association is expected to set the direction of Catholic education and decide ways of handling educational issues.

B   The Catholic Bishops' Conference of Korea (http://www.cbck.or.kr/)

a) Establishment of Committee on Education

In October 1972, the CBCK established the Committee on Education with a view of fostering gospel values based on the Catholic educational philosophy and contributing to the development of the Korean education system. As the importance of youth ministries grew, the conference separated the Committee on Youth Ministry from the Committee on Education in 2008.

b) Charter of Catholic School Education

The CBCK realized that despite historical contributions to the Korean educational system by Catholic education, the Church failed to make a relevant assessment of the role of Catholic education from historical and educational perspectives. Even official documents of the Church that help to establish Catholic educational philosophy and to operate schools did not exist. Given this reality in October 2006, the CBCK issued the Charter of Catholic Schools in Korea as a kind of *magna carta*.

The Charter defines Catholic schools with two characteristics: one is the ecclesial characteristic which means that "stakeholders take Christ's life as an example, hold Christian perspective and commit themselves to the Church's evangelization mission"; the other is a general characteristic which "just like other schools conveys knowledge and information, passes on cultural heritage and cultivates deep personality." (para. 1.1) The Charter states that the mission of Catholic schools is "to be committed to evangelization and whole-person education." (para. 1.2)

c) Guidelines on Catholic School Education in Korea

In 2011, the CBCK promulgated the final version of "Guidelines for Catholic School Education in Korea" with hopes that the spirit of the Charter would be realized in every Catholic school. The guidelines are an enlarged version of the Charter of Catholic School Education with more detailed information and contents.

The guidelines aim to make stakeholders such as students, parents and teaching and administrative staff understand the advantages and uniqueness of Catholic schools and to help Catholic foundations disseminate the Catholic educational spirit consistently and effectively. In addition, the guidelines provide the legal basis so that Catholic foundations and individuals can make adequate responses to any public and private attempts to compromise Catholic educational philosophy and autonomy of the schools.

d) Guidelines on Catholic Education in Kindergarten

The CBCK is drafting "Guidelines for Catholic Education in Kindergarten." Resonant with the Charter of Catholic School Education, the guidelines provide instructions on how to run Catholic kindergartens in the spirit of the Catholic faith.

C Response of the Society of Jesus: Sogang University (http://www.sogang.ac.kr/english/)

a) The Jesuit Education Philosophy

Jesuit schools had a unique feature in that Jesuits integrated two models of schools into one: the medieval university for the training of the mind and the Renaissance humanistic academy for character formation. (A Pocket Guide to Jesuit Education, Why Were Jesuit Schools so Successful?). Several features of Jesuit education methods would account for their success in education as follows:

- Self-knowledge and discipline,
- Attentiveness to their own experience and to others',
- Trust in God's direction of their lives,
- Respect for intellect and reason as tools for discovering truth,
- Skill in discerning the right course of action,
- A conviction that talents and knowledge were gifts to be used to help others,
- Flexibility and pragmatism in problem solving,
- Large-hearted ambition, and
- A desire to find God working in all things.

Two crucial Jesuit axioms began to shape the face of the modern Jesuit education arena. One is "men-and-women for others." The 28th Superior General of the Society of Jesus Fr. Arrupe stressed in his address to the Jesuit alumni of Europe in 1973: "Today our prime educational objective must be to form men-for-others…" (Arrupe, p. 9). The other is "the service of faith and promotion of justice." In 1975 the 32nd General Congregation of the Society made a compelling statement on the essence of its mission of the day: its mission is "the service of faith, of which the promotion of justice is an absolute requirement" (Decree 4, #2) and "[the service of faith doing justice] should be the integrating factor of all our ministries…" (Decree 2, #9). Now these two Jesuit adages touched on a thread that ran through many writings and speeches and set the tone of Jesuit education today. They are the modern charter of Jesuit education and became a litmus test that identifies a school as Catholic and Jesuit.

The mission of Sogang is an offspring of this Jesuit philosophy of education that forms the whole person with traditions flowing from Catholic, Jesuit and Korean tenors to commit themselves to human development and the world.

b) Programs Within Sogang and Beyond

In 2005, on the occasion of the 50th anniversary of the Korea Province of the Society of Jesus, Fr. Kolvenbach (2005) gave a speech to the Sogang family, which encapsulated the Jesuit educational goal: "Ultimately, the goal is to promote that full growth of the person so that he or she becomes a leader of service to the community. Ignatian education seeks to prepare men and women of competence, of conscience, of compassion." With this set of facets of Jesuit education and its goal, Sogang has been providing a range of academic and service programs.

b.1 Curriculum at a Jesuit University

At its beginning, for the sake of character education, Sogang required general education that constituted a half of the total 160 credits. In the 1970's, the required credits for general education decreased and the range of choice for selective courses of general education widened. At present, students should take a minimum of 22 credits to a maximum of 31 credits of general education.

b.2 Campus Ministry (http://kyomok.sogang.ac.kr/)

The Office of Campus Ministry with 5 Jesuits, 2 religious members and 2 lay staff orchestrates diverse programs and activities of 4 categories that precisely mirror the Jesuit educational philosophy.

b.2.1 Formation

Catechism classes, bible study for students, and bible study in English, Spanish and French are available. Now 21 Bible classes for students and 2 for foreigners are in operation. Since 2010, "Stepping Stone for Love," targeting freshmen and their parents, is a program in which the parents recommend books on life lessons along with hand-written letters for their kids.

b.2.2 Student/Staff Organization

On-campus organizations for stakeholders are formed: altar boys, FIAT choir, Sunday Youth Community for Sunday Mass, Gracias choir, liturgy committees for the Sunday English Mass, and Ignatius for voluntary services. Legion of Mary is for faculty and staff. In addition, liturgical dance and meditative yoga also welcome people.

b.2.3 International Immersion Experience & Voluntary Service

Sogang has been running immersion experience programs in Cambodia and the Philippines to experience the history and culture of the underprivileged in the third world and live out "men and women for others" through voluntary services.

The "AJCU-AP Service Learning Program" was initiated in 2008 and is a service learning space where students from Jesuit universities in the region learn for 3 weeks how to apply Ignatian Pedagogy in their everyday life with practical experience through community service.

Two domestic voluntary services are also available. One is for children of North Korean defectors (Firefly Teachers Council) and the other is for Hansen's disease patients.

b.2.4 Center for Voluntary Social Service

Echoing what Fr. Kolvenbach (2001) stressed, the future whole person must be educated with "an educated awareness of society and culture with which to contribute socially, generously, in the real world. … [with] *a well-educated solidarity*," (Kolvenbach, 2001,pp. 23-24), in terms of planning and financial support, the Center has taken care of 6 voluntary service teams. What is more, they opened a community service course and run a community service certification system.

b.3 Ignatius Night School

Finally, since 1978, this school has been a place for underprivileged students to get the opportunity to learn from Sogang students as teachers. The rector of the Sogang Jesuit Community has been helping the school as principal.

c) The Future of Sogang

Since its foundation in 1960, Sogang University has played a leading role in the Korean higher education arena and has become an exemplary educational model by introducing revolutionary schemes. Sogang's inherent nature such as internationalized and systematized curriculum, compulsory general education that focuses on fostering the whole person, strict academic management and *cura personalis* for students has helped Sogang to grow into a prestigious university in such a short time. However, the consequence of a high degree of compressed economic growth and globalization has impacted the identity and sustainability of Sogang as well in the wake of fierce competition with larger and more competitive local universities. Sogang is planning three major projects not just to enhance excellence in education, but to keep the Jesuit education philosophy vibrant.

c.1 Restructuring of General Education and *Chulwoo* Manresa Center for Spirituality[8]

Sogang will expand courses about community service, leadership and experiential general education to form the whole person with intelligence, personality and spirituality. One way of achieving this plan is building the Chulwoo Manresa Center for Spirituality on the outskirts of Seoul. The center, with a total of 96 classrooms and dormitory rooms, will be used to provide all freshmen with opportunities for spiritual formation from the academic year 2015.

c.2 The 2nd Campus: GERB Campus

Sogang's main campus in Seoul is currently running short of space. Sogang plans to build a new GERB (Global Education Research & Business) campus at Namyangju in the eastern suburbs of Seoul as an advanced educational facility to strengthen the cohesion of an education-research-culture-industrial environment.

c.3 SOWUUS (Sogang World University of Underprivileged Students)

To contribute to the human development of the third world, Sogang is planning to establish a world university, Sogang World University of Underprivileged Students, on the 2nd campus site which will provide college education at no cost for a certain number of socio-economically underprivileged students per year from all over the world. The

30th Superior General of the Society of Jesus Fr. Nicolás (2010) laid stress on the importance of working together in order to construct "a more humane, just, sustainable, and faith-filled world." (Nicolás, p. 13) Sogang will provide a new paradigm to Korean universities by actively utilizing the asset Sogang has as a Jesuit university and the asset is with no doubt the global network of Jesuit universities. Sogang, in collaboration with UNESCO and UN, will invite young students and offer them avenues of learning that feature Korea's development experiences in education, science and technology so that when they return home, they can contribute to the economic and human development of their home countries. The key to this project will lie in collaboration with the wide network of Jesuit universities, UN, UNESCO, NGO's and business companies.

IV   Issues of Catholic Education for Future Consideration

Catholic Education in Korea has been taking an important but difficult road to fulfill its vision and mission to uphold the value and meaning of whole-person education and evangelization. The myriad of problems and their causes and effects have alerted them to the urgency of an endeavor for creative solutions. Assessing the reality of Korean Catholic schools, it will be a long path to finding a reasonable but committed way to fulfil their unique and particular mission of Catholic education. Keeping in mind the core mission of Catholic schools, there is a real need for a genuine and measured understanding of the reality of Catholic education and for solutions. The following suggestions are put forward to generate discussion.

A   New and Deeper Understanding of the Roots and Traditions

It is argued that "the only condition [the Catholic school] would make, as is its right, for its continued existence would be remaining faithful to the educational aims of the Catholic school" (The Catholic School, #85). There can be little doubt that the educational aim of an institution radiates its mission, vision and educational philosophy, which are the most important indicators that direct the course of the institution by identifying the contents and characteristics of all policies that the institution is planning and implementing.

However, it is necessary for the educational aim to be revisited in order to make it possible for an institution to have a more effective role and service through a deeper reflection on a new context in which the institution is currently located and how its educational mission corresponds to this new context that brings in a difference to its stakeholders and societies so as to reappropriate the essence of its founding spiritual heritage. Danger always resides in the tendency to remain unquestionably loyal to the *status quo* without considering a new atmosphere.

B Dialogue with the Market

What is important is to maintain a dialogue with the market rather than shunning it. Working at the university, the Jesuit vocation is "to live on the borderline where the Church meets the world and the world meets the Church"; the challenge is that "the borderline is ever shifting" (Murray, 1966, p. 10). When Pope Francis had an interview with the editor-in-chief of *La Civiltà Cattolica,* he warned against the temptation to stay at *status quo* or "to tame the frontiers" (Spadaro, 2013,):

> When I insist on the frontier, I am referring in a particular way to the need for those who work in the world of culture to be inserted into the context in which they operate and on which they reflect. There is always the lurking danger of living in a laboratory. Ours is not a 'lab faith,' but a 'journey faith,' a historical faith. God has revealed himself as history, not as a compendium of abstract truths. I am afraid of laboratories because in the laboratory you take the problems and then you bring them home to tame them, to paint them artificially, out of their context. You cannot bring home the frontier, but you have to live on the border and be audacious.

How can leadership preserve and enhance educational ideals and values without being swept away by market forces? It is more dangerous and damaging to remain in the cozy and unchallenged ivory tower than to engage the market force in an effort to create an educational environment for a better education that produces citizens of service and compassion. The issue is how the leadership at the university should find the balance between market power and the public responsibility of the university.

C Local, Regional and Global Networking

At the local level, networking should be developed to foster a collaborative partnership among Catholic schools and stakeholders. Networking will be conducive to insightful and different perspectives on a problem and leave better impacts on society as a way of securing constructive synergy.

Sogang can expand its international engagement through the Jesuit network. Fr. Nicolás (2010) requested "deeper analysis, reflection, and discernment" in order to tackle the challenges of "the globalization of superficiality – superficiality of thought, vision, dreams, relationships, convictions" (p. 9). He continued to suggest a more universal, creative and effective international network of Jesuit higher education:

> If each university, working by itself as a *proyecto social*, is able to accomplish so much good in society, how much more can we increase the scope of our service to the world if all the Jesuit institutions of higher education become, as it were, a single global *proyecto social*? (p. 15)[9]

In the Jesuit Conference of Asia Pacific, the Association of Jesuit Colleges and Universities in Asia Pacific (AJCU-AP) for higher education and JEC-AP for pre secondary and secondary education are good examples of networking. The Service Learning Program (SLP) initiated by AJCU-AP for students and faculty of several AJCU-AP members as well as SOFEX for sports and the cultural exchange between Sophia University and Sogang are other examples.

D Legal Legislation and Social Affirmation for the Justification of the Catholic Educational Philosophy

As stated, religiously-affiliated private schools have been exposed to the excessive interference and control of the government through stifling laws, conventions and policies. This control by laws endangered the realization of the founding philosophy of Catholic education. Irrespective of revisions of the Private School Act in 2005 and 2007, the autonomy of religiously-affiliated schools is still hardly at hand. The development of Catholic education is partly dependent on a legal measure that occupies a unique role of religiously-affiliated schools. In order to guarantee more autonomous operation and differentiated education of Catholic schools, efforts to amend related laws such as the Private School Act are greatly needed.

E Enhancement of The Role of Foundation/Corporation

There are three major roles and responsibilities of any school corporation: 1) to provide financial support to the school, 2) to check whether the founding education philosophy is secure, and 3) to try to answer some questions with its mission in mind.

- What are the strengths and weaknesses of the school at the moment?
- What opportunities and threats is the school facing?
- What is the strategic planning for the school in the long run?
- What policies does the school provide in order for the school leadership to promote and deepen the Catholic/Jesuit education philosophy and character?
- What human and financial resources does the school secure in order to empower the school leadership?

F Paving the Way for Sharing the Mission of the Church with Lay Colleagues

The Church does not fail to appreciate the role and presence of lay people in the mission of the Church. As coworkers in the salvific mission of the Church, each lay person is always "a sharer in the priestly, prophetic, and kingly functions of Christ" and their apostolate is also "a participation in the saving mission of the Church itself" (Lay Catholics in Schools, 1982, #6). In the same vein, the 34th General Congregation of the Society of Jesus highlighted the role of lay people in the fulfillment of the mission of the Society of Jesus: "Cooperation with the laity is both a constitutive element of our way of proceeding and a grace calling for individual, communal, and institutional reward. It invites us to service of the ministry of lay people, partnership with them in mission, and openness to creative ways of future cooperation" (Decree 13, #26).

However, in sharp contrast with these declarations of the roles of teachers and laypeople, in reality, it was stunning to recognize how little presence lay people have in the Catholic Church in Korea at the level of deciding the direction or vision of an organization. For instance, as indicated earlier, no layperson sits on the Board of the Federation of Catholic Educational Foundation in Korea. More participative engagement from lay people through collective intelligence and collaborative mechanism should be in place within or around an institution to facilitate this engagement. At the same time, leadership at the school including the Corporation should consider programs that help staff and teachers to be immersed into the educational philosophy of the schools and to live it out on a daily basis. Examples of the programs can include workshops for newly-hired and appointed staff and teachers as well as programs for alumni/ae.

G Creative Civic Engagement

A sincere reflection regarding the extent of how the Catholic school education system makes the most of its potentiality in terms of civic engagement is also needed. The current education system in Korea which does not allow diversity leaves little room for differentiated education which is not directly pertinent to examination preparation. Catholic schools should consider a different model of schooling packed with diversity, choice and caring, which will eventually enhance the value of Catholic education. Some questions are presented for consideration:

- What is the best way to utilize religious education in order to enhance social justice, peace and environment in societies?
- How can the underprivileged be helped to increase their education assets?
- What adequate provisions are available, particularly for children from multicultural families?

How can the cultural and educational gap in marginalized areas such as rural areas be narrowed down?

Notes

1 During the 1960s, labor-intensive light industry was a focus, with numerous manual workers supplied through the universalization of primary education. During the 1970s, capital-intensive heavy and chemical industries were a focal point. Secondary education and technical and vocational education were emphasized. During the 1980s, a subsequent shift of the leading industries to technology-intensive and knowledge- and information-intensive industries took place and, thus, higher education experienced rapid expansion.
2 Shadow education is defined as "fee-based lessons outside of school that provide supplementary instruction to students in academic subjects they have studied or will study in school to help prepare them for high-stakes exams administered in the public education system" (Lee & Jang, 2010, p. 514).
3 Among the 34 OECD members, Korea ranked third behind Denmark and Iceland in terms of ex-

penditure on educational institutions as a percentage of GDP in 2010. Korea spent 7.6% of their GDP on education, higher than the OECD average of 6.3%.

4   The Korean government took note of the vicious effects of education fever on society and family expenditures. In order to address the problems that shadow education brought about, the government introduced a series of policies: (1) abolition of the middle school entrance examination (1968), (2) the high school equalization policy (1973), (3) educational reform measures (1980. 7.30), (4) the reform of the college entrance examination system and the public education system (1980s-1990s), (5) policies for enhancing public education (2000-2004), and (6) increases in school autonomy (2009).

5   In 2012, Korea was sending the third largest number of students to the United States after China and India.

6   The Ministry of Education proposed that 1) all universities should be categorized into 5 groups starting from 2015; 2) the 1st group will remain intact while the remaining four will be forced to cut their quota; 3) the lower the evaluation, the more quota cut; and 4) the 5th group will be penalized to the point of closure.

7   The abolition of the middle school entrance examination (中學校無試驗入學, 1969), the equalization policy of high school (高等學校平準化政策, 1973), revision of the constitutions of private schools' corporations (私立學校定款改正, 1975, 1981, 2006), and institutionalization of high school grades (內申制, 1981).

8   Mr. Lee, Chulwoo, alumnus of Sogang Catholic Advanced Management Program, donated a large property to Sogang in the hope that the site will be a place for education of character based on the Jesuit education philosophy.

9   In regards to the term *proyecto social* that was coined by Ignacio Ellacuría, a Jesuit theologian killed by the government of El Salvador in 1989, Fr. Nicolás (2010) defines it as a university that "with its rich resources of intelligence, knowledge, talent, vision, and energy, moved by its commitment to the service of faith and promotion of justice, seeks to insert itself into a society, not just to train professionals, but in order to become a cultural force advocating and promoting truth, virtue, development, and peace in that society." (p. 14)

References

Ahn, B.C. (1998) 가톨릭 학교 운영의 현황과 문제 및 미래 전망 [Catholic School Management: Current Status, Problems and Prospect], 사목 [Samok], 8: 71-89.

Anderson, T.M. & Kohler, H-P. (2012). *Education Fever and the East Asian Fertility Puzzle: A case study of low fertility in South Korea.* Retrieved 20 September 2013 from http://repository.upenn. edu/cgi/viewcontent.cgi?article=1037&context=psc_working_papers

A Pocket Guide to Jesuit Education (n.d.). Retrieved September 23, 2013 from http://www.bc.edu/ content/bc/offices/mission/publications/guide.html

Arrupe, P. (1973). *Men for Others: Education for Social Justice and Social Action Today.* Rome: S.J. Press and Information Office.

Chang, K.S. (1999). Compressed modernity and its discontents: South Korean society in transition. *Economy and Society,* 28 (1), 30-55.

Chung, J.Y. (2010). Social Dynamics and Educational Change in Korea. In C.J. Lee, S.Y. Kim & D. Adams (Eds.), *Sixty years of Korean Education* (pp. 444-475). Seoul: SNU Press.

Han, M.S. (2007, May). 가톨릭 학교의 교육 현실 [Status of Catholic School Education]. Symposium conducted at the meeting of the Education Week Seminar. Nonsan, Korea. Retrieved October 5, 2013 from http://edu.cbck.or.kr/index.php?mm_code=708&sm_code=733&tab_code=&board_mode=list&board_no=&board_search_keyword=&board_page=1&board_search_head_word=&board_search_part_subject=Y&board_search_part_content=Y&board_search_part_writer=N&board_mode=view&board_no=41

John Paul II (1992). *Ex Corde Ecclesiae*. Retrieved September 28, 2013 from http://www.vatican.va/holy_father/john_paul_ii/apost_constitutions/documents/hf_jp-ii_apc_15081990_ex-corde-ecclesiae_en.html

Kang, T.J. (1999). 교육개혁과 가톨릭 학교교육 [Education Reform and Catholic Education]. In the Federation of Catholic Educational Foundation (Ed.), 한국의 가톨릭 학교교육 [Catholic Education in Korea] (pp. 135-156). Seoul: Catholic Cultural Center.

Kim, J.Y. (2013, March 7). Education spending gap reaches a 10-year high, *The Korea Joongang Daily*.

Kim, M. (2003). Teaching and Learning in Korean Classrooms: The Crisis and the New Approach. *Asia Pacific Education Review*, 4 (2), 140-150.

Kim, Y.H. (2010). Education and Economic Growth in Korea 1945-1995. In C.J. Lee, S.Y. Kim & D. Adams (Eds.), *Sixty years of Korean Education* (pp. 326-359). Seoul: SNU Press.

Kolvenbach, P-H. (2001). The Service of Faith and the Promotion of Justice in American Jesuit Higher Education. *Studies in the Spirituality of Jesuits*, 31(1), 13-29.

Kolvenbach, P-H. (2005). Speech at the 50th Anniversary of Sogang University, Seoul, Korea.

Kolvenbach, P-H. (2005, September 10). Interview with the Sogang Alumni Newspaper. 서강옛집 [The Sogang Alumni Newspaper].

Lee, C.J. & Jang, H.M. (2010). The History of Policy Responses to Shadow Education in Korea: Implications for the Next Cycle of Policy Response. In C.J. Lee, S.Y. Kim & D. Adams (Eds.), *Sixty years of Korean Education* (pp. 512-545). Seoul: SNU Press.

Lee, C.J. & Jung, S.S. & Kim, Y.S. (2006). 한국교육의 발전 전략과 새로운 과제 [The Development of Education in Korea: Approaches, Achievement and New Challenges]. 教育行政學研究 [The Journal of Educational Administration]. 24 (4), 1-26.

Lee, C.J., Kim, S.K., Kim, W.J. & Kim, Y.S. (2006). A Korean Model of Educational Development. In C.J. Lee, S.Y. Kim & D. Adams (Eds.), *Sixty years of Korean Education* (pp. 53-106). Seoul: SNU Press.

Lee, K.H. (2013, November 12). 대학평가 5 등급 체제로… 재정지원도 차등화 [5 Levels of the University Evaluation]. 아시아 경제 (*The Asia Economy Daily*).

Murray, J.C. (1966). The Vatican Declaration on Religious Freedom. *The University in the American Experience* (pp. 1-10). New York: Fordham University.

Nicolás, A. (2010) Depth, Universality, and Learned Ministry: Challenges to Jesuit Higher Education Today. In F. Brennan (Ed.), *Shaping the Future: networking Jesuit higher education for a globalizing world* (pp. 7-21). Washington, DC: Association of Jesuit colleges and universities.

O'Brien, D.J. (2008). Conversations on Jesuit (and Catholic?) Higher Education: Jesuit Sí, Catholic....Not So Sure. In G.W. Traub (Ed.), *A Jesuit Education Reader* (pp. 217-231). Chicago: Loyola Press.

OECD (2001). *The Well-Being of Nations: the Role of Human and Social Capital*. Paris: OECD.

Park, C.U. (2009). 다문화 교육의 탄생 [The Genesis of Multicultural Education]. Ansan: Borderless village press.

Piderit, J.J. (1999). Managing Jesuit Universities After GC 34. In M.R. Tripole (Ed.), *Promised Renewed: Jesuit Higher Education for a New Millennium* (pp. 43-61). Chicago: Loyola Press.

Seth, M.J. (2002). *Education fever: Society, Politics, and the Pursuit of Schooling in South Korea*. Honolulu: University of Hawaii Press.

Seth, M.J. (2005). "Korean Education: A Philosophical and Historical Perspective". In Y.K. Kim-Renaud, R.R. Grinker & K.W. Larsen (Eds.), *Korean Education* (pp. 3-15). Retrieved September 30, 2013 from http://www.gwu.edu/~sigur/assets/docs/scap/SCAP24-KoreanEd.pdf

Spadaro, A. (2013, September 30). A Big Heart Open to God. *America*. Retrieved October 4, 2013 from http://www.americamagazine.org/pope-interview

Statistics Korea (2013). 2012년 사교육비조사 결과 [Survey Results on the Expenditure for Shadow Education]. Retrieved September 24, 2013 from http://kostat.go.kr/survey/pedu/pedu_dl/1/index.board?bmode=read&aSeq=271849

The Catholic Bishops' Conference of Korea (2006). *Charter of Catholic School Education*.

The Catholic Bishops' Conference of Korea (2011). *Guidelines for Catholic School Education in Korea*.

The Catholic Bishops' Conference of Korea (n.d). *Guidelines for Catholic Education in Kindergarten*.

The Federation of Catholic Educational Foundation (1999). 한국의 가톨릭 학교교육 [Catholic school education in Korea]. Seoul: Catholic Cultural Center.

The Federation of Catholic Educational Foundation (2007). 가톨릭 학교 관련 법제의 현황과 발전 방안 [The Current Status of Laws related to Catholic Schools and Suggestions]. Seoul: Catholic Cultural Center.

The Ministry of Education (1998). 교육 50년사 : 1948-1998 [50 years of History of Education: 1948-1998]. Seoul: Author.

The Ministry of Education & Human Resources Development (2007). 사립학교 재정결함지원 제도개선 방안 [Proposal for Improvement of Financial Deficit Subsidies for Private Schools]. Retrieved October 10, 2013 from https://www.google.co.kr/url?sa=t&rct=j&q=&esrc=s&source=web&cd=9&ved=0CHsQFjAI&url=http%3A%2F%2Finno.jje.go.kr%2Findex.php%2Fcontents%2Finfo%2Flawinfo%2Fadministrator%2Fjjedurole%3Act%3Ddown%26seq%3D55609%26serial%3D1%26bd_bcid%3Dedu_jjedurole%26page%3D9%26page%3D&ei=vyJ8UqToPOiaiAfrqYHICQ&usg=AFQjCNFdB5jfDb84OUH36SWaLX7BKud0wg&

sig2=haEBzzNu1SSntc06l4OybA&bvm=bv.56146854,d.aGc&cad=rjt

The Sacred Congregation for Catholic Education (1977). *The Catholic School.* Retrieved September 23, 2013 from http://www.vatican.va/roman_curia/congregations/ccatheduc/documents/rc_con_ccatheduc_doc_19770319_catholic-school_en.html

The Sacred Congregation for Catholic Education (1982). *Lay Catholics in Schools: Witness to Faith.* Retrieved September 23, 2013 from http://www.vatican.va/roman_curia/congregations/ccatheduc/documents/rc_con_ccatheduc_doc_19821015_lay-catholics_en.html

The Society of Jesus (2009). *Jesuit Life & Mission Today: The Decrees & Accompanying Documents of the 31st-35th General Congregation of the Society of Jesus.* St. Louis: The Institute of Jesuit Sources.

Part 2

Comments and Discussion

Part 2   Comments and Discussion

Comments

Commentator: **Michael Calmano SVD**
⟨Nanzan University⟩

Introduction

I would like to start my comments with a few remarks on two phrases I perceive to be an appropriate framework for our symposium on the Role of Jesuit Universities in Asia—the motto that expresses what Sophia education is all about: *Men and Women for Others, with Others*; and the official theme for the 100th anniversary celebration of Sophia University: *Bringing the World Together*.

I like both—because they do make sense—but I'm also somewhat uneasy. Asia surely represents an important part of the world, but the only people speaking today are six males from two religious orders—a member of the Society of the Divine Word, commentating on the presentations given by members of the Society of Jesus. I do believe, however, that the (perhaps a bit presumptuous) names of these two religious orders are concrete signs of what our mission in Asia and in the rest of the world is all about: to project an image of what it means to join with other persons who work with and for Jesus; to work with and for persons who listen to the Divine Word.

As one might expect, in order to articulate this mission, Societas Jesu and Societas Verbi Divini are pointing in the same direction but using different words to do so. One of the things I will try to do with my comments is to show that the reverse can also be true: when we talk about the role of Jesuit universities, we may be using the same words but actually talking about different realities. We do have a common mission, but, at the same time, whenever we come together to talk about a common topic, expressed by common terms and concepts, we discover that we may be talking about different things altogether even though we are, without doubt, moved by the same Spirit (with a capital S).

The presentations today showed clearly that much of this is due to the simple fact that our various efforts to put into practice a Catholic spirit of higher education are happening in very different, even hostile environments. There is, therefore, always the temptation to take an easy escape route by focusing on the differences. For example, we all know that Japan is completely different from, and unintelligible for, people from Western countries.

I have played the "Japan is different" card myself, e.g., when I was making a presentation at a symposium organized by the International Federation of Catholic Universities (IFCU).[1] A "One Size (Mission) Fits All" approach doesn't work, nor is this the main message of *Ex Corde Ecclesiae*. However, I think we also realized today that, for all the differences in history and environment, we need a family to keep up the spirit. We are a community moved by the same Spirit and I'm sure that today was a good opportunity for us to experience this Spirit working among us. We are doing much more than just exchanging information because, with our information, we are also sharing the same Spirit.

■ Comments on the Presention by Dr. Jose M. Cruz (Ateneo de Manila)

"The school was established quite by accident; or, as some of us deeply believe, by providence." I was very glad to see this remark by Dr. Cruz at the very beginning of the first presentation. This is, I believe, precisely the point of view, the dimension needed for talking about Catholic Higher Education anywhere, Jesuit or otherwise. Realistic goal-setting and sound financial management are very important but, at the same time, there is always the challenge to redefine and renew the Jesuit commitment to the education ministry. There is no doubt that religious orders can make a difference through their commitment to the learned ministry, but the implications of such a commitment need to be discussed and reviewed on a regular basis.

Another point that drew my attention was the remark about the colonial past as a part and burden of higher education ministry in the Philippines. There can be no doubt that this kind of history, together with persisting economic inequalities, creates a "hostile" environment that will continue to be a real challenge for Catholic higher education in the foreseeable future.

Part 2 Comments and Discussion

■ **Comments on the Presentation by Dr. Benedict Kan-Yup Jung** (Sogang University)

Catholic universities and colleges in Korea are facing a different kind of hostile environment. Characterized by rather strict government regulations and by a culture of extremely competitive entrance exams (called "education fever"), Catholic higher education's challenge is to find ways of expressing its special mission against this emphasis on uniformity. Additional factors are an extremely low birthrate, a high rate of international marriages and a great number of immigrants looking for work in Korea.

Yet, even within these very limiting conditions, Jesuit universities are initiating programs that make real contributions to society. I want to draw special attention to the SOWUUS (Sogang World University for Underprivileged Students) program that brings together underprivileged students from inside and outside Korea. The openness required for such programs within the confines of a globalized market economy is expressed by what Pope Francis said in an interview—words that, I believe, merit repeating. "Ours is not a 'lab faith,' but a 'journey faith,' a historical faith. God has revealed himself as history, not as a compendium of abstract truths….you have to live on the border and be audacious."

■ **Comments on the Presentation by Dr. Louis Gendron** (Fu Jen University)

So far, examples of hostile environments could be traced mainly to outside factors beyond the control of educational institutions. Sometimes, however, the challenges faced by Catholic institutions of higher education also derive from internal problems as, e.g., a lack of cooperation among the founding members (religious orders and the diocese) of a university. The situation is made worse by the fact (due, perhaps, to a worldwide decline in vocations) that there are simply not enough qualified Jesuits to work in higher education. At the same time, the example of Fu Jen University also showed some of the opportunities that exist for a focused Jesuit engagement as, e.g., the important role played by the theological faculty (the only one in Taiwan) across the road from Fu Jen University, and the efforts to create a Jesuit Liberal Arts College in Hongkong.

One point that struck me as really important was the emphasis on a common core (general education) for Catholic colleges and universities, the concerted effort to create a common basis that allows our students (and our faculty) to initiate a dialogue across the borders of the various disciplines taught at our universities. This may actually be one of the roles Jesuit universities are asked to fulfill in Asia: to emphasize, again and again, the importance of a common human (humanistic) core while doing in-depth teaching and research in the various faculties and disciplines.

■ Comments on the Presentation by Dr. Kuntaro Adi (Sanata Dharma)

This emphasis on the core values of a Catholic university is, quite often, expressed by a phrase that was used by Dr. Adi—"Jesuit Education: Educating the Whole Person." Needless to say, Jesuit universities are not the only ones using this phrase for giving direction to educational activities and, in his resume, Dr. Adi stated this very clearly: "We share the same identity: Catholic Jesuit University." While I read this as an unambiguous affirmation that you can be both Catholic and Jesuit at the same time, there was also a particular question that arose in my mind: is it possible to keep the same identity in the many different environments represented by our panelists today? As I suggested at the beginning, the term "Catholic University" or "Jesuit University" points to very different realities, depending on the environment where we have established our universities.

I think it is quite possible to maintain, and reaffirm again today, a common identity that connects our endeavors and I will use the presentation by Dr. Kawamura to make my point.

■ Comments on the Presentation by Dr. Shinzo Kawamura (Sophia)

Dr. Kawamura characterizes Christianity as a disrupting factor in Japan, a point of view that disturbed the policies promoted by the Japanese government, which emphasized the all-important the role of the Emperor within the framework of traditional Shinto religion. In a sense, this is what I feel is the mission of our universities in any country we work in. To use an expression coined by Clayton Christensen, our mission is "disruptive innovation"[2] in a society that seems to be caught in tradition. I'm quite sure we haven't always been aware of this aspect of the Catholic spirit. Instead, we tend to view the hostile environments we encounter as something that "disrupts" the things we really would like to achieve or see happen.

Examples abound. The 1890 Imperial Rescript (教育勅語) had a great influence on religious education in mission schools, and the militaristic government's Yasukuni shrine policy created a severe problem for Sophia University students. At the same time, as Dr. Kawamura points out, the anti-communism attitude created some kind of a link between the government and the Church. In hindsight we could say that a Catholic university should have been an even more disruptive force for both atheistic communism and narrow military nationalism.

The globalized market economy dominated by multi-national corporations presents a similar challenge and opportunity for our institutions. A very good example, I think, is the Ateneo Institute for Sustainability, which seems to be in perfect tune with the 4 challenges given by Jesuit Superior General Nicolás. This is a role that will always fit a Catholic university, especially in 21st century Asia with all the diverse political, historical, and economic environments. Such a stance will not necessarily assure the survival of a Catholic university as an institution, but, personally, I don't see any immediate scenario that would force a choice between keeping the Catholic spirit and the continued existence of an institution. However, the challenge will always be there: to define the spirit that makes us Catholic—and to ensure that we are true to this spirit.

I very much liked the conclusion of Dr. Kawamura's presentation. At the end of our presentations there are questions[3] and dilemmas, not conclusions. Yet, but, since our universities were created not by accident but by providence, there is no need to be pessimistic. As long as we keep asking questions—which might entail letting go of answers that have served us well in the past—we should be able to continue as a disruptive force serving humankind.

Notes

1. "The Catholic University Today: Nanzan University." Actes du premier symposium du projet: Université, Eglise, Culture. D'un paradigme à un autre, l'Université catholique aujourd'hui. Université Saint-Paul, Ottawa, 20 avril 1999. (Pierre Hurtubise, editor), pp. 213-236. Paris: Fédération internationale des universités catholiques, 2001.
2. Christensen himself applied this view to education in Clayton M. Christensen, Michael B. Horn, Curtis W. Johnson, *Disrupting Class: How Disruptive Innovation Will Change the Way the World Learns*, 2008.
3. A favorite saying of mine, discovered in a Peanuts cartoon, is "If you don't know the answer, question the question."

International Cooperation of Higher Education in Asia and the Role of the Jesuit Universities

Moderator: **Miki Sugimura**
〈Sophia University〉

Introduction

Since the 1990s, Asian countries have been carrying out reforms in higher education due to the need of meeting educational demands and manpower development. Amid these reforms, there is a growing trend for universities and governments to try to make their countries' university programs more appealing by globalizing their campuses through cooperation and connections with universities overseas. Meanwhile, higher educational institutions based on Christian missions had been developing educational activities that cross borders for a long time before globalization came into focus. Christian universities have developed their educational achievements and traditions in this globalizing world. The universities of the Society of Jesus as a missionary religious order conduct various international apostolic activities and place education and research among them.

This paper, firstly, investigates the way in which the internationalization of higher education in Asian countries accelerates international competition while it also possesses new possibilities for higher education arising from international connections. Secondly, it examines Christian university networks with the mission of Christianity and international cooperation, and clarifies the significance of Christian universities with international connections. And finally, one possible model with inter-disciplinary/trans-disciplinary liberal arts education will be proposed in light of the Global Leadership Program of five Jesuit universities in East Asia[1].

I Two Aspects of Internationalization
——Competition and International Cooperation

Several factors have underlay the development of the internationalization of Asian higher education from 1990 onward. The first factor is the popularization of higher education and the trend to go on to higher stages of education. In East Asia, where we find greater stability in political regimes and social developments than in other regions in the world, the rise in economic power has made people expect much of the education of their children and their grandchildren's generations, leading them to invest in it. As more people sought higher education, those who could not find an institution to go to within their country began to look overseas. This caused the problem of 'brain drain'. Each government came out with policies to create hubs of international and educational cultural exchange to expand and develop their country's higher education and to cope with the domestic demand for education. At the same time, they aim to accept competent students from overseas to create the base explained above. This changed the nature of 'brain drain' into 'brain circulation', and higher education came to be regarded as a means to strengthen international competitiveness and develop human resource.

In planning policies, each government began to promote the privatization of their national or public universities. They also began to allow the private sector to open private universities and to enter the educational market. The entry of such private organizations led to drastic changes in higher education. The higher education sector, which used to be intended for a small elite group, began to accept a wide range of people. At the same time, diverse and flexible curricula became possible. These programs were often implemented by connecting them with programs of other universities overseas. This created cross-border/transnational programs, which clearly enable students to participate in curricula of universities overseas while remaining their own countries. This diversification of programs reinforces their research/ educational strength and raises the universities' and governments' international competition. The goals for their policies are to form centers of excellences or regional hubs, as Knight (2014) pointed out as "Education Hubs".

Meanwhile, the internationalization of higher education brought a movement of international cooperation. The actors are each university or institution, governments and regional organizations. Besides many partnership agreements among universities, there are several higher education networks in Asia, i.e. 'Campus Asia' by China, South Korea and Japan, ASEAN International Mobility for Students Program (AIMS) by the Regional Centre for Higher Education and Development (RIHED) of the Southeast Asian Ministers of Education Organization (SEAMEO), ASEAN University Network, and the South Asian University (SAU) by the South Asian Association for Regional Cooperation (SAARC). At the same time, there are networks that support cooperation to guarantee educational quality. They include the Asia-Pacific Quality Network (APQN), ASEAN Quality Assurance Network (AQAN) and University Mobility in Asia and the Pacific (UMAP) with current credit compatibility. They form a multi-layered higher education scheme (Sugimura, 2013).

II The Mission of Christianity and International Cooperation in Higher Education

As stated above, Asia is experiencing internationalization in higher education in various forms today, and as a result, while the global competition of nations and institutions intensifies, international cooperation also grows. On the other hand, practical activities involving education around the globe, which are based on religious missions, have existed since long ago. Christian education reached East Asia in the 15th century, when the art of navigation developed and many missionaries were dispatched from Europe to the American continent and Asia. This is because people considered education to be an important tool to propagate Christianity. Yet their work did not end with mere missionary activities, but aimed at stimulating the development of regional society itself by spreading education and raising manpower[2]. International cooperation among Christian universities developed to convey their message, based on their educational philosophy, their concept of the human being and of the world which stem from Christianity[3].

II-1 The Association of Southeast and East Asian Catholic Colleges and Universities (ASEACCU)

The Association of Southeast and East Asian Catholic Colleges and Universities (ASEACCU) is a case of cooperation among universities with a Christian mission in

Asia. ASEACCU is a regional league of Christian universities in Southeast and East Asia which was inaugurated in 1992. Its purpose is to develop higher education based on Christianity and to strengthen its relationship with the Catholic Church. As of 2013, it has 69 institutions from eight countries and regions: two Australian universities, ten Indonesian universities, eleven Japanese universities, five South Korean universities, thirty-four Philippine universities, three Taiwanese universities, three Thai universities and one Cambodian university. Their activities include: sharing information via newsletters and the like, holding general meetings once a year, and exchanging students and teaching and clerical staff. They aim at contributing to discussions on international education across borders in Southeast Asia or East Asia. The ASEACCU member universities form a network involving exchange programs among them. Member universities are connected by mutual linkages, and the educational exchanges promote mobility of students and of the teaching and clerical staff.

II-2 The Association of Christian Universities and Colleges in Asia (ACUCA)

Another Christian university network is the Association of Christian Universities and Colleges in Asia (ACUCA), which includes both Catholic and Protestant universities. ACUCA was inaugurated in 1976. There are current member Christian universities in Indonesia, South Korea, Thailand, Taiwan, Japan, the Philippines and Hong Kong. This association first launched as the Christian Universities' Chancellors' Conference in the 1950s, was established in December, 1976 by the United Board for Christian Higher Education in Asia (UBCHEA) with the objective of enhancing mutual cooperation and the quality of Christian higher educational institutions. Activities mainly target chancellors and those engaged in administering universities regarding teaching staff exchange programs, staff exchanges, short-term exchange programs, and student camps. The current members are three universities in China and Hong Kong, eleven in Indonesia, eleven in Japan, ten in South Korea, ten in the Philippines, eight Taiwanese universities and four Thailand universities.

With the reinforcement of mutual exchange and mutual understanding, ACUCA holds one general meeting and one mass meeting every two years, and has sent out and accepted students based on the Student Mobility System (SMS) since 2002. This SMS mainly contains programs that conduct classes in English and accepts students into summer sessions or general classes. Also, besides exchanging students, they also hold a Management Conference, gathering representatives of the member universities/ institutions.

II-3 Association of Jesuit Colleges and Universities in Asia Pacific (AJCU-AP)

Among Christian educational institutions, those established by or associated with the Catholic religious order, the Society of Jesus (the Jesuits), possess a network organization that binds together their higher educational institutions and schools. There are academics at Jesuit universities and schools[4] around the globe and 185 higher educational institutes are members.[5] Jesuit institutions in Europe (including Lebanon), Latin America (Mexico, Central America, and South America), North America and South Asia have their regional networks[6]. The Society of Jesus traditionally places great importance on higher education and aims to offer an education of values in the 21st century. It aims to produce "men and women for and with others", striving for world peace and social justice, caring for those margins of society, and creating knowledge that aims at constructing a sustainable environment.

Castañeda and Koso eds. (1993) point out that a recent trait of education in the Society of Jesus is "Education for the 21st century to build personalities that serve others within today's society, especially in international society." (p. 3) In order to do so, there is a need to cultivate "First of all, the ability to think seriously about oneself and the world and truly understand them. Secondly, the ability to accurately judge people's behavior and social situations from a human point of view. And thirdly, the ability to willingly join the process of improving society and constructing a world that is more fair and a better place to live for everyone." (ibid, p. 3) They say this is exactly where we need education aiming at uniting the various abilities of people, which enable us to develop intelligently and with feeling. International cooperation of the universities of the Society of Jesus is a network of people who pursue this educational vision together.

In the Asia Pacific region, there is the Association of Jesuit Colleges and Universities in Asia Pacific (AJCU-AP). This AJCU-AP, formerly known as the Association of Jesuit Colleges and Universities in East Asia and Oceania (AJCU-EAO), was formed by the 16 Jesuit institutions in East Asia/Oceania: China, Indonesia, Japan, the Philippines, South Korea, and Taiwan[7]. AJCU-AP also develops services and learning programs that aim at combining "research and education in a university with service to regional society (especially in developing countries)", under the Ignatian educational goals of the Society of Jesus. Here, programs are designed to make a place where participating students share their knowledge and experience of 'development', and to link academic research to practice in the regional society. Ignatian pedagogy tries to promote understanding through five steps: context, experience, reflection, action and evaluation. When students from Catholic universities in the East Asian region gather, their common language is English.

III The Significance and Challenge of International Cooperation
──The Global Leadership Program for Jesuit Universities in East Asia (GLP)

III-1 Outline of the Global Leadership Program

International cooperation among universities with a Christian mission in Asia is special in that they cooperate on the basis of the mission of Christianity, which is different from most cases of international cooperation. The 'Global Leadership Program (GLP)' reflects the characteristics of the Society of Jesus and five universities have joined it: Sogang University in South Korea, Ateneo de Manila University in the Philippines, Fu Jen University in Taiwan, Sanata Dharma University in Indonesia and Sophia University, which originally proposed the program. The Global Leadership Program for the Jesuit Universities in East Asia started in 2008, but Santa Dharma University in Indonesia joined in 2013.

The participating universities of the Society of Jesus are mainly influenced by the way participants actively take part in planning, training, and administration around a common problem with group discussion, fieldwork and presentations. This makes the program a student-centered and active learning program for international exchange. It aims to raise the level of manpower with global leadership by gathering students of different nationalities and different backgrounds and letting them discuss global issues, specifically issues and resolutions for international understanding and the creation of a symbiotic society. Students prepare details beforehand for a one-week seminar at a training camp in August. They prepare for the camp within each university by learning about the chosen theme in advance. The training camps are held every year, and member schools take turns hosting them. The first camp was held by Sophia University in

2008[8], the second one by Sogang University in 2009, the third one by Ateneo de Manila University in 2010 and the fourth one by Fu Jen University in 2011. Then in 2012 Sophia University was in charge again. Sogang University and the Ateneo de Manila University and Fu Jen University followed respectively in 2013, 2014 and 2015, taking their second opportunity to be in charge.

III-2 The Character of the 'Global Leadership Program' and the Significance of International Cooperation

What is most important in the leadership seminar is that students choose a theme on the basis of the mission of the Society of Jesus, and have an opportunity to discuss it actively. For the Society of Jesus' mission of "Men and women for and with others", it is important that people from various regions and with diverse cultural backgrounds discuss global issues focusing on poverty, environment, education and ethics. In addition, it is also important for them to have young people, who will lead the next generation, share issues through discussion and seek solutions for a symbiotic society amid political and social differences. This international cooperation supports their mission: internationalization itself is not their primary goal.

At the same time, another important point this seminar raises is that, in order to deal with global issues, people need to approach them on an interdisciplinary level, where several fields intersect, as well as on each separate academic/ research field. This seminar is constructed so that the students can actually feel the need of approaches from various directions. In the first program, 'inequality' was chosen as the theme, and the following themes chosen by the schools in charge all involved inter-disciplinary/ trans-disciplinary approaches: "Intercultural Communication" by Sogang University in 2009, "Reconciling Ourselves with Creation: Environment and Social Involvement Specific Theme: Biodiversity" by Ateneo de Manila University in 2010, "Character Education" by Fu Jen University in 2011, "Recovery and Reconstruction (Recovery from the natural disaster: How people overcame it)" by Sophia University in 2012, "Technology and Human Values" by Sogang University in 2013, and "Building Inclusive Societies through Social Entrepreneurship" by Ateneo de Mania University in 2014. These themes cannot be seen globally unless people cross borders, discuss and learn from one another. This indicates once again that international cooperation is inseparable from interdisciplinary learning.

Part 2   Comments and Discussion

This 'interaction of learning' becomes a very interesting issue once people actually experience the program. Indeed, at the first Global Leadership Program, students faced a situation where their opinions were mutually incompatible. Students from two universities discussing their theme of 'inequality' were critical of globalization. However, each member university took a totally different view and evaluated globalization positively. If the members of these three universities had not met, each would be trapped in its own opinion without making progress. Fortunately, people from the fourth university listened to the opinions of both sides and even suggested yet another opinion, leading to a multi-layered discussion, and making it possible to share various opinions constructively.

This kind of learning is exactly what the education of the Society of Jesus has pursued. Koso (1993) clarifies six aspects in 'The Characteristics of Jesuits Education' edited by the International Commission on the Apostolate of Jesuit Education in 1986 and published by the Society of Jesus in Rome. The six aspects are: 1) positive attitude towards the world and consideration of each person, 2) nurturing the strength to learn by oneself and the role of teachers, 3) formation of leaders and the pursuit of excellent human education, 4) constructive criticism directed at the real world and the formation of those who can change the world, 5) focus on the educational community and the possible curricula, and 6) continuing reforms and practices of lifelong study. Castañeda and Koso eds. (1993) also suggest that "In schools of the Society of Jesus, education of high quality has been aimed at, and while they train competent members of society, those who learn will reflect on the human significance of what they learn and come in contact with truth in the most profound meaning, thus being led to become responsible members of the human family. Education is not meant to create people who will unconditionally and blindly devote themselves to their nation or business, nor is it a tool to guarantee only their own future." (p. 4) Moreover, they stress the importance of being engaged in volunteer activities, where people hold out helping hands to those in need in various forms, and the significance of interacting with those who live totally different lives, with different cultures and various backgrounds.[9] These indicate that it is not just intellectual activities that count, and also that it does not count whether the activity takes place within or outside of one's own country. This shows why the GLP is a program formed from the core of the educational mission of the Society of Jesus.

III-3 Challenges of International Cooperation

There are also challenges to international cooperation carried on among universities. First is the problem of how to run the program. Although international cooperative programs are of great significance, the reality is that when universities try to cooperate with each other, making adjustments and having contacts become all the more complicated, and processes become troublesome because of diversity of opinions. In the case of the GLP for the Jesuit Universities in East Asia, the first problem was about the academic calendar, and choosing a suitable period when everyone can gather. The seminar was held in Tokyo for those from the Ateneo de Manila University in the Philippines in August, which was a time of vacation. The Ateneo had to make special arrangements to allow students to participate in the seminar during the academic semester. Other typical problems stem from the structure of the program itself and are not specific to this program. There were problems in regard to the guarantee of the program's quality, for example, what they should do to certify and evaluate the program, and what steps to take to authorize academic credits. The GLP was conducted in English, and although it did not qualify for credits at first, Sophia University began to give credits for this program starting from the academic year 2013.

A second challenge is maintaining international cooperation. The success of cooperative programs depends on the relationship among the participating organizations. In the case of the GLP, the teaching staff in charge and those in charge of the international exchange staff of the university prepare for the program through close contact. However, with international cooperation, differences in each participating institutional and national organization as well as political relationships complicate the task. One important point about international cooperation is that it should not end up being something transient, but placed as a framework with sustainability, as it will be of significance only after continuous operation. For this reason, in developing real programs, they should take into full consideration issues of the budget and staff that sustain the programs. Also, there is need for each participant to be fully aware of the publicity and social responsibility of international cooperation.

Conclusion

This short paper summed up the flow of the strategies of higher education and international cooperation, which have been a trend in this globalizing world, especially since the 1990s, and classified the traits of international cooperation focusing on that based on Christian mission, which universities have developed until today. The approaches of Christian universities are different from those which other universities of Asian nations have taken as higher educational strategies. Christian universities crossed borders for a long time before internationalization came into fashion. In particular, when we look at the international cooperation of Christian universities, they form a platform where people accept each other's different value systems or cultural differences and discuss social problems and regional issues while respecting diversity.

What is specific to international cooperation among universities of the Society of Jesus is that learning here focuses on global issues that cross borders and need to be analyzed and dealt with by crossing academic fields. These global issues include poverty, the environment, education and ethics. These topics can be approached through international networks. They also require inter-disciplinary/ trans-disciplinary education, such as liberal arts education and human education with significance throughout the increasingly globalizing world. This accords with what Stewart (2013) said in an international seminar on the secondary education of the Society of Jesus. He stated that what matters was how schools of the Society of Jesus enable their students to become leaders of the global world, and make themselves generally accepted in the world. In order to do so, he continues, schools should make use of international networks, recognize the possibility of joint research or joint learning by students from various nations, and expand relations with other schools and service learning programs, while developing suitable subject materials.

Today the international cooperation among Asian universities is not limited to the Asian region, but is spreading to cooperation with other regions and cooperative networks. In addition, those who visit countries for international cooperation include not just the students who are at the center of education, but also the teaching and clerical staff that sustains the programs. This trend can be seen in the educational institutions and systems themselves. Along with globalization, strategic international competition and international cooperation are to be fostered. Educational institutions must remember: what kind of students they wish to produce, and in order to serve this object, what kind of programs can they should provide. In other words, in order to achieve their goal, can they provide them with a platform that promotes interaction of learning? The mission and the way of education of the universities of the Society of Jesus have already relied on such international cooperation. Today, our world is increasingly globalizing, and higher education has found new opportunities in international higher education. The education of the universities of the Society of Jesus has been devoted to producing leaders for the next generation with knowledge and understanding that come from the networks. The cornerstone here is understanding and sympathy for people of different cultures, and respect for diversity, and not reducing higher education to a mere strategy for international competition. Now is the time for the education of the universities of the Society of Jesus to prove its true value as a model for new international higher education.

Notes

1 This paper is based on Oto,Y. and M. Sugimura (2014). The co-author of this article, Prof. Oto consented to this substantial correction and revision.
2 Anthropologist Junzo Kawada (2007) regards the global occurrence of "the change of culture due to mobility and interaction of groups of people" as 'globalization', which "began in the era of expansion by the Silk Road, after the era of Game and Columbus at the end of the 15th century". It was in this era of 'globalization's first stage' that the propagation of education by missionaries developed.
3 Besides the international cooperation of Christian universities in Asia, there is the Japan Association of Catholic Universities. This Association was established in 1975 by 11 Catholic universities within Japan, and currently includes 20 universities. They hold their vision as the following; "The basic missions of the universities are to constantly seek truth through research and to preserve and convey knowledge for the benefit of society. While Catholic universities possess these missions, they have been working on education and research activities with their own traits and objectives. Beneath this activity lie the values and ethics of the Catholic Church, and the philosophy for education, which nurtured over its history of 2000 years, and shared by people around the globe", which promote cooperation among Catholic universities in Japan to accomplish the goals of Catholic education.
4 For universities and schools of the Society of Jesus, refer to: http://www.ajus.org/about-us.php (Accessed on August 10, 2014).
5 For higher education institutions of the Society of Jesus, refer to: http://www.ajus.org/institutions.php (Accessed on August 10, 2014).
6 For the outline of the educational institutions of the Society of Jesus around the globe, refer to: http://www.ajus.org/institutions.php (Accesed on August 10, 2014.)
7 The Society of Jesus is spread out around the globe, which can be divided into 10 Assistancy, namely Africa, North Latin America, South Latin America, North Europe, West Europe, East Europe, Central Europe, East Asia/ Pacific, South Asia, America. The Japan Province belongs to the "East Asia/ Pacific" Assistancy, and this region includes the jurisdictions of China, South Korea,

the Philippines, Vietnam, Indonesia, Australia, Malaysia/ Singapore, East Timor, Myanmar and Cambodia.

8   The details of the first GLP are summarized in Overseas Liaison Center ed. (2008), *Final Report of the first Global Leadership Program for the Jesuit Universities in East Asia,* The contents of this paragraph were cited from Miki Sugimura, "Reviewing the Program (Japanese version: pp. 81-83, English version: pp. 141-144).

9   The educational missions of the Catholic Church, in particular of the Society of Jesus, was also discussed in the international symposium at the Pontifical Gregorian University (2014), Between Past and Future, the Mission of the Catholic Church in Asia: the Contribution of Sophia University on the Occasion of the 100th Anniversary of Sophia University (International Symposium, March 14-15, 2014) , which was held the at Pontifical Gregorian University (2014) reports the results.

References

Castañeda, J. and Toshiaki Koso eds. (1993). *Iezusukai kyoiku no kokoro: sekaijin wo hagukumu nettowaku* (*Mission of Jesuit Education: Network for Global Citizen*), Mikuni Publisher.

International Commission on the Apostolate of Jesuit Education (translated by Toshiaki Koso) (1988). *Iezusukai no Kyoiku no Tokucho* (*The Characteristics of Jesuit Education*), Chuo Shuppansha.

Kajiyama, Yoshio tr. and Jesuit Secondary Education Committee ed. (2013). *The Characteristics of Jesuit Education,* Don Bosco.

Kawada, Junzo (2007). "Gurobaruka ni chokumenshita jinrui bunka: mukei bunka isan hogo no igi". (United Nataions University, the 7th Global Seminar, Shona Session, Keynote Speech). In Kawada, Junzo, *Bunka no Sankaku Sokuryo* (*Triangulation of Culture*) , Jinbun Syoin, 2008, pp. 97-137.

Knight, Jane ed. (2014). *International Education Hub: Student, Talent, Knowledge Innovation Models*, Springer.

Koso, Toshiaki (1993), "Iezusukai no Konnichiteki Kyouiku Riso: Saikin no 'Iezusukai no Kyoiku no Tokucho' wo Tegakari ni (The Ideal of Jesuit Education in Contemporary world: Based on the Characteristics of Jesuit Education)", In Castañeda, J. and Toshiaki Koso eds. (1993), *op.cit.*, pp. 235-251.

Kuroda, Kazuo ed. (2013). *Ajia no Koutoukyouiku Gabanansu* (*Asian Regional Governance of Higher Education*), Keisou Shobo.

Oto Yoshihiro and Sugimura Miki (2014). "Ajia ni okeru Kirisuto kyokei daigaku no kokusai renkei (Regional Cooperation among Christian Universities in Asia)", *Comparative Education*, 48, Japan Comparative Education Society, Toshindo, pp. 104-115.

Pontifical Gregorian University (2014). "Between Past and Future, the Mission of the Catholic Church in Asia: the Contribution of Sophia University on the Occasion of the 100th Anniversary of Sophia University" (International Symposium, March 14-15, 2014), *Gregoriana* 8, Gregorian & Biblical Press.

Social Justice and Ecology Secretariat ed. (2014) *Special Document: Promotion of Justice in the*

Universities of the Society, Promotio Institiae, No. 116, March 2014. (Japanese translation version published in 2015.)

Stewart, V. (2013). "Sekai wo Kyoshitsu ni (A classroom as wide as the world)", *Shingaku Digest*, 114, pp. 44-61.

Sugimoto, Hitoshi (2014). *Toransunashonaru Koutou Kyouiku no Kokusai Hikaku: Ryugaku Gainen no Tenkan* (*Comparative Study on Transnational Higher Education: Change of Concept of Study Abroad*), Toshindo.

Sugimura, Miki & Kuroda, Kazuo eds (2009). *Ajia ni Okeru Chiiki Renkei Kyouiku Fremuwaku to Daigakukan Renkei Jirei no Kensho* (*Regional Coopration Framework and University Cooperation in Higher Education in Asia*), Ministry of Education, Science, Culture and Sports, Support Center Project of Fiscal Year 2008.

Sugimura, Miki (2013). "Ajia no Kotokyouiku ni okeru Chiiki Renkei Nettowaku no Kouzou to Kinou (Structure and Functions of International Higher Education Networks in Asia)", *Jochi Daigaku kyouikugaku Ronshu* (*Sophia University Studies in Education*), No. 47, pp. 21-34.

Umemiya Naoki (2009), "Tonan Ajia chiiki ni okeru chiikiteki na koutou kyouiku no Shitsu no hosho: sono tokucho to gendouryoku (Regional Quality Assurance Activity in Southeast Asia: Characteristics and Driving Forces)", *Comparative Education*, 37, Japan Comparative Education Society, Toshindo, pp. 90-111.

Part 2 Comments and Discussion

Panel Discussion

A panel discussion and Q&A Session followed the paper presentations from each university, led by Dr. Antoni Ucerler SJ, Director of Asia Wing, University of San Francisco and Dr. Miki Sugimura of Sophia University.

Ucerler Now that you have heard all the presentations, I am sure there are issues, things that you may be stimulated to talk about concerning your own institutions in the light of what you heard. We would like to go back to the five initial speakers before going into further discussion.

Cruz The comments of Dr. Sugimura made me reflect on internationalization as a phenomenon in the community of universities, and how it affects the Ateneo de Manila. Filipino people are international. 10% of the labour force at any given time are out of the country, and about 22% of mariners in commercial shipping are Filipino. But many people tell us that we continue to think in insular ways, and that somehow we bring our "Philippino-ness" to places we go to. Even in our university, many of the questions we attend to, and the ways we do so are in very local terms. So we are facing tensions as we seek globalisation for its many benefits, and education comes at a cost. Globalisation puts us at a risk of homogenising us, making all universities eventually look alike. If we are not careful, in the end we will give shape to what we are according to these globalising forces and lose our traditions, and the spirit for which we were created in the first place. How does one become a global university and at the same time keep our traditions? I would propose that one way of addressing the challenge is to see ourselves as global universities by attending to global problems. To look at local problems is of infinite importance, but to also invest in the reality that transcends our borders, and to change the way we teach and learn by looking at different regions with love. So for us, it is training students to be global citizens with global awareness, global competencies and commitment to global outreach. For Filipino students, to let them understand that what happens to us happens elsewhere too, and that problems and solutions are shared by humanity. That is the kind of university that we would like to be.

Kawamura In my talk this morning I talked about Catholicism, the role of Jesuits in Catholic education and Sophia University, dividing the history into three phases. What I wanted to stress the most, however, was the fact that missionaries always started their evangelization from the very bottom of society. But there were certain things they had to do in order for them to be accepted in Japan, which Alessandro Valignano called adaptation. Mateo Ricci also insisted on this in China. Then, the direction of their evangelization always changed. They tended to forget their initial purposes and started to approach high-ranking intellectuals. I wanted to point out that this repeatedly happened in Japan, from the 16th century to the 19th century under the new Meiji government, and in the 20th century after the war.

Also, as Prof. Calmano said, we probably should have worked more as disruptive forces in our society. We should not always have followed the social trend. There is no sense in being Catholic if we cannot have a strong belief in our way of living or live as leaven in society.

When we reflect on our own university to see if we are playing such a role, I personally sometimes feel that we are only following the majority. The future of Catholic universities depends on whether we can realise this role of leaven or light in our educational programmes.

Gendron Prof. Calmano spoke about the disruptive impact of Catholic universities. In my talk this morning I mentioned that Catholic universities in China were too disruptive and they had to close. The same thing happened with our Faculty of Theology. Nothing was left, but then it started again in a different place, in Taiwan. This morning I asked how concretely the mission of the university can be fulfilled. At Fu Jen University, when we really decided to work on it, we learned from Catholic universities in the US. Many of the non-Catholic, Protestant universities in the US have lost all their Christian savour, but we were able to keep something.

About 20 years ago, the Ministry of Education in Taiwan gave permission to Buddhist groups to start universities. I think now there are about six Buddhist universities in Taiwan, and they have a required course for all students in Buddhism. In Catholic universities in Taiwan we never dared to do this. First of all, it was against the law to provide a required course in any religion. And then the government said we could give a course on religion as long as we introduce different religions. A couple of years ago, a representative of the Catholic congregation at the Vatican came to Taiwan to the Ministry of Education, to negote for an agreement between the Vatican and the Taiwan government about Catholic higher education. Since then the government allowed us to open courses introducing Catholic thinking and Catholic theology and the basic spirit of our faith. Students do not have to accept it, but they are expected to have understanding of a philosophy of life. The board of trustees, however, has been very prudent in seeing how to implement this at the level of the whole university.

Adi Let me say two things. The first is about students and the second is about Igantian pedagogy. In the university, I am in charge of student affairs and most of the students are high-tech students. Therefore, they use a lot of gadgets and their language is different or incomplete, although they understand each other. My question is: how can we promote depth of thought and imagination for this type of students? When I come here I wonder what happens because in Taiwan, Korea and Japan I am sure all your students are very high-tech.

Secondly, education is about spirit. One day the government questioned whether to give funds for the institution because we were trying to implement Ignatian pedagogy. The government wondered what kind of pedagogy this is. Is it possible to implement it in public schools, not just Jesuit schools? The person in charge of Ignatian pedagogy is not a Jesuit. And they are trying to express this in a very different language to the public, which is very interesting. It is very challenging because most of our Jesuit schools do not have many Jesuits working for the institutions. For example, in our case, we have about 25 Jesuits working in the university among about 300 faculty members.

Ucerler Now we will enter into some questions and I have been trying to formulate a question which makes sense. I was also very stimulated by what Prof. Sugimura said in her presentation about international cooperation of Catholic universities and its significance. We have heard a lot about local realities in each of these five countries, and this is very important because one has to be, especially in the Catholic tradition, incarnated in the place that we are so each one of these contexts are different socially, politically, religiously, and culturally. However I was struck by both what Dr. Jung said and at the beginning what Dr. Cruz said. In different ways you spoke about the difference between global and local reality. Maybe one could also speak about the difference between global and provincial realities, provincial ways of thinking, and I wonder whether this is still not a problem or a challenge. We talk a great deal about globalisation and internationalisation, but what does it really mean? When we look at lay or secular universities that are doing joint programmes with other countries or have a campus in another country, they are marketable because of what they do and the opportunities that they offer. Is there a possibility of Jesuit joint degrees? Why can't we have a degree issued by Sophia, Sogang and Fu Jen at the same time? Of course the bureaucratic and legal complications of such an idea is immense, but wouldn't that really be a disruptive innovation, which is also very marketable?

The political conflict over the islands between China and Japan, and Korea is also involved in this. Would it not be a testimony to show that "we do something together to promote peace and to work in very close networks?" These are just some transnational ideas that could really be disruptive and creative innovations.

Calmano   Sometimes when I hear the expression "double degree," it sounds like getting two for the price of one. I think this is not what we are talking about. A joint degree by three different Jesuit universities should involve studies of the person at all the universities. How to count the credits, and how to make sure that the degree is also recognised by the local authorities, is a little difficult but can be solved. I agree that studying for a degree at three different locations might actually give the degree much greater worth than getting three for the price of one.

Ucerler   I did not intend it to be three for the price of one but one degree that would actually have three components in it so that it will be a joint degree.

Jung   I think your idea is fantastic. However, when I was working for the Jesuit Conference of Asia Pacific, the least functioning body is the Association of Jesuit Colleges and Universities. So that is the reality. But on the other hand there is a great need for universities to work together. Having said that, I think what is more important is to notice that these days education is a buyer's market, not a supplier's market, which means we have to get to know what students need and want. We have to crack open what young people are thinking about and wanting to have. If we get these things mapped out, I think it is a feasible plan. I think we can get over the bureaucratic hurdles.

Cruz   Prof. Sugimura mentioned that the academic calendar in the Philippines is quite misaligned with that of Asia and actually that of the rest of the world. Next year the Philippines will be the only country with a June to March academic calendar. In response to that challenge, Ateneo de Manila will probably shift its calendar to August-May in 2015. Having said that, we remind the academic committee that having an aligned calendar will be helpful but will not be sufficient either to bring in students or to generate programmes with other universities. At our university we have to create programmes that are useful and attractive to others. We need to choose a programme that is significant not only to ourselves but to others as well, attractive to people, so that despite inconveniences they would want to work with us. We have at the moment 220 institutions of higher learning associated with the Society of Jesus, but the level of international cooperation is relatively low. I explain the situation by saying that we have not done sufficient work in finding out what sort of programmes work for all of us.

Gendron Two related sharings. In our university, the college of management is creative. They have a programme with a university in China and a Jesuit university in the US. Students study in three places, China, Taiwan and the United States. At the end they get two degrees, none from Taiwan. But we are the bridge because we can easily work with Chinese universities and Jesuit universities. This programme is all in English. It is an innovative programme.

Second, I mentioned this Liberal Arts College in Hong Kong. Some Jesuit universities in Europe, Latin American and the US are very interested because graduates from that programme in Hong Kong are likely to go to these Jesuit universities for further degrees. It is not a joint degree but it is linked.

Adi It is interesting to know why Indonesian students want to go to Korea; they tell us they want to learn Korean pop culture, K-Pop. And why do students want to go to Indonesia? They do not want to learn language nor culture. But most of them want to know what dialogue is, especially with Muslims. So to this kind of need of students, we try to respond by a short two weeks programme or a 1-month programme. This semester Sogang University invited us to think about cooperation for four years because we are trying to send a proposal to the Korean government for four-year cooperation programmes and we are trying to identify what the need is, who might be interested in the programme, whether students or the faculty... so we are trying to have a joint degree for specific needs.

Sugimura Dr. Jung mentioned that the context of each country and region needs to be respected. Another thing that struck me was Dr. Kawamura's point on learning from history. I think you all know that the Society of Jesus is establishing St. Ignatius University in East Timor, a university for teachers' training. I had a chance to see the school. East Timor won independence only 10 years ago. Jesuits priests were providing what people need for the reconstruction of their country, using the local language of Tetum. What I saw was completely different from what is being commercialised. I had thought that such activities were done in the 16th century. When I saw them working with and for the local people, I was reminded of the social responsibility of universities. Dr. Kawamura said that Catholic education has to keep its traditions, but would you please elaborate on the social responsibilities of Jesuit universities in the Japanese context?

Kawamura Dr. Sugimura and Dr. Ucerler both talked about joint degrees, but I understood this as taking advantage of the international network of the Society of Jesus. We always talk about degrees or achievements, but whose degree are we talking about? They are for students or faculty members. The Society of Jesus has a network that can bridge their experience. Private enterprises and other public schools do not have this. I think this Jesuit network has a tremendous value.

Ucerler Now I am going to ask another disruptive and provocative question. I have been staring at the sign "The Role of Jesuit Universities in Asia" and the word that stands out more than anything else is Asia. We did not include India, which is a very large reality in Asia, or South Asia in this conversation. We talk a lot about East Asia, North Asia, and South East Asia. Is there such a category as the Jesuit University in Asia? Is there something really common between these realities or is this something artificial? It is a bit of a provocative question. We talk so much about common points, but if there are common points, what do you think they are? Or are these realities so different that it is difficult to talk about something that is common? What do you think Asia means in this context?

Gendron Let me say something. First, I think we should have written here something like Asia Pacific. In the Society of Jesus we used to have East Asia and Oceania. Now this name is changed to Asia Pacific. I think what we are actually talking about is Asia Pacific. I was Provincial of the Chinese province for six years and the provincials of Asia Pacific including Australia, Japan, Korea, Philippines and Micronesia, Indonesia and so on used to meet every six months for five days. There is a tremendous amount of variety, I think more than in any other section of the Jesuit order.

One example. I think there are six schools of theology, and we do not really have the resources to run so many schools of theology. So it would be nice to have at least one Jesuit scholastic theology all together in one place, but we found this is not possible because we cannot close out the only school of theology in China. If all the young Jesuits disappear, it's a loss. But on the other hand, half of the Jesuits studying theology in the Asia Pacific region are concentrated in Manila. So there is a degree of collaboration possible. It might be different from Europe or Latin America, but there is all that diversity. I just gave one example from the view of the Society of Jesus but I think this is also valuable for other universities.

Q&A Session

Ucerler I thought that before we open the questions, I will first ask the three speakers maybe to begin with their questions. As you have listened to other speakers you have issues that may have come up or things of interest that you wish to ask further.

Cruz Catholic schools and universities are private institutions, and rarely, if ever, get government support. The possible exceptions are tax waivers where institutions are not taxed as long as the profit they gain from operation is brought back to the institution. In terms of challenges faced by Catholic universities, however, in my view, the older generation has less and less understanding of the young, and we have to find a way to reach a full understanding of the experience of the young in the way they think. In the case of the Philippines I hope I am not too alarmist, but the challenge is not so much the varieties of religious traditions, Christianity and Islam for instance, but the matter of belief and unbelief. I see a lot of young people growing up with a cultural apparatus, a cultural distraction of religious faith. But perhaps many of them do not have the opportunity to encounter faith struggles necessary to grow in faith. So for churches and for Catholic institutions like universities, there are of course varieties of institutions, but I think even more importantly, forms of unbelief.

Gendron I would be interested to know more about how Sophia University is trying to deepen and nurture its Catholic mission, concretely how you do it. The second question is that we heard that the Ateneo de Manila is an elite university but the Society has four or five other universities. How do they stand to each other?

Kawamura That is a very difficult question. The Catholic population in Japan is even less than a minority, but Catholic universities have always had a major influence on society and that is a fact. Even if one does not believe in Catholicism, people come to realize Catholic values. So there are non-believers that do not join the Church, but the Catholic Church has little by little exerted some influence. That is as much as we can hope to achieve. A major change is not something we can hope for, but I think the only thing we can do is to keep up with the small efforts that we have been making up until now.

Koso I can discuss this from different angles. After the war up until today Sophia

University achieved a certain development. One major factor is that after the war very competent Jesuits came from various parts of the world and joined Sophia, and they served to connect Japan with other countries of the world. They all emphasized the attractiveness and connectedness of human beings. They made great contributions to nurture such people here at the university. In addition to this intermingling, at Sophia, philosophy, ethics and religious studies have been combined to create one area of study called Christian humanism. For those who are shallow in thought and knowledge this is difficult, but once they accumulate experience they come to realize the importance of what they learned here. This was a major factor.

But this perspective is such that in this age when globalization is progressing, we are being challenged. The past framework of humanistic studies does not work anymore. We cannot deal with the problems that the world presents just with anthropology alone. We have to be able to focus in order to achieve our mission. Fr. Nicolás mentioned this in 2008 when he made a presentation here at the university to commemorate the 100th anniversary of the Jesuits' return to Japan. He mentioned four challenges that universities are facing. One is poverty. To achieve peace we have to resolve the problem of poverty. Secondly, the issue of the environment. For sustainable development how do we involve ourselves in environmental issues to make that possible? Third, developing countries face the issue of education. If you do not have sufficient education, you will not be able to communicate well and you cannot make your own choices in your own life. In order to function as a human being, education is important. The fourth point is the way of life for human beings. Up until now, based on capitalism, we were very consumption-oriented, consuming large amounts, but from now on we have to value human beings and the earth more. Sophia takes these four challenges as a focal point of education or research, our contribution to society, to international society.

Cruz The Ateneo de Manila is an interesting place. It works for diversity, and one of the ways it does so is to set aside 15% of the tuition revenue from the very beginning for scholarships. The idea is that even if the university wishes to form leaders among its students, if the only students trained are from a particular social class, those students will find great difficulty being leaders of the entire country. So diversity is our priority because it is our way of making sure that the education we provide will affect the entire country. If the representatives of the four other Jesuit universities were here, I am sure that they would insist that they are the most influential in their regions, and I would accept that. The Ateneo de Manila, despite its name, functions as a university for the entire country. But the other four, although they excel in many areas such as engineering and have solid strengths, were set up and they continue to serve for the region where they exist. Ateneo de Zamboanga University located in the southwestern part of the country, for instance, is there to facilitate dialogue between Christians and Muslims. Davao in the north and in the southeast, Xavier University in the northern part of Mindanao, are both there to make sure that the local people are trained properly. They certainly serve a very important function in the country and in the Church.

Sugimura This has been a wonderful symposium so far. As Professor Koso said what sort of education we have to build from now on is I think one of the larger missions of Catholic universities. Catholic education, even before globalisation, had missions and tasks within the international network. Now with globalisation, what specific plans do you have in your research or in your daily work?

Ucerler We can probably discuss this further in the panel discussion. Let us open questions to the floor.

| Question 1 | This is a question addressed to Prof. Kawamura. In Japan, Sophia University, Sacred Heart College, Seisen University, and Nanzan Universisities are all called Catholic universities, because they were founded by religious congregations. Is it possible to have a thoroughly Catholic university like the Gregorian University in Japan?

Kawamura I did talk about the historical background in Japan and I did mention that evangelisation and education were separated. There was a separation between Catholic teaching and education per se. Therefore in 1913, Sophia University, which is a Jesuit university, could not have been called a Catholic university although they may have wanted to do so. How do we define a Catholic university? Is it a university for nurturing Catholic followers? Is it a university with a lot of Christians? Or is a Catholic university about informing the general public about the universe of Catholicism? I think Sophia University is the last one. In other words, we are targeted toward non-Christians. We were not strictly a Catholic university per se. Some may disagree, but that was the historical background in Japan, so if we are going to be

Part 2 Comments and Discussion

called a Catholic university, I believe we do not have to follow the Gregorian University.

Question 2 I was missioned to Taiwan between 2003 and 2007 by the congregation I belong to. I hear that actually there are now mainland sisters studying together with Taiwanese students in the Faculty of Theology at Fu Jen University. If I am not mistaken, our international leadership also decided to support some mainland students financially and our local community in Taiwan is involved in this movement. Is there any tension over the fact that mainland students and Taiwanese students are studying together in the field of theology?

Gendron Universities in Taiwan are now taking students from mainland China. Fu Jen University has 26,000 students and about 200 are from mainland China. But we take only the best students from mainland China, those who could enter the best universities in China. As a result, in Fu Jen University they are always the first in their class and they are very good. In the Faculty of Theology, this is not the case. Sisters and seminarians and priests are not intellectually very special. However, they do quite well and they mix well with local theology students. About 1/4 of our students in theology are lay students, Catholic lay students, and the mainland religious seminarians are very impressed by the quality of these lay students. It shows that the Church in Taiwan has been developing according to the idea of Vatican II in forming the lay students in their faith.

In China there is a problem of the underground unofficial Church. All these problems seem to disappear once they leave their country so they all become good friends when they are outside China. This is very good because they talk together and so I think this is a service to Chinese churches.

Ucerler Could you tell us when Taiwan allowed mainland Chinese to come to Taiwan to study, live or work there?

Gendron This has been going on now for about three years. It is still very much controlled. The Taiwanese government does not want mainland Chinese students to be more than 2 or 3% of the student population. But it is increasing slowly. In the case of theology, half of our students are from mainland China. This is a special case so we have a special arrangement between the government and the Vatican representative in Taipei to allow as many as we can take from China because there is a need of good formation in faith for those people from the Church in China.

Question 3 I would like to ask Fr. Gendron about the Catholic Faculty at Fu Jen which now has a number of mainland sisters and seminarians and priests. What is, if any, the relationship between the Fu Jen Faculty and seminaries or theology faculties in China? For example, Shanghai would be a good example to talk about.

Gendron The seminary in Shanghai has been closed for more than a year because the government is unhappy. The Shanghai diocese ordained a bishop and then the bishop decided to leave the patriotic association so they punished the diocese by closing the seminary. None of the seminaries in China are a faculty of theology. So we are the only ecclesiastical faculty that can give a recognized degree. In Hong Kong, the Holy Spirit seminary can give a theology degree and licentiate in dogmatic theology. So the development of seminaries in mainland China is very weak. That is one reason we take them. We also are beginning a post-doctoral programme. We are going to take professors from seminaries who already have a degree in theology and invite them to our faculty so that they will have an occasion to do more research and progress in their field.

I think our situation is more or less like that of Sophia. 1% of our students are Catholic, and 5% of our professors. However, I remember a group of 10 to 12 professors reading the Chinese translation of the Constitution on Catholic Universities from Pope John Paul II. I think 60 of our professors completely agree with its contents and really identify with the mission of the Catholic university. The only point that was different from our actual situation was that the constitution says that Catholic professors should be about half the number of professors, which is totally impossible. But it is very positive that many of our professors completely agreed with the ideas and goals of Catholic higher education.

Question 4 My question is addressed to Dr. Benedict Jung. Frankly I found your talk very fascinating, particularly when you spoke of a world university where you offer free education to youngsters from all over the world. Do people in your university also talk about online education?

Jung Have you heard about MOOC? As you know, Korea is probably the most advanced in terms of Internet technology at the moment and about 80% of people who are using mobile phones are using smart phones. I think we have two different ways of learning emerging at the moment. First, e-learning through the Internet and now Smart learning. If you have an iPad, you have access to anything through the Internet from your mobile. Sogang has a very good potentiality in this light. Recently our current president had an interview with a newspaper and he presented a very interesting plan to make Sogang a hub among Korean universities who are very good at MOOC. I think we are interested in online degrees and Smart learning including mobile gadgets.

Question 5 In each of the Jesuit universities you described Catholicism and the local cultures of your countries have come together to shape a particular sort of Catholic Jesuit university. I wonder what elements of your cultures have come together with the Catholic identity, particularly elements of education, merged with Catholicism to shape something unique that each of your universities offers.

When we speak of integrating Ignatian identity into the institutions, how do universities reflect, create and discuss Ignatian identity and put it into practice in concrete ways in the institution?

Cruz If I may provide a very small piece of a broader answer, references made to Philippines being a Catholic country, there are many Catholics, but I would not be surprised if many of the Catholics have a form of faith that is locally closed, pure, secured and formally articulated. Catholicism for the young is strong in its ability to dialogue with other religious traditions. So we will remain Catholic but our Catholicity will be expressed quite pronouncedly in terms of a contemporary need of facility for dialogue and in deep respect of other religious traditions. I would be very happy if our young people grew up as Catholics who can do so.

Jung I do not have a concrete Korean case that exemplifies the good blending between Catholic and another identity which was enhanced by some other cultural elements. I would like to quote a very famous novelist who was a Catholic. He said, "My head is formed by Catholicism. My blood is formed by Buddhism. My heart is formed by Confucianism." I think a Korean Catholic identity has something to do deeply with our cultural background and identity. But as Prof. Kawamura said, the Catholic culture or Catholic religion was a very disruptive factor in Korean society in the 18th century because it denied our filial respect for our ancestors, which the government at the time regarded as undermining the stability of society. Later on, the antagonism or conflict between Catholicism and the government faded out, but I am very proud of our Catholic identity in Korea. We are religiously a very complex country, full of different religious groups including Islam and other religions. I do not see any big news about conflicts between religions because we share all religions in Korea. Coming from outside or coming from within, we share the same cultural elements. That is a particular case for Korean Catholic identity.

At Sogang, the board of trustees is trying to help staff members and professors as well as alumni to be immersed into the Jesuit Catholic educational philosophy. For instance, imitating Georgetown University, we are going to have a Jesuit heritage week during which we want to have an Ignatian lecture. We have some DVD programmes which show the history of the Society. We can have pizza conversations with Jesuits and students. Also with the school corporation we have workshops for newly hired and appointed staff members and administrative members. The workshop usually lasts two or three nights, and helps people who newly come to the university to understand why the Society of Jesus was sent to Korea to educate young people and why the educational philosophy of the Society is still relevant even though its history dates back more than two centuries.

Interestingly, when I returned to the school corporation I found it strange we did not have any brochures or DVD programmes which show our identity or Jesuit educational philosophy. Now we are making brochures and a DVD which will be circulated around the university and to the alumni.

Finally, now Sogang has a lay president. By the rules of the board, the president has to be Catholic. That means from the beginning we can guarantee a minimum level of understanding of Jesuit education from the lay president. But this is not enough to preserve our Jesuit Catholic identity, so we have frequent conversation with the chairperson of the board, myself and the president and two vice-presidents who meet every month. That is for us a very good tool to understand each other mutually. The chairperson of the board, the provincial of the Society of Jesus in Korea and the president also meet regularly. They make arrangements and adjustments, or converse on important issues. The focal point of their talk is how we can make our Jesuit educational philosophy as vibrant as possible. Conversation and dialogue are very important.

Part 2   Comments and Discussion

Adi   I would like to answer your question about Jesuit identity for lay persons, for the institution and for students. We started to introduce Ignatian pedagogy five years ago. We agreed to implement it for the curriculum as well as for extra-curricular activities. We not only identify but also state that our goal is competence, conscience and compassion. It is interesting that we started from a small group of faculty. We measured these three factors with indicators. At the end of the semester we have reflection among faculty and students and we have a symposium to see what is going on, whether it is easy or difficult to implement this Ignatian pedagogy. This type of symposium is a way of trying to spread Ignatian pedagogy slowly but continuously. It has only been five years but it is interesting that not only Jesuits or Catholic faculty members but also non-Catholics are able to implement, understand, and see difficulties in measuring how students develop conscience and compassion.

■執筆者一覧／Writers List

髙祖敏明 ／ Koso Toshiaki　SJ
上智大学総合人間科学部教授、上智学院理事長（日本）
Professor of the Faculty of Human Sciences, Chair of the Board of Sophia Corporation (Japan)

ホセ・クルス ／ Jose M. Cruz　SJ
アテネオ・デ・マニラ大学社会科学部教授、副学長（フィリピン）
Professor of the School of Social Sciences, Vice President of Ateneo de Manila University (Philippines)

川村信三 ／ Kawamura Shinzo　SJ
上智大学文学部教授（日本）
Professor of the Faculty of Humanities of Sophia University (Japan)

ルイス・ジェンドロン ／ Louis Gendron　SJ
輔仁大学神学部教授（台湾）
Professor of the Faculty of Theology of St. Robert Bellarmine of Fu Jen University (Taiwan)

クントロ・アディ ／ C. Kuntoro Adi　SJ
サナタダルマ大学科学技術学部教授、副学長（インドネシア）
Professor of the Faculty of Science and Technology, Vice President of Sanata Dharma University (Indonesia)

ベネディクト・カンユップ・ユン ／ Benedict Kang-Yup Jung　SJ
西江大学常任理事（韓国）
Executive Director of the Board of Trustees of Sogang University (Korea)

ミカエル・カルマノ ／ Michael Calmano　SVD
南山大学学長、東南・東アジアカトリック大学連盟（ASEACCU）会長（日本）
President of Nanzan University, President of the Association of Southeast and East Asia Catholic Colleges and Universities [ASEACCU] (Japan)

杉村美紀 ／ Sugimura Miki
上智大学総合人間科学部教授、副学長（日本）
Professor of the Faculty of Human Sciences, Vice President of Sophia University (Japan)

アントニ・ウセレル ／ Antoni Ucerler　SJ
サンフランシスコ大学人文科学部教授、東アジア研究科長（アメリカ）
Professor of the College of Arts and Science, Director of Asia Research Wing, University of San Francisco (USA)

サリ・アガスティン ／ Sali Augustine　SJ
上智大学神学部教授（日本）
Professor of the Faculty of Theology of Sophia University (Japan)

アジアにおけるイエズス会大学の役割

2015年12月30日　第1版第1刷発行

共　編：髙　祖　敏　明
　　　　サリ・アガスティン

発行者：髙　祖　敏　明
発　行：Sophia University Press
　　　　上　智　大　学　出　版
　　　　〒102-8554　東京都千代田区紀尾井町7-1
　　　　URL：http://www.sophia.ac.jp/

制作・発売　㈱ぎょうせい
〒136-8575　東京都江東区新木場1-18-11
TEL　03-6892-6666　FAX　03-6892-6925
フリーコール　0120-953-431

〈検印省略〉　　URL：http://gyosei.jp

Ⓒ Eds. Toshiaki Koso and Sali Augustine
2015, Printed in Japan
印刷・製本　ぎょうせいデジタル㈱
ISBN978-4-324-09945-2
(5300241-00-000)

[略号：(上智) イエズス会大学]
NDC 分類 377.2

Sophia University Press

　上智大学は、その基本理念の一つとして、「本学は、その特色を活かして、キリスト教とその文化を研究する機会を提供する。これと同時に、思想の多様性を認め、各種の思想の学問的研究を奨励する」と謳っている。

　大学は、この学問的成果を学術書として発表する「独自の場」を保有することが望まれる。どのような学問的成果を世に発信しうるかは、その大学の学問的水準・評価と深く関わりを持つ。

　上智大学は、(1) 高度な水準にある学術書、(2) キリスト教ヒューマニズムに関連する優れた作品、(3) 啓蒙的問題提起の書、(4) 学問研究への導入となる特色ある教科書等、個人の研究のみならず、共同の研究成果を刊行することによって、文化の創造に寄与し、大学の発展とその歴史に貢献する。

Sophia University Press

One of the fundamental ideals of Sophia University is "to embody the university's special characteristics by offering opportunities to study Christianity and Christian culture. At the same time, recognizing the diversity of thought, the university encourages academic research on a wide variety of world views."

The Sophia University Press was established to provide an independent base for the publication of scholarly research. The publications of our press are a guide to the level of research at Sophia, and one of the factors in the public evaluation of our activities.

Sophia University Press publishes books that (1) meet high academic standards; (2) are related to our university's founding spirit of Christian humanism; (3) are on important issues of interest to a broad general public; and (4) textbooks and introductions to the various academic disciplines. We publish works by individual scholars as well as the results of collaborative research projects that contribute to general cultural development and the advancement of the university.

The Role of Jesuit Universities in Asia

ⓒEds. Toshiaki Koso and Sali Augustine, 2015
published by
Sophia University Press

production & sales agency : GYOSEI Corporation, Tokyo
ISBN978-4-324-09945-2
order : http://gyosei.jp